ASTRO-WISDOM

THE KNOWLEDGE, LOVE AND POWER IN YOUR STARS

Lyn Birkbeck

BOOKS

New York, USA
Alresford, UK

Copyright © 2003 O Books
46A West Street, Alresford, Hants SO24 9AU, U.K.
Tel: +44 (0) 1962 736880 Fax: +44 (0) 1962 736881
E-mail: office@johnhunt-publishing.com
www.johnhunt-publishing.com
www.0-books.net

US office:
240 West 35th Street, Suite 500
New York, NY10001
E-mail: obooks@aol.com
Text: © 2003 Lyn Birkbeck

Design: Nautilus Design (UK) Ltd

ISBN 1 903816 56 4

A CIP catalogue record for this book is available from the British Library.

Printed in the USA by Maple-Vail

TO THE SUN

Greatest of Greatest Hearts
Life-Truth blazed in the Sky
Mysterious streams of Space Desire
Impressing you and I

O Greatest of Greatest Hearts
Who can look You in the Eye
Love is Your Core, hard to resist
So hard to resist yet we try

Our eyes squint, our skin burns
Our zone layers melting away
By the smoke screens we raise resisting the Love
That You unfold everyday

In the Always Sky that You always are
From morning's first greeting gleams
To Your farewell flicker in the gloaming
Throughout the night, enlightening dreams

As Your Soulmate Moon's soft reflection
In this sweet way to the heart is revealed
Your bright mystery - Your intense intention
That ripens corn - warms starry field.

Now I feel the Sun burst in my heart
Exploding blazing petals free
Streaming beams to darkened reaches
Unfolding golden endlessly

Listen to Song Sun is singing
And the Music of the Spheres you'll hear
Through Twelve great Zodiacal verses
That resonate around our year

Impressing and impregnating
Making you a servant of the One
Whose Greatness pulses as our heartbeat
And in us Love shall have begun

To celebrate our remembering
As we run around the Sun
That we are members of one Race
You and I are One - You and I are One.

ASTRO-WISDOM

The Knowledge, Love and Power in Your Stars

CONTENTS

Looking at your Sun-Sign or Star-Sign in terms of how you may emotionally connect and align yourself with the living energy and power that your Sun-Sign actually is. Also the mental dynamics of your personality and how by following the positive ones you can become a happier you.

The ways in which each Sign relates, and what issues predominate in their relationships. How to get the best out of relationship through being true to your own laws of relating, and by avoiding the pitfalls.

Straightforward and practical descriptions of how all the Signs interact with one another, and how you can make the most of a relationship.

4. Planetary Cycles – Laws for Living & Loving ....page 89

5. Planets of Love – Laws for Living and Loving ......page 255

This shows you how life is a cosmos – that is, an ordered and intelligent system. Through being aware of this system, you can begin to see your own and others' parts in it, as well as finding some explanation of the basic scheme of things and why they are like they are at this present time in history.

6. Appendix ....page 281

7. The Age Index..page 293

1. SUN-SIGN POWER

The Sun is The Life Force. The Sign that It was
travelling through when you were born (your Sun-Sign
or Star-Sign) therefore tells you the nature of your individual life-
force. Be true to this, your true potential, and It will energise and
guide you. Each Sun-Sign has a double-page spread, set out like this:-

LEFT-HAND PAGE

This is for your right-brain or FEELING side, the visual or intuitive side of your perception and understanding. Through interacting with this page you are emotionally and physically aligned with the essence of your being. Quite simply, the Force will be with you! First is given your part in The Zodiacal Life-Stream (the whole of which is shown on pages 33-36) which ideally you should memorise or record and then go with it, eyes closed and looking up into your brow, thereby increasing the alpha waves in your brain and connecting you to your higher intelligence. Then there is your Emotional Intent. You can just study this or use it as an affirmation, but it is far better to mime it, line by line, in a very free and feeling way - not like charades though! You are conveying the meaning of yourself to yourself, not anyone else. However, you can do the mime in a group or one-to-one. The magic of the mime is the mime of the magic. This page ends with a suitable quote as a motto for your Sign.

RIGHT-HAND PAGE

This is for your left-brain or THINKING side, the logical and deductive side of your perception and mind. Here your personality is seen in terms of key dynamics, not just character traits that cannot be changed. There are good dynamics and bad ones; the good ones lead to positive outcomes, the bad lead to negative outcomes. These are like 'Divine Do's and Don'ts', cosmic affirmations. The upward arrows with the header 'Accentuate the Positive' are those Do's or good dynamics and their positive results. The downward arrows with the footer 'Eliminate the Negative' are the Don'ts or bad dynamics with their negative consequences. Through being a positive thinking expression of your Sun-Sign in accordance with these 'Divine Do's and Don'ts' you provide a clear path for your Emotional Intent and for going with the flow of the Life-Stream given on the left-hand page. In this way you may simply come a happier person.

FEELING ARIES

Still yourself as much as possible, perhaps put on a favourite piece of instrumental music, and picture and immerse yourself in your particular stretch of...

THE LIFE-STREAM

~ I am the first, straight from the Source, energetically emerging from the hidden depths of the Earth and Primordial Waters, fresh and sparkling. I tumble onward – impetuously and enthusiastically. When strong in flow, I feel independent, and lead others, showing them the way to push on. When the flow is weak, I admit to it, tarry awhile, and allow more energy to accumulate until I can once more exert and assert myself ~

Repeat (or better still, tape and playback) several times.

Then, line by line, study, and then mime (with feeling) this, your....

EMOTIONAL INTENT

I act in order to be make things happen
Exciting body and soul
I make my life secure through mobilising
And find enlightenment in simply being
I am empowered and directed by the Spirit of Independence

Now, if you wish, immerse yourself once again in the Life-Stream.

**"Courage is not merely one of the virtues,
but the form of every virtue at its testing point"**

KNOWING ARIES

ACCENTUATE THE POSITIVE

My assertive style and uncomplicated approach
CREATE
freedom of expression and blaze a trail for others to follow.

My spontaneity, decisiveness and willingness to act
ENERGIZE
people and occasions, showing the way forward.

My direct and straightforward manner of expression
ILLUMINATES
situations because it removes obscuring and inhibiting agendas.

Being headstrong, too wrapped up in my own version of what is happening
BLINDS
me to what is really happening, paving the way for failure.

Forcing issues, or not thinking delicate ones through
DESTROYS
what is of most importance and value to me.

Impatience, which is an inappropriate sense of time and reality,
EXAGGERATES
the need for what I believe is wanted, making me even more impatient.

ELIMINATE THE NEGATIVE

☿ FEELING TAURUS ☿

Still yourself as much as possible, perhaps put on a favourite piece of instrumental music, and picture and immerse yourself in your particular stretch of...

THE LIFE-STREAM

~ I now encounter the richness and resistance of the Earth. I savour and ponder Her nature and worth, and in so doing, realise my own talents and abilities. When strong in flow, I feel abundant and fertile, and bring the pleasure and reassurance of Nature's goodness to myself and others. When the flow is weak, in order to avoid becoming bogged down, I allow chance and change into my life, freeing and refreshing me ~

Repeat (or better still, tape and playback) several times.

Then, line by line, study, and then mime (with feeling) this, your....

EMOTIONAL INTENT

I produce in order to enjoy
Blending body and soul
I make life secure through maintaining definite values
And find enlightenment in Nature's laws
I am empowered and directed by the Spirit of Plenty

Now, if you wish, immerse yourself once again in the Life-Stream.

"Nature does nothing without purpose or uselessly"

KNOWING TAURUS

ACCENTUATE THE POSITIVE

My sensuous awareness of what pleases and my sense of wholesome values
CREATE
appealing and substantial things that attract wealth and happiness.

Making definite, necessary and timely changes in my life
ENERGIZES
myself and my projects for it removes inhibiting and compromising situations.

My down-to-earth philosophy of life and my ability to recognise quality
ILLUMINATE
and make obvious what is of practical worth in people and things.

Refusing to see the more psychological or symbolic reasons for issues
BLINDS
me to the truth, keeping me stuck and unable to see a way through.

Resisting change, or even just denying the possibility of change,
DESTROYS
what chances there are of improving the quality of life.

Pursuing physical pleasures or material rewards at the expense of the spiritual
EXAGGERATES
the need for such, leading to ever more dissatisfying situations.

ELIMINATE THE NEGATIVE

11

⚏ ⚏ FEELING GEMINI ⚏ ⚏

Still yourself as much as possible, perhaps put on a favourite piece of instrumental music, and picture and immerse yourself in your particular stretch of...

THE LIFE-STREAM

~ I now divide and criss-cross with other streams. And so I bubble and froth with the diversity of Life and the amusement and knowledge that it brings. When the flow is strong, I tirelessly make more and more connections, informing and delighting myself and others. When the flow is weak, I allow myself to slow down a little, that I might appreciate my multi-faceted expression of the Life-Stream's possibilities ~

Repeat (or better still, tape and playback) several times.

Then, line by line, study, and then mime (with feeling) this, your....

EMOTIONAL INTENT

I circulate in order to communicate
Connecting body and soul
I make life secure through being friendly to all
And find enlightenment in variety and humour
I am empowered and directed by the Spirit of Enquiry

Now, if you wish, immerse yourself once again in the Life-Stream.

"Hail to thee, blithe Spirit!"

KNOWING GEMINI

ACCENTUATE THE POSITIVE

My versatility, quick wits and readiness always to learn something new
CREATE
in me a youthfulness and openness that forever refreshes all and sundry.

My ability to make contacts and to create interest with words and ideas
ENERGIZES
any and all situations, be they private, professional, intellectual or emotional.

My flexibility, lightness of touch, and ability to see both sides
ILLUMINATE
matters because they show how things simply are, not how they 'ought' to be.

Evading or and rationalising away emotional issues
BLINDS
me to how I actually feel and so attracts even more emotional problems.

Fearfully refusing to see the whole picture
DESTROYS
my sense of where or who I actually am – a dangerous place to be.

Any fear of being tied down and the consequent difficulty in committing
EXAGGERATES
relationship problems, making them appear more difficult than they are.

ELIMINATE THE NEGATIVE

FEELING CANCER

Still yourself as much as possible, perhaps put on a favourite piece of instrumental music, and picture and immerse yourself in your particular stretch of...

THE LIFE-STREAM

~ I now settle into a pool of safety and security where I may prosper from Nature's surrounding bounty, and dream in my silent depths. When clear and therefore maintained and fed by the Stream's input and output, I am able and willing to nourish myself and others. When clogged by the silt of stale memories and unnecessary emotions, I become aware of those fresh thoughts and feelings that are readily offered, allowing myself to receive them and be restored by them ~

Repeat (or better still, tape and playback) several times.

Then, line by line, study, and then mime (with feeling) this, your....

EMOTIONAL INTENT

I nurture in order to prosper
Comforting body and soul
I make life secure through creating a sense of belonging
And find enlightenment through being receptive
I am empowered and directed by the Spirit of Caring

Now, if you wish, immerse yourself once again in the Life-Stream.

"Home is where the heart is"

KNOWING CANCER

ACCENTUATE THE POSITIVE

My ability to sense and meet immediate practical and emotional needs
CREATES
a safe environment and a warm and reassuring atmosphere.

My sympathetic and protective instincts
ENERGIZE
everyone, making them feel they are 'family' and that they all belong.

My talent for being tender and responsive
ILLUMINATES
how myself and others truly feel, ensuring true security.

Being afraid of confrontation and not being emotionally direct enough
BLINDS
me to how myself and others feel, thereby undermining everyone's security.

Blaming myself or others, being overly apologetic, or feeling resentful,
DESTROYS
my own and others' chances of peace and happiness.

being too sensitive and over-reacting
EXAGGERATES
situations to the point of them being as bad as I feared them to be.

ELIMINATE THE NEGATIVE

FEELING LEO

Still yourself as much as possible, perhaps put on a favourite piece of instrumental music, and picture and immerse yourself in your particular stretch of...

THE LIFE-STREAM

~ now the Force rises and accumulates as much as It can, and I overflow and burst forth to show myself to the World – full and ebullient. Being so strong in flow I readily and easily express how it feels to have the Force coursing through and around me, showing and reminding others of Its greatness. When, inevitably, this tide of enthusiasm ebbs, I gracefully and happily languish until once more the Force rushes through ~

Repeat (or better still, tape and playback) several times.

Then, line by line, study, and then mime (with feeling) this, your....

EMOTIONAL INTENT

I radiate in order to be express
Celebrating body and soul
I make life secure through being open to good advice
And find enlightenment in listening to my heart
I am empowered and directed by the Spirit of Generosity

Now, if you wish, immerse yourself once again in the Life-Stream.

"All the World's a stage"

KNOWING LEO

ACCENTUATE THE POSITIVE

My confident aura and generous heart
CREATE
an atmosphere and response that benefit everyone, myself included.

My dramatic, romantic and convincing expression of self
ENERGIZES
everything and everyone that it touches.

My powerful, elevated and unequivocal view of things
ILLUMINATES
areas of doubt and darkness, dispelling fears, clarifying the path ahead.

Vanity, snobbishness, affectation or brazenly showing off
BLINDS
me to how others see me, and therefore what I truly am, need and feel.

Being domineering and demanding
DESTROYS
the loyalty and respect that I am actually seeking.

An unexamined or unconscious need for attention
EXAGGERATES
the importance of that need, thereby making it progressively harder to satisfy.

ELIMINATE THE NEGATIVE

♍ ♍ ♍ FEELING VIRGO ♍ ♍ ♍

Still yourself as much as possible, perhaps put on a favourite piece of instrumental music, and picture and immerse yourself in your particular stretch of...

THE LIFE-STREAM

~ now the Stream is checked by difficult terrain, and it becomes critical as to how I proceed. And should I lose a sense of the Flow altogether, I simply remain true to myself and before long I am once more aware of the Stream coursing through me and within me, guiding me and buoying me up. Such experiences create in me sound methods and an intricate knowledge of the nature of things, enabling me to help others through difficult times ~

Repeat (or better still, tape and playback) several times.

Then, line by line, study, and then mime (with feeling) this, your....

EMOTIONAL INTENT

I work in order to perfect
Purifying body and soul
I make life secure through listening to my conscience
And find enlightenment through acting upon what it tells me
I am empowered and directed by the Spirit of Service

Now, if you wish, immerse yourself once again in the Life-Stream.

"Man will err while yet he strives"

KNOWING VIRGO

ACCENTUATE THE POSITIVE

My analytical and discerning mind, and my eye for detail,
CREATE
an ordered life and a healthy environment.

My industriousness, helpfulness and conscientiousness
ENERGIZE
whatever or whoever they are applied to, including my own life.

My pure intentions, keen observation and studious nature
ILLUMINATE
issues and thereby resolve difficulties.

Trying to find a logical reason and answer to everything all of the time
BLINDS
me to how things really are, and so sabotages my reasoning and wellbeing.

Fear of failing and being too critical of everyone and everything
DESTROYS
the very projects and relationships I wish to improve or further.

Wanting to fix everyone and everything when it is not required
EXAGGERATES
difficulties and creates more problems – a vicious circle.

ELIMINATE THE NEGATIVE

FEELING LIBRA

Still yourself as much as possible, perhaps put on a favourite piece of instrumental music, and picture and immerse yourself in your particular stretch of...

THE LIFE-STREAM

~ now I meet another Stream of equal strength and importance ~ and so I sense the natural give and take that must now take place at this place of confluence. Both have equal right of way, and turbulence arises as alternately we each separate and unite, surrender and hold on to our individual identities, yet knowing that merging is inevitable. And so naturally I balance as the Stream swings between separateness and unity ~

Repeat (or better still, tape and playback) several times.

Then, line by line, study, and then mime (with feeling) this, your....

EMOTIONAL INTENT

I harmonize in order to please
Balancing body and soul
I make life secure through being true to my principles
And find enlightenment in what or who has beauty
I am empowered and directed by the Spirit of Fairness

Now, if you wish, immerse yourself once again in the Life-Stream.

"Beauty is Truth, Truth is Beauty"

KNOWING LIBRA

ACCENTUATE THE POSITIVE

Expressing wholeheartedly my sense of beauty, harmony and justice
CREATES
a happier life and a more peaceful world.

My pleasant, sociable and diplomatic manner
ENERGIZES
any occasion, be it personal or public, romantic or professional.

Pursuing and upholding worthwhile values and principles
ILLUMINATES
the minds of anyone in my sphere of influence.

Viewing life in solely conventional or superficial terms
BLINDS
me to the truth of the matter, making true happiness impossible to attain.

Trying to please everybody
DESTROYS
my chances of pleasing anybody, and of knowing who I truly am.

Being afraid of making the wrong decision
EXAGGERATES
the problem, making the decision even harder to make.

ELIMINATE THE NEGATIVE

FEELING SCORPIO

Still yourself as much as possible, perhaps put on a favourite piece of instrumental music, and picture and immerse yourself in your particular stretch of...

THE LIFE-STREAM

~ the merging of two Streams now becomes imperative and so my former and lesser self has to die. Should I resist this merging or attempt to coerce others solely for my own ends, then inevitably I shall be cast out, alone, drowned in my own undercurrent. Yet when I sacrifice to the true intimacy of truly joining, the power of the Life-Stream is doubled. With such combined Flow the strength of my inner convictions can move mountains ~

Repeat (or better still, tape and playback) several times.

Then, line by line, study, and then mime (with feeling) this, your....

EMOTIONAL INTENT

I penetrate in order to be intimate
Merging body and soul
I make life secure through being true to my depths
And find enlightenment by going through darkness
I am empowered and directed by the Spirit of Authenticity

Now, if you wish, immerse yourself once again in the Life-Stream.

"Yea, though I walk through the valley of the shadow of death,
I will fear no evil "

KNOWING SCORPIO

ACCENTUATE THE POSITIVE

My persistent and penetrative emotional insight and charisma

CREATE

a genuine and profound sense of what really matters, despite resistance.

My intense physical vibration and magnetically charged aura

ENERGIZE

anyone or anything that comes close to me, healing and transforming them.

My unflinching approach and uncompromising opinions

ILLUMINATE

the psychological landscape, clarifying motivations and empowering feelings.

Too much covert behaviour and emotional manipulation

BLIND

me to issues to such a degree that no-one knows what I actually want or fear.

Fears of betrayal amounting to intense jealousy and insecurity

DESTROY

the very things that I am afraid of losing or not attaining.

Mistaking sensitivity for weaknesses and then hiding or suppressing it will

EXAGGERATE

such sensitivity to the point of making me really vulnerable.

ELIMINATE THE NEGATIVE

FEELING SAGITTARIUS

Still yourself as much as possible, perhaps put on a favourite piece of instrumental music, and picture and immerse yourself in your particular stretch of...

THE LIFE-STREAM

~ with the crisis of merging now passed, the Stream is freed on to the open plain, where it runs wide and majestic. Upon both banks may be seen sweeping vistas of opportunity and adventure which I am called to take up and explore. So as the Stream proceeds it gathers many experiences that allow me to learn and teach, teach and learn. And lest I flood the banks with excesses or arrogant enthusiasm, I always remember my small and trickling origins - and again the Stream is good ~

Repeat (or better still, tape and playback) several times.

Then, line by line, study, and then mime (with feeling) this, your....

EMOTIONAL INTENT

I speculate in order to accumulate
Rejoicing in both body and soul
I make life secure by being adventurous yet wise
And find enlightenment through seeking
I am empowered and directed by the Spirit of Joy

Now, if you wish, immerse yourself once again in the Life-Stream.

**"It never matters how hard the road ahead might look,
for it is still road, and roads go places!"**

KNOWING SAGITTARIUS

ACCENTUATE THE POSITIVE

My optimistic openness
CREATES
the very vistas and opportunities that give rise to it.

My sense and belief that there is always a new horizon beckoning
ENERGIZES
me and mine, drawing me forever on.

My far-flung vision of a glorious future
ILLUMINATES
the present, the very road that is bound for that future.

Assuming an over-optimistic outlook and a self-justifying attitude
BLINDS
me to what is truly great and honourable in myself and others.

Believing that I have got as far as I can go, or that I know all I need to know,
DESTROYS
my chances of going any further, of gaining wisdom, of receiving grace.

It is a false sense of confidence or an unexamined belief that
EXAGGERATES
my prospects or sense of being right. And over-inflated bubbles always burst.

ELIMINATE THE NEGATIVE

FEELING CAPRICORN

Still yourself as much as possible, perhaps put on a favourite piece of instrumental music, and picture and immerse yourself in your particular stretch of...

THE LIFE-STREAM

~ the Stream, having become full, is now tested as I endure Its course through the narrow divides of the canyon. Hemmed in by the steep cliffs of Earthly conditions, I use my natural senses of resourcefulness and ambition to amount to something through negotiating the cataracts of adversity that I now encounter. My power to progress is not in question, for it is inescapable; but my ultimate achievement is to exercise only the control necessary to remain upright and aware of my emotional depths ~

Repeat (or better still, tape and playback) several times.

Then, line by line, study, and then mime (with feeling) this, your....

EMOTIONAL INTENT

I build in order to achieve
Integrating body and soul
I make life secure through shouldering responsibility
And find enlightenment by accepting what I cannot control
I am empowered and directed by the Spirit of Order

Now, if you wish, immerse yourself once again in the Life-Stream.

"The opposite to the devil you know is the god that you don't"

KNOWING CAPRICORN

ACCENTUATE THE POSITIVE

When my innate sense of responsibility serves a higher purpose, it
CREATES
in me a deep understanding and trust in the processes of life.

My disciplined, organised and resourceful nature
ENERGIZES
and galvanises myself and others to action, leading to accomplishment.

My earthy, pragmatic, matter-of-fact awareness
ILLUMINATES
mundane issues that can totally flummox so many others.

Only believing what I can see with my eyes, or sense with my senses,
BLINDS
me to the whole, undermining my ability to maintain control.

Trying to impose rules and limitations in order to hold back what I fear
DESTROYS
the soul of what and who makes up my life, which includes myself.

Not giving emotions and other intangible factors enough attention
EXAGGERATES
negative feelings and imaginings in others, thus provoking very real problems.

ELIMINATE THE NEGATIVE

FEELING AQUARIUS

Still yourself as much as possible, perhaps put on a favourite piece of instrumental music, and picture and immerse yourself in your particular stretch of...

THE LIFE-STREAM

~ the Stream is now liberated on to the wetlands and the delta, bringing irrigation and refreshment to all flora and fauna. And so I bear the precious water of knowledge and life, distributing it evenly and impartially ~ never resisting or shrinking from the truth, for I know it spreads inexorably. And as all beings are thus nourished and informed with the truths of life, eventually a great awakening occurs amongst the people as the accumulated knowledge that the Stream brings frees us from fear ~

Repeat (or better still, tape and playback) several times.

Then, line by line, study, and then mime (with feeling) this, your....

EMOTIONAL INTENT

I endeavour in order to become aware
Liberating body and soul
I make life secure through being cool and non-judgemental
And find enlightenment by acting upon my ideals
I am empowered and directed by the Spirit of Progress

Now, if you wish, immerse yourself once again in the Life-Stream.

"A paradox is the truth standing on its head to attract attention"

KNOWING AQUARIUS

ACCENTUATE THE POSITIVE

My idealistic and reformist spirit
CREATES
a humanistic environment and ultimately a more intelligent world.

My broadminded and impartial input and perception
ENERGIZE
myself and others because they are refreshing and liberating.

My inventive and forward-thinking mind
ILLUMINATES
issues and gives hope for the future.

Judging people and things according to some theory of how they ought to be
BLINDS
me to the truth of what is happening, and makes me appear hypocritical.

Being dismissive of what I do not understand or think I know already
DESTROYS
my chances of discovering a solution to what most disturbs me.

Suppressing, detaching from, or rationalising away my own or others' feelings
EXAGGERATES
difficulties to the point of them exploding into the very thing I wished to avoid.

ELIMINATE THE NEGATIVE

)( )(FEELING PISCES)( )(

Still yourself as much as possible, perhaps put on a favourite piece of instrumental music, and picture and immerse yourself in your particular stretch of...

THE LIFE-STREAM

~ at last all the many individual streams of the one Stream empty into the Ocean. We realize that our individual longings are ultimately a longing for the same thing - the mysterious sea of peace & acceptance. And so I feel all the life-streams within me as the one Life-stream, and I am faithfully led forever on to inspire and relieve - or I merely crave some non-existent shortcut. For as vapour from the sea rises up into the sky, and falls as rain, or sleet or snow, so too shall we go, and return to the Source ~

Repeat (or better still, tape and playback) several times.

Then, line by line, study, and then mime (with feeling) this, your....

EMOTIONAL INTENT

I suffer in order to inspire
Healing body and soul
I make life secure through being compassionate
And find enlightenment in acceptance
I am empowered and directed by the Spirit of Sensitivity

Now, if you wish, immerse yourself once again in the Life-Stream.

"Obstacles - I either use them or go around them"

KNOWING PISCES

ACCENTUATE THE POSITIVE

Employing my profound sensitivity and imagination
CREATES
things and situations that are relieving, enlightening or entertaining.

My compassionate acceptance of the way things are
ENERGIZES
myself and others for it forestalls needless resistance, stress or strain.

My subtle perception and awareness of things
ILLUMINATE
matters because they sense the way things naturally want to go.

An inclination to see things only how I want to see them
BLINDS
me to the way things actually are, leading to ever more confusion.

Taking what appears to be the easy way out, when it
DESTROYS
what or who is near and dear to me, is a way to be resisted.

Feeling a victim, being too self-effacing, or feeling sorry for myself
EXAGGERATES
such feelings of inferiority, further attracting abuse and disregard.

ELIMINATE THE NEGATIVE

31

THE ZODIACAL LIFE-STREAM

"Then the angel showed me the river of the water of life, as clear as crystal, flowing down from the throne of God and of the Lamb down the middle of the great street of the city. On each side of the river stood the tree of life, bearing twelve crops of fruit, yielding its fruit every month. And the leaves of the tree are for the healing of the nations".

- St. John the Divine, from Revelation chapter 22 verses 1-2

Popular and well-known as Sun-Signs are, they are not usually appreciated for making up a cycle in themselves – even though everyone is aware of that cycle's name: the Zodiac.

The Zodiac is traditionally seen as a cycle that parallels the unfolding of the four seasons, embracing Nature's budding, blooming, fruiting, dying, sleeping, rebirth process. However, this seasonal analogy, beautiful as it is, does not quite satisfy when wanting to view it from one's position in the human drama of thinking, sensing, feeling and doing. Moreover, it does not apply to the seasons of the Southern Hemisphere.

To this end, here is another metaphor for the Zodiac: that of a river from source to ocean to source. This analogy, I hope you will find, contains the emotional flow that is necessary for a healthy life, a sense of going on a meaningful and eternal journey, and the understanding that in being part of some whole there lies a good reason for why you are like you are.

Above all, there is a spiritual and even romantic quality to this river analogy, for it creatively places us all in that great production where 'all the world's a stage'.

I call this The Zodiacal Life-Stream, and you will find it depicted and explained overleaf. Sign glyphs are as follows:

♈ = Aries	♋ = Cancer	♎ = Libra	♑ = Capricorn
♉ = Taurus	♌ = Leo	♏ = Scorpio	♒ = Aquarius
♊ = Gemini	♍ = Virgo	♐ = Sagittarius	♓ = Pisces

♒ ~ the Stream is now liberated on to the wetlands and the delta, bringing irrigation and refreshment to all flora and fauna. And so I bear the precious water of knowledge and life, distributing it evenly and impartially - never resisting or shrinking from the truth, for I know it spreads inexorably. And as all beings are thus nourished and informed with the truths of life, eventually a great awakening occurs amongst the people as the accumulated knowledge - that the Stream brings - frees us from fear ~

♓ ~ at last all the many individual streams of the one Stream empty into the ocean. We realise that our individual longings are ultimately a longing for the same thing - the mysterious sea of peace and acceptance. And so I feel all the life-streams within me as the one Life-stream, & I am faithfully led forever on to inspire and relieve - or I merely crave some non-existent shortcut. For as vapour from the sea rises up into the sky, and falls as rain, or sleet or snow, so too shall we go, and return to the Source ~

♈ ~ I am the first, straight from the Source, energetically emerging from the hidden depths of the Earth and Primordial Waters, fresh and sparkling. I tumble onward - impetuously and enthusiastically. When strong in flow, I feel independent, and lead others, showing them the way to push on. When the flow is weak, I admit to it, tarry awhile, and allow more energy to accumulate until I can oncemore exert and assert myself ~

♉ ~ I now encounter the richness and resistance of the Earth, I savour and ponder Her nature and worth, and in so doing realise my own talents and abilities. When strong in flow, I feel abundant and fertile, and bring the pleasure and reassurance of Nature's goodness to myself and others. When the flow is weak, in order to avoid becoming bogged down, I allow chance and change into my life, freeing and refreshing me ~

♑ ~ the Stream, having become full, is now tested, as I endure Its course through the narrow divides of the canyon. Hemmed in by the steep cliffs of Earthly conditions, I use my natural senses of resourcefulness and ambition to amount to something through negotiating the cataracts of adversity that I now encounter. My power to progress is not in question, for it is inescapable; but my ultimate achievement is to exercise only the control necessary to remain upright and aware of my emotional depths ~

The Zodiaca

We must now remember that we all are Sons and Daughters of the Sun. As Mother Earth travels the year around Father Sun, She and we Her Children follow the Course of the River of Life, the Zodiac, beginning in Aries ♈, through Taurus, on anti-clockwise and around to Pisces, and then to begin again. According to our date of birth, each one of us embodies and plays out a certain stretch of the Life-Stream.

♊ ~ I now divide and criss-cross with other streams. I bubble and froth with the diversity of Life and the amusement and knowledge that it brings. When the flow is strong, I tirelessly make more and more connections, informing and delighting myself and others. When the flow is weak, I allow myself to slow down a little, that I might appreciate my multi-faceted expression of the Life-Stream's possibilities ~

♐ ~ with the crisis of merging now passed, the Stream is freed on to the open plain, where It runs wide and majestic. Upon both banks may be seen sweeping vistas of opportunity and adventure which I am called to take up and explore. So as the Stream proceeds It gathers many experiences that allow me to learn and teach, teach and learn. And lest I flood the banks with excesses or arrogant enthusiasm, I always remember my small and trickling origins - and again the Stream is good ~

ife Stream

Through simply being true to our Sun-Sign, our part in the Life-Stream, the Essence of Life itself shall guide and support us, vitalize and protect us.
The Stream flows inexorably on, around and around, year after year, through the Earthly Seasons that correspond to them. And so we too, like the River, through keeping to our part of the Course, will inevitably find our true Path.

♋ ~ I now settle into a pool of safety and security where I may prosper from Nature's surrounding bounty, and dream in my silent depths. When clear and therefore maintained and fed by the Stream's input and output, I am able and willing to nourish myself and others. When clogged by the silt of stale memories and unnecessary emotions, I become aware of those fresh thoughts and feelings that are readily offered, allowing myself to receive them and be restored by them ~

♏ ~ the merging of two Streams now becomes imperative so my former and lesser self has to die. Should I resist this merging or attempt to coerce others solely for my own ends, then inevitably I shall be cast out, alone, drowned in my own undercurrent. Yet when I sacrifice to the true intimacy of truly joining, the power of the Life-Stream is doubled. With such combined Flow the strength of my inner convictions can move mountains ~

♎ ~ now I meet another Stream of equal strength and importance I sense the natural give and take that must now take place at this place of confluence. Both have equal right of way, and turbulence arises as alternately we each separate and unite, surrender and hold on to our individual identities, yet knowing that merging is inevitable. And so naturally I balance as the Stream swings between separateness and unity ~

♍ ~ now the Stream is checked by difficult terrain, and it becomes critical as to how I proceed. And should I lose a sense of the Flow altogether, I simply remain true to myself and before long I am once more aware of the Stream coursing through me and within me, guiding me and buoying me up. Such experiences create in me sound methods and an intricate knowledge of the nature of things, enabling me to help others through difficult times ~

♌ ~ now the Force rises and accumulates as much as It can, and I overflow and burst forth to show myself to the World - full and ebullient. Being so strong in flow I readily and easily express how it feels to have the Force coursing through and around me, showing and reminding others of Its greatness. When, inevitably, this tide of enthusiasm ebbs, I gracefully and happily languish until once more the Force rushes through ~

2. Laws Of Relating

These Laws apply to how your Sun-Sign relates and functions within a relationship, as well as how your Sign tends to influence the nature of a relationship. Note that the singular form 'relationship' is used here, but in some cases it might mean 'relationships'. Also, rather than an assume that the other person is a partner, I have used the term 'Other' to denote whoever it may be that you are in relationship with.

Apart from using the Laws just for your own or your partner's Sun-Sign, all of these Laws of Relationship can apply to your/their Moon-Sign or Rising Sign (see Resources on page 290). Furthermore, whatever your Sign is, these Laws can act as a general guide to relating in that they are universally applicable.

Aries	38	Libra	50
Taurus	40	Scorpio	52
Gemini	42	Sagittarius	54
Cancer	44	Capricorn	56
Leo	46	Aquarius	58
Virgo	48	Pisces	60

LEANINGS

INDEPENDENCE - In a relationship, it is vitally important that you feel free to do your own thing by following your own individual impulses, seeking Other's approval first of all purely as a formality. However, this should not preclude relying upon one another for support.

ARTLESSNESS - You relate in a childlike way, and are without agenda or guile. This could make for a 'Babes in the Wood' scenario where your naivete is a liability, but this ingenuousness can, if it hasn't already, evolve into an innocent and straightforward nature that Other finds refreshing to be around.

ACTIVITY - Leading an active and physical lifestyle with Other is important to you- that is, you need to be doing things together like sports, walking, dancing, etc. You do not like to stand still, so some competitiveness between you and Other acts as a healthy fillip to making all-important advances.

ADVANTAGES

COURAGE - If there is a battle to be fought or some challenge to be met, you have the guts and push to face the music. Significantly, this includes being prepared to take an honest look at the reason for any difficult circumstances you may be in with Other, and act upon them - as a couple or individually.

LEADERSHIP - In some respect or other, you like to lead the way for Other. Relationship for you should be a pioneering issue in that you could be exploring untried methods of being together, discovering the rules of the game or inventing your own as you go along.

SPONTANEITY- At a moment's notice, you are quite capable of changing your tack or dropping everything and taking off in another direction. So in a relationship, you like to travel light, not be weighed down by unnecessary ties. You can turn the unexpected into an exciting surprise or adventure.

WEAKNESSES

IMPETUOSITY - You leap into relationship before you have a proper look at what you might be getting yourself into, but the chances are it will act as a challenge to be more or less independent. But unless you make the most of your Advantages, such wantonness could also find you leaping equally quickly out of relationship (and into another)!

COMBATIVENESS - You can have quite fierce battles. If the above qualities, like Independence and Activity are not exercised then this could continue to be the case, with destructive consequences. You have to appreciate the difference between a 'good' fight and a 'bad' one.

UNSOCIABILITY - Because you often tend to be into your own thing and ways of doing things, involving other people in your life can be deemed compromising, frustrating or awkward. But this can find you uninvited, bored and lonely at a later date.

TAURUS

LEANINGS

SUBSTANCE - A firm grip and appreciation of the actual facts and possibilities of your being together with Other hold sway. This means that if your relationship works it proves itself simply by enduring and producing something of worth. Conversely, if your relationship lacks a sense of reality, it will not fit in with it and fail to exist to any substantial degree.

POSSESSION - It is important that you and Other feel that you belong to one another and that you have something material, like property, to call your own too. It is as if the proof of and testament to your relationship lies in this 'having and holding' of one another - for better or worse.

TERRITORY - This is inextricably linked with Possession in that you have to have some physical area to call your own. It also means that you need to have clear, uncomplicated boundaries regarding 'right & wrong', and what parts each of you is playing in, and contributing to, the relationship.

ADVANTAGES

STABILITY- You provide a good base for creating and maintaining anything - particularly a family. There is also an relaxing, unhurried atmosphere about you, and others see you as something permanent which endures amidst the storms of life in general.

SENSUALITY - You have a strong sense and appreciation of the physical and aesthetic pleasures of life, qualities which probably attracted Other to you in the first place. And you would continue to be sensual with one another, possibly despite any decline that might occur in other areas of relating.

PRODUCTIVITY - Ultimately, the whole point to your being with someone is to create something more that what you are as an individual. As well as this meaning the likelihood of raising a family or being in a business partnership, you probably actively pursue arts or crafts together or individually, and pass it on to your kin.

WEAKNESSES

OBSTINACY - You are slow or resistant to any kind of change or anything 'newfangled' or suggestive of transformation. This could be regarded as the necessary downside to being so stable and enduring, but if taken too far such stubbornness can lead to a stagnation within your relationship itself.

JEALOUSY - Because you invest a great deal of yourself into your relationship with Other in order to create that all-important dependability, you are understandably sensitive to any third party upsetting the apple cart. But should this occur it would be owing to your resisting change on other levels - that is, the third party or a chance event could be merely an agent of change.

GULLIBILITY - Wholesome and uncomplicated as your relationship might be, at least on the outside, such can give rise to a psychologically rather unsophisticated attitude - a bit like the farmer and his wife. This can find you precariously uninformed and open to being taken advantage of - or just plain bored.

GEMINI

LEANINGS

INTEREST - You depend upon a constant stream of various interests to stimulate you. It is as if you are a pair of lungs that has to breathe in order to live, taking in all sorts of ideas, people and experiences. Such curiosity also makes for being an interesting as an individual, in one way or another.

COMMUNICATION - Having plenty to talk about, both with Other and people outside of your relationship, is very likely and quite essential. In fact, without this intellectual stimulation, a relationship could flag. Consequently, you will endeavour to ensure that a supply of contacts and information is always forthcoming - even if it irritates Other at times.

LIGHTNESS - You do not as a rule like to get too heavy or bogged down through looking too deeply into the whys and wherefores of your being with Other - not unless you really have to. You like to tread lightly across the surface of things and not look under every emotional stone.

ADVANTAGES

EASY-GOING - The laid-back and friendly quality that is the product of that Lightness above, is pleasant and refreshing for Other to be around. As a person you are therefore popular, although possibly very few would really know you. Be that as it may, such affability is priceless.

YOUTHFULNESS - You are quite young in the way you behave with Other. Unless there's some really heavy jelly going down, you usually have a skip in your step, and can put one into Other's as well. You are able to tune into the latest fashions and possibly use your creative wits to contribute to and profit from such.

HUMOUR - You see the funny side of life and probably create fun have a good laugh with Other. In company you will bring out the wit and brilliance of others, making for highly stimulating gatherings. At your best, you can see your own joke, but not take yourself or your relationship too lightly either.

WEAKNESSES

FLIPPANCY - This, the shadow of your Lightness, may not become a problem - but it could attract a situation that forces you to dig deeper into your feelings, or to understand why you are with Other. You may be able to coast along unperturbed for quite some time - but not indefinitely.

FRIVOLITY - This would be an excess of the Lightness mentioned above, and as such can degenerate into a dangerous disrespect for your own and Other's feelings. Ironically, this breeziness may have been initially what Other found so attractive about you - like a light relief.

DISTRACTION - Another irony of the inherent inclination of your Sign to seek variety and avoid difficult emotions is that you get into a rut of never being with an Other long enough. Something or someone is always getting the attention of one or the other of you. For the same reason, flirtatiousness born of a reluctance to commit can also be a weakening influence.

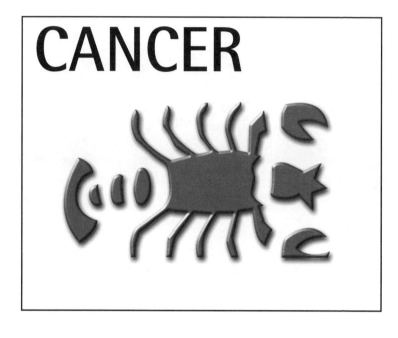

LEANINGS

SECURITY - The outright ruling need of your Sign is to feel safe and comfortable with Other and in the sense of your being a couple who together feel protected from the hard cold world outside. Needless to say, a home or place of retreat is your primary material requirement for a relationship to exist.

FAMILIARITY - You form yourself and Other into a private, family-oriented unit quite instinctively, with all the plusses and minuses of such a state. You also like a definite measure of routine and predictability in your relationship, for this maintains a feeling of certainty and natural rhythm.

DREAMINESS - When in relationship, you live quite close to the unconscious. This can mean anything from being driven by conditioned needs or fears, to being pleasantly wistful and vague, to being actively concerned as a couple with the whole realm of dream-life and the workings of the unconscious mind.

ADVANTAGES

SENTIMENTALITY - You have a childlike, romantic way of being in relationship with Other. Nostalgia and the value of the past play an important part in your manner of relating. People who have associated with you from the beginning of your relationship have a special place in your heart.

PROTECTION - This has primarily to do with your natural ability to raise a happy family - or at least, a family that has a strong family feel to it. This is founded upon a sympathy and concern that you have for Other's welfare. This may, or should, persist despite any falling out.

TENACITY - You are able to hang in with Other through decidedly tough circumstances. This will be mainly because of the need to keep family together, or simply to continue what you are both so accustomed to. You are probably tied to one other by bonds stronger than you may appreciate - which is why you could keep testing them, or having them tested.

WEAKNESSES

HABIT - Your need for the familiar and predictable can insidiously amount to doing things together purely because you have got into the habit of doing so. These things may actually become negative or stress-producing. Make a conscious effort to identify and break such habits for there is an ultimate danger of the relationship itself becoming one.

BLACKMAIL - Owing to the strong needs for Security and Protection, there is unfortunately an inclination on one or both of your parts to use guilt and/or indispensability to keep the other where you want them. Indeed, this is a cancer that can be the death of a relationship - so root it out.

MOODINESS - Being so feeling and needs-oriented, it is not surprising that your being with Other can create an emotional swell that has you (both) lurching from high to low, from desperate to hopeful - and reacting to one another to perpetuate this. You should contact the inner child in yourself and in Other and heal its hurts - or you'll 'drown'.

LEANINGS

PLAYFULNESS - A sense of drama and of the game of life is vital to your Sun-Sign. Playing in the way that children do (make-believe, costumes, characterisation, pet names, etc.) creates a sense of relationship being fun and romantic, and not just a lack-lustre, day-to-day business. Parties, passions and highs and lows are what your Sign thrives upon.

CREATIVITY - Art or some other form of self-expression, individually or together with Other, gives and maintains the sense of personal uniqueness and self-esteem that creates the all-important mutual respect essential to your relationship. Having and bringing up children is also regarded as creativity.

HIERARCHY - Who's in charge of what is a serious issue, so you and Other must consciously and deliberately devise and agree upon individual duties, positions and rights - or else chaos can reign. Having a sense of respect for one another - and respect for and from others generally - is important.

ADVANTAGES

STYLE - Your Sun-Sign usually attracts a comparatively upmarket lifestyle, even if it is slightly down-at-the-heel in itself - paupers in a stately home kind of thing. Others find your relationship exciting or eventful to be around for you make sure that as a couple you exude a sense of occasion, this all being part of the Creativity.

WARMTH - There is a good-heartedness you create within your relationship which also radiates out to friends and family. There is also an enthusiastic appreciation and recognition of talent or class in those around you, especially your children. Hospitality is granted to those that are gracious, and always graciously received.

DIGNITY - Your Sun-Sign demands that high standards of behaviour be set and maintained. Consequently, shady or shoddy goings-on are not tolerated - or they shouldn't be. Respect for Others' time and situation is strongly linked to the respect shown for your own time and situation.

WEAKNESSES

PRIDE - This is really an over-sensitivity towards having your dirty laundry aired in public. You do not like the world to see any cracks in your relationship. But ironically, what are regarded as shortcomings by you are probably regarded as quite normal by ordinary, lesser mortals.

MELODRAMA - This is a case of making a crisis out of a what could have been simply passed over as an everyday emotional hiccup. Such a reaction stems from your sense that life should always be larger than it actually or usually is. Such a crisis can turn into a real disaster.

ELITISM - There is a sense of specialness that you imbue your relationship with that can unfortunately devolve into an exclusiveness that allows very few people into it. This can eventually result in a somewhat incestuous affair that drowns in an excess of itself, and suffocates for lack of external input.

VIRGO

LEANINGS

PURITY - This is a much misunderstood concept which you can fall foul of because it is central to your Sun-Sign. The Latin virgo refers to something which is 'nothing but itself' - that is, not sullied by anything or missing anything. So a relationship for you has to have a distinct quality and purpose which must be identified so that it may be worked upon, improved, and kept in tact.

HEALTH - The promotion and maintenance of a healthy relationship - be it mentally, physically, emotionally or spiritually - is an issue that should concern you. Such health, and the helpfulness you have toward Other which characterises it, becomes a mainstay to the whole of your relationship.

ORDER - Legendary Virgoan tidiness is one of the issues here. You like a relationship to have a sense of order about it, so both of you maintaining domestic and personal tidiness and hygiene is important, as too is being precise in what you say to one another or discriminating in what you do together.

ADVANTAGES

SOBRIETY - This may sound like a rather dull asset but it does in fact go a long way towards keeping a relationship on an even keel. And should there be an indulgent streak in you too, you are aware of it and keep it within healthy bounds.

IDIOSYNCRASY - There is a quality to your relationship that is both complex and unique. Others may find it difficult, in some respects, to see what you have going for you as a couple, but that is because you have this link which is exquisitely personal. An aspect of love you could call the 'glass slipper'.

HARDWORKING - For you, industriousness is an integral part of the fabric of a relationship. You do not mind time apart spent working, and ideally you can work together quite happily too. Moreover, you are of service to Other, and you (should) also work hard at improving the relationship itself.

WEAKNESSES

FUSSINESS - Avoid a neurotic need for Order, for this would be counter-productive. This is most likely to manifest in being over-critical of Other, or of those around you. Underlying such a corrosive inclination as this is a lack of acceptance of something within yourself as an individual.

INHIBITION - You may not notice it, but lurking somewhere within you is a fear of doing or saying something. This may well be sexual in nature. It is as if you are afraid to expose or plunge into some issue - but failing to do this could cause this very thing to go critical.

PARSIMONY - In relationship you should have a natural sense of economy. Unfortunately, this can devolve into a stinginess with yourself and Other. Really, this is emotional in nature for it smacks of being afraid or reluctant to give something of yourself to Other. You probably think there is something about you that is too personal or would be censored - but you would be wrong in thinking this - or at least, in allowing Other to judge you so.

LIBRA

LEANINGS

HARMONY - 'Don't let the Sun go down on your wrath' could be a very apt motto for you with regard to maintaining a relationship. Striving for a pleasant and peaceful atmosphere is vital to your well-being in a relationship. As such, your Sun-Sign is the most effective for maintaining a positive partnership.

JUSTICE - Having a sound sense of what is right and wrong with regard to one person's behaviour towards another is of paramount importance to you. It is as if you are innately aware that there is such a thing as 'establishing right relations' and you strive morally to achieve this.

ART - Life without Art is for you is a life which is not worth living. So in your daily lives together it is imperative that you have beauty and elegance around you for most of the time, especially where you live. If you don't already, pursue some form of artistic practice or appreciation.

ADVANTAGES

CONSIDERATION - You take time out to weigh the pros and cons, and the best way of going about relating to Other. You have the sensibility to take into consideration the emotional and social positions of Other with a view to alleviating or improving their situation.

AESTHETICS - You have an awareness of how to please Other. The look, taste, smell, sound and feel of things is something which you deem highly desirable and significant. You use music and fine food to good effect, to entertain or simply live amidst.

SOCIABILITY - You should be quite popular for you grace your social environment to one degree or another. Most significantly, when in relationship you are, or at least appear to be, an item in the accepted sense of the term. You are a testament to the fact that a harmonious couple create harmony around them.

WEAKNESSES

INDECISIVENESS - Being merely a social response to your social environment finds you lacking in the direction and principles needed to determine what you want in a relationship as something in its own right. Choosing an emotional objective and progressively striving toward it is the answer.

TIMIDITY - Because of your need to be liked, appreciated, understood or approved of, you can lack the identity that is spirited and sure enough of its own integrity not to be manipulated or compromised by Other. Forge your own strengths and do not compromise them because of Other's.

SUPERFICIALITY - If you find your life getting meaningless, or that you are merely have a relationship in name only, then it is because you have settled for a semblance of compatibility, for being in a relationship for fear of being alone. Dig beneath the surface for your true motivations and a true relationship will eventually follow.

SCORPIO

LEANINGS

INTENSITY - With your Sun-Sign there is no danger of your relationship being insipid. You are drawn to Other initially by powerful urges such as sexual desire or emotional hunger. It is also likely that you will at some time have these feelings re-intensified by some factor, like a third party.

INVOLVEMENT - The chemistry between you and Other is such that you become automatically and progressively more involved. This is an all-or-nothing kind of thing, and you will make a bond increasingly inextricable through the establishing of joint finances, shared investments, and more to the point, unconscious ties that are kept intact by certain taboos. For you sex is more psychological than physical, that you are sharing more than just body fluids.

CRISIS - Your Sign does not make for a smooth, uneventful partnership, however much you may want or pretend to have such a thing. In fact, pretence and compromise would quicken the process whereby you are plunged into profound emotional experiences, from grief to great intimacy.

ADVANTAGES

INSIGHT - The more you are involved with someone, the greater your sense of what lies beneath the surface of not just each other but anyone that spends any time with you. In relationship you can develop a penetrating insight into the inner truths of life. This could, in some cases, lead to an interest in the occult.

GENUINENESS - You can be trusted to express yourself in a manner that is unalloyed by formality. Such emotional authenticity can act like a magnet to Other, as well as giving any children you might have a deep sense of the worth of (their own) feelings.

COMMITMENT - The dynamics of your Sign guarantee, through one means and another, that your relationship has emotional substance and a lasting psychological bond. Where priorities are concerned, sentiment, romantic love and social niceties fall way behind your 'urge to merge'.

WEAKNESSES

MANIPULATION - Much as, or rather because, you want to be involved with another body and soul, there is also the temptation to use underhand means to achieve this objective. Using Other's desires and fears to keep them where you want them can do this, but the price you pay is being in bondage rather than having a loving bond.

SECRETIVENESS - A feature of Manipulation is enabled by having the 'dope' on Other. But this means that you and Other will then keep certain things to yourselves which effectively undermines the relationship because such secretiveness is denying access to one another. A cold war, in fact.

DESTRUCTIVENESS - This is the 'nothing' part of the above-described 'all or nothing' quality of your Sun-Sign. If, along with Manipulation and Secretiveness, the negative aspects of distrust and suspicion - the hazards of intimacy - are allowed to get out of control, a relationship dies a death. And because of an inherent lack of forgiveness it might be a lingering one.

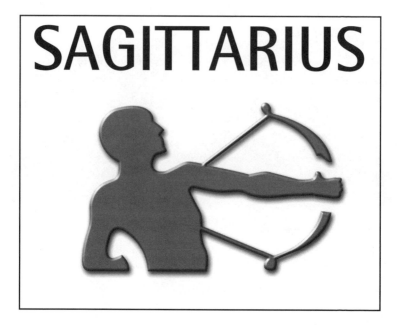

LEANINGS

IDEALISM - You feel and know that there is something that you are seeking. This could be finding the meaning of a sound and healthy partnership, raising a wholesome family, or even striving toward some religious objective together. Whatever it might be, you have a sense of there being something you have to make or discover as a couple that is higher and better.

FURTHERANCE - This springs from the Idealism. Because you have this expansive sense of life, and of yourself and your partner, going somewhere, you pursue various projects or programs that are in aid of educating, promoting and furthering you and yours - or you just travel/explore a lot together.

ETHICS - You like to share with Other a sense of there being a right and a wrong way of relating. Possibly you devise a set of 'laws' for your relationship to steer itself by. Or, your relationship itself may raise some moral issue that you have to contend with, which in turn determines its success or failure.

ADVANTAGES

CONFIDENCE - There is an innate sense of sureness within and about you. Whatever the status of your relationship or the feelings between you and Other, there exists a certain positivity, or at least an absence of neurosis. Consequently, you go about things with an enthusiasm and optimism that breeds success.

ADVENTUROUSNESS - In relationship, you make for being an outgoing couple, meaning that you can be active together in the field of sports, outdoor pursuits, travel, partying or anything that takes you out of yourselves. You do not get cooped up and gloomy together. You see the world as your oyster and make the most of it.

CONTEMPORARY - You are in tune with the culture you are living in and therefore make an advantage out of it; you know who or what is 'in'. So in a relationship you are also 'in flow' with the times, giving you a sense of where things are bound politically, morally, religiously, educationally, etc..

WEAKNESSES

SMUGNESS - This is the downside of being so positive and with it. You can get carried away on the wave of your own sense of enjoyment or of being right. Like a hot-air balloon, you get so 'high' that you do not notice you have left reality and Other - or people in general - way behind. So eventually you disappear into nothing or come crashing down to Earth.

NONCHALANCE - Negatively, your essentially broad and expansive nature as can reach a point where you lose sight of you and Other as ordinary emotional people with their 'little' problems and concerns. Realise this and you will restore your feelings for one another.

TRENDINESS - There is a danger of mistaking what most people appear to be doing as being right merely because that is the general trend. Being 'in the know' is another possible pitfall. You may even flip this over and be disdainful of what's in vogue. In either case, you can lose sight of the importance of having your own values as a relationship - and ultimately of each other.

CAPRICORN

LEANINGS

RESPONSIBILITY - Without a serious purpose to a relationship which must be observed and adhered to, one would not exist at all. This can mean that a relationship has responsibility as an inherent part of it, or that this is precisely what is imposed upon you in order that you may learn from it.

TRADITION - You are inclined to follow a quite conventional route in your relationship - namely marriage, officially or unofficially. But whether you remain together because you want to or have to is another matter, as too is how it appears on the outside not necessarily concurring with how you are in private.

REGULATION - An order and pattern to your life with Other is something that seems to get installed one way or another. Possibly you are in a business together which dictates this. Whether it is this, or running home and family, you make it into a businesslike affair with routines, economy, etc.

ADVANTAGES

DUTIFULNESS - Because you conduct your relationship in such a responsible manner, you come to rely upon one another more and more as time goes by. And with time comes trust and the learning of valuable lessons which enable you to build your relationship into something lasting.

OBJECTIVITY - You are not one to let emotions get the better of you to a point where you overlook the practical realities of your relationship and the situation in which it exists. Whether it is a family, a business or anything else you are responsible for, you see what has to be done, and do it.

CONSTRUCTIVITY - Being practical and aware of material issues - or at least when the relationship has made you be so - you set about ensuring that you and yours amount to something in the world at large. Professional plans and activities (should) come high up on your list of priorities.

WEAKNESSES

COLDNESS - Not surprisingly, a disadvantage of the above-described practicality and Objectivity is that your inner feelings get over-looked or suppressed. In time, this could find you seriously out of touch with the very feelings that endeared you to Other - and them to you - in the first place.

RIGIDITY - Whatever pattern or order you have devised, possibly over years, to create stability and security, could devolve into tramlines that you have to keep to day-in and day-out. If this has made your relationship stale and into a meaningless drudge, then consciously introduce some change and flexibility.

AUSTERITY - Economy is one thing, but denial is another. An almost Dickensian set of values can creep up on you, causing you, either emotionally or materially, to be mean with yourself, and Other too. This would reflect the degree to which the love and soul had drained from your relationship owing to that Coldness and a need to control.

AQUARIUS

LEANINGS

LIBERATION - Through your relationship you look for the true reason for being in a relationship at all. It is essential that you have an openness with Other as only this can grant you the freedom to find out why you are together as a unique couple of two unique human beings. Ultimately, yours is an issue of finding the right amount of freedom within a relationship - neither too much nor too little.

UNUSUALNESS - This goes hand in hand with Liberation because without being unusual in some way, your relationship would conform to some stereotype which stifles freedom and originality. Relatively at least, you should be involved with Other in some out of the ordinary or awakening pursuits.

EQUALITY - The presence of any kind of discrimination between you and Other is an abomination for it goes against the basic fabric of your relationship, whether you know it or not. Any thought of one of you being better or less than the other would automatically destabilise the whole relationship.

ADVANTAGES

ORIGINALITY- Like a distinct individual, your relationship is one that follows its own star, is true to itself. This will also be evidenced in the actual circumstances of your being together having a unique and unprecedented quality. You can inspire other couples to be this way too.

BROAD-MINDEDNESS - There is an openness and spirit of experimentation about your being with Other. You not only tolerate odd traits and circumstances, but may even venture into unusual and ground-breaking ways of discovering your sexual and emotional parameters.

FRIENDLINESS - This quality of your Sun-Sign is highly valuable in a relationship because it is actually more reliable than say passion or what passes for love. This is because friendliness is non-possessive and non-judgmental, and you bestow it upon Other and whoever else is involved with you.

WEAKNESSES

INDIFFERENCE - Because your relationship inclines toward cool impartiality rather than fiery passion, there is an incipient tendency to 'de-emotionalise' your interaction with Other so that gradually an absence of motivation or meaning can beset you as a couple - or at least, your half of it.

ALIENATION - In relationship, you stand in danger of cutting yourself off from Other and the society or culture in which they live. When your qualities of Unusualness and Originality are not recognised or positively expressed, you tacitly or actively turn yourself - or yourselves as a couple - into misfit or outcast.

REBELLIOUSNESS - This is really the Shadow of your specialness and uniqueness . Rather than living and expressing your sense of Freedom and Originality, you attract the 'petty tyrant', that is, someone who suppresses you, causing you merely to rebel or be bolshy. Then again, rebellion may be your only way to free yourself.

PISCES

LEANINGS

IMAGINATION - Relationship for you, whether you are aware of it or not, is largely determined by what you imagine it to be. As you feed Other's imagination, you progressively make them into what you hope or fear them to be. If you have a positive vision, then that is what they and the relationship shall develop into. If vague, negative or unconscious however - then chaos could descend.

SACRIFICE - There is something about the energy of your relationship that attracts, sooner or later, a need to make a sacrifice. This could occur willingly or unwillingly, and be accompanied by great suffering. When this is consciously surrendered to, a great sense of peace or bliss envelopes you.

SENSITIVITY - This, arguably the definitive human quality, runs through your relationship like a river through a valley, bringing it life and beauty. Great care must therefore be taken that it never dries up through denying, suppressing or over-rationalising it. Being ever sensitive to one another, without being hysterical, will elevate and refine your relationship.

ADVANTAGES

COMPASSION - This, the ultimate product of Sensitivity, is something you extend to not just Other but all those around and about you. You may even be actively involved in some charitable organisation together. Somehow, your relationship may cause one or both of you to pursue some 'good work'.

ARTISTRY - It is quite possible that you are involved in some form of artistic expression. In any event, the way that you relate and live could be an art-form in itself. One way or another, the creative flow and process is, or should be, central to your relationship, for this vitalises it.

PSYCHISM - You are highly attuned to Other's thoughts and feelings. At its most evolved, this can find you living and acting as one. The experiencing of psychic phenomena - be it discarnate entities, significant coincidences or whatever - should and could give your relationship guidance and spiritual meaning.

WEAKNESSES

FANTASY - Owing to the influence of so much Sensitivity and Imagination, there is a danger of you pretending your relationship is something that it is not. This may even include believing you have a viable relationship when you don't. The only remedy is to determine the truth of what you are together actually is - and gracefully accept it.

EVASIVENESS - Again, owing to your innate Sensitivity, there can be a reluctance to take a good look at what is actually happening in your relationship. Trust, that by following and being true to that river of feelings, you will both find a way through to the 'ocean' of peace and healing.

ADDICTION - If one or both of you is any way addicted to a substance or a distracted or compulsive way of being, or to the other or another person, then Fantasy and Evasiveness have done their worst. Here, the best, and maybe only way is one of you seeking spiritual help and redemption.

3.SIGN-TO-SIGN INTERACTION

Simply go to the double-page spread that has the heading which refers to your Sun-Sign, i.e. (SIGN) INTERACTS WITH, and find below it a simple and helpful description of how you interact with any other Sign, (including your own) along with a suggestion of how to be positive about any such relationship. The single adverb that is used to sum up how any two Signs interact (e.g. Virgo Interacts with Pisces Humbly) is sometimes also used to suggest how those two Signs are advised to relate. Also each Sign is matched in terms of an archetypal quality, like Aries=Leader, Taurus=Banker, etc.

If you happen to know you and your partner's Sign positions for the Moon, all the Planets and your Ascendant (Rising Sign)* then you can compare them in the same way but with regard to the Planet in question. That is, how you interact emotionally will be your Moon-Signs; how you communicate: Mercury-Signs; romantically/socially: Venus; sexually/physically: Mars; morally/growing together: Jupiter; durability/responsibility: Saturn; spontaneously: Rising Signs.

*To discover these and more, see my books Do It Yourself Astrology, and Dynamic Synastry (which goes into the complex subject of relating in far more depth and detail).

ARIES interacts with

ARIES *impulsively*

TWO LEADERS - Everything depends upon your sharing the same goals and principles. At the positive extreme, you will charge through life together in an uncomplicated way, getting where you want to get to as a couple, and as independent beings. If your directions are too dissimilar though, you are probably one of the record-holders for short-lived relationships!

TAURUS *compromisingly*

THE LEADER AND THE BANKER - Your criteria are so different. Aries sees life in terms of going ahead no matter what; Taurus in terms of weighing the cost and hanging on to what they've got. Meeting halfway could create a relationship that satisfies both basic needs and the urge go forward. But a forceful ego and a stubborn one are, as a rule, never about to.

GEMINI *easily*

THE LEADER AND THE JESTER - This is a youthful pairing with the highs and lows that such speed, enthusiasm and self-interest engender. So as far as it goes, this can be stimulating and uncomplicated. You are both agile and freedom-loving enough to avoid a heavily passionate or intense involvement. Outside attractions could change all this however.

CANCER *uncomfortably*

THE LEADER AND THE MATRIARCH - Such classic extremes as Arian independence and Cancerian dependence can only find anything approaching harmony in a very traditional set-up where the Aries is male and wins the bread, and the Crab is female and keeps the home Failing this, Arian selfishness and Cancerian neediness can only torment one another.

LEO *heroically*

THE LEADER AND THE MONARCH - Much can be achieved and with plenty of fun and excitement too. But this can become a problem if the interaction turns into a competition to see who can dominate or win the most. When both of you are directing your prodigious energies towards a common goal, guided by similar principles, all goes well.

VIRGO *inappropriately*

THE LEADER AND THE ADVISOR - The problem for Virgo is that Aries will not listen and jumps in headfirst, and then, maybe, will listen when its too late. So Aries should learn to listen, weigh Virgo's advice carefully, and then act - or not. Virgo is learning to be more forceful, be more sure of their own counsel, and ultimately to act upon it themselves.

ARIES interacts with

LIBRA confrontationally

THE LEADER AND THE DIPLOMAT - You can work as a team as long as Aries is allowed to forge ahead in their straightforward way, while Libra irons out the bumps caused by this. Also, Libra's pleasantness and Aries' forcefulness can temper one another. But without recognising how different you are, it can be felt as uncouthness and niceness grating horribly.

SCORPIO explosively

THE LEADER AND THE SPY - This is rather like fire and ice meeting up; a lot of passionate hissing and melting at first, but inevitably your elemental natures compromise one another, causing rage and resentment. Scorpio comes disdainfully to see Aries' straightforwardness as stupid, and Aries cannot abide Scorpio's covert behaviour. Gut-wrenching honesty is needed.

SAGITTARIUS enterprisingly

THE LEADER AND THE PRIEST - This marries together a strong sense of being after something in life with the justification for getting it. Consequently, you have the wherewithal to go far and achieve a great deal. If this sounds more like an enterprise than a relationship, then you have spotted that a sense of personal intimacy could be amiss - but what matter?

CAPRICORN conflictingly

THE LEADER AND THE PRESIDENT - Together you have the makings of success, but it is unfortunate and more likely that one of you feels superior to the other - usually Capricorn over Aries. So ultimately, as neither of you is one to be bested, rebellion or resistance, or locked horns, is a strong likelihood. A common goal, or enemy, might help to unite you.

AQUARIUS progressively

THE LEADER AND THE REFORMIST - This is a relationship that can really go places, change things, set new standards, etc.. You are both independent and freedom loving, and so respect each other's space and wishes. There is a dark side to such undeniable brightness and lightness however: the little needy child hiding in one or both of you can get overlooked.

PISCES inappropriately

THE LEADER AND THE MESSIAH - Aries wants to win, Pisces is prepared to turn the other cheek. Aries takes direct action, Pisces uses passive resistance. It might initially seem that one of you is saving the other - but later it gets confusing as to who is saviour and who is victim. A case of tragically mistaken identities - unless you explode your respective myths.

TAURUS interacts with

ARIES compromisingly

THE BANKER AND THE LEADER - Your criteria are so different. Aries sees life in terms of going ahead no matter what; Taurus in terms of weighing the cost and hanging on to what they've got. Meeting halfway could create a relationship that satisfies both basic needs and the urge go forward. But a forceful ego and a stubborn one are, as a rule, never about to.

TAURUS solidly

TWO BANKERS - Hopefully you started off together on the right foot, because if you didn't it is unlikely to get any better. Why? Because two Bulls are twice as unlikely to change as one of them! But Nature and Her rhythms being what they are, you are likely to attract or encounter some-one or something that forces you to change. This way lies true prosperity.

GEMINI awkwardly

THE BANKER AND THE JESTER - The image here is of the Bull peacefully grazing his field when along comes a bee to buzz around his head. Taurus provides and abides, while Gemini stops things from getting too settled. You both need what the other supplies, but a failure to realise and accept this would attract greater threats to Taurus' stability and Gemini's freedom.

CANCER comfortably

THE BANKER AND THE MATRIARCH - This is a bit like the farmer and his wife; a natural, traditional and productive arrangement of things. There will also be other timeworn elements as well though - like possessive and jealousy, and classic gender roles with their plusses and minuses. But these are as Nature's price for this wholesome combination.

LEO difficultly

THE BANKER AND THE MONARCH - This is a solid and lasting combination, but it is unlikely to be without it storms. It is essential that you both appreciate what each is providing. Taurus could be seen as providing the 'stage' or steadiness, and Leo the 'drama' or excitement. Without such an agreement no amount of pleasure or wealth will compensate.

VIRGO agreeably

THE BANKER AND THE ADVISOR - This is a very harmonious combination. Taurus provides and Virgo maintains - and should Taurus get too bogged down in material things, Virgo coaxes them towards the finer things of life in the delicate manner they appreciate. The Bull's part is kindly to keep Virgo mindful of the wood when the trees get in their way.

TAURUS interacts with

LIBRA indulgently

THE BANKER AND THE DIPLOMAT - Because you both like set procedures and ways of doing things, it would be a wonder if you ever gelled in a natural, emotional sense. Yours is more of an arrangement that has the pleasures of the flesh and society as a substitute for anything more profound. As far as this goes, you can enjoy this sedate and stable... arrangement.

SCORPIO powerfully

THE BANKER AND THE SPY - The Bull wants to keep things stable and as they are; the Scorpion wants to get down to the hidden emotional roots of why they are. The Earth and the Underworld are embedded together, yet they jealously guard their own realms. For this passionate involvement to work each must respect how different yet interdependent they are.

SAGITTARIUS disagreeably

THE BANKER AND THE PRIEST - At first Sag looks like an exciting prospect to the Bull, but before too long they just don't deliver what Taurus thought they were promised. To Sag, Taurus initially seems to be the anchor they need, but they wind up feeling tethered by them. A healthy exchange could occur, if your different currencies or value systems would allow it.

CAPRICORN prosperously

THE BANKER AND THE PRESIDENT - You make a stable, industrious and eventually affluent couple, and enjoy together the pleasures of the flesh. Both of you have a style of living that is power-based, with Cap initiating projects and Taurus maintaining funds. As long as neither of you becomes greedy or philistine, you will last and last, happily and securely.

AQUARIUS unsuitably

THE BANKER AND THE REFORMIST - As Taurus effectively 'invests' in a relationship, they get extra-possessive when Aquarius shows signs of going out on a limb, as is their wont. Earth and Air co-exist rather than unite as seen in the differing priorities of Taurean physical needs and Aquarian mental abstractions. Both being stubborn, you persist - mostly in vain.

PISCES symbiotically

THE BANKER AND THE MESSIAH - This has all the joy and security of a fertile island set in a mysterious sea. You provide one other with what each needs: Fishes get something solid to contain and feed them; the Bull is kept alive to the wonders of life. Only your egoistic extremes of playing it too safe or of being too evasive could scotch this potentially fine match.

GEMINI interacts with

ARIES easily

THE JESTER AND THE LEADER - This is a youthful pairing with the highs and lows that such speed, enthusiasm and self-interest engender. So as far as it goes, this can be stimulating and uncomplicated. You are both agile and freedom-loving enough to avoid a heavily passionate or intense involvement. Outside attractions could change all this however.

TAURUS compromisingly

THE JESTER AND THE BANKER - The image here is of the Bull peacefully grazing his field when along comes a bee to buzz around his head. Taurus provides and abides, while Gemini stops things from getting too settled. You both need what the other supplies, but a failure to realise and accept this would attract greater threats to Taurus' stability and Gemini's freedom.

GEMINI nimbly

TWO JESTERS - This can be a case of who's fooling who as you both weave in and out of contact. As long as neither of you crave anything more emotionally profound and do not look too deeply into things, life can be a breeze. But should such avoiding of each other's heartland cease to satisfy, then that breeze could stiffen into an icy gale. Two butterflies.

CANCER tentatively

THE JESTER AND THE MATRIARCH - Like blossom and fruit respectively, one must leave the tree and the other must stay on it until ripe. You are part of the same process but you do not gel at all easily. Gemini being off and about to bring home fresh ideas and people, while Cancer keeps the home, could work. But if Crab cling, Twins no come home at all.

LEO good-naturedly

THE JESTER AND THE MONARCH - This is a playful interaction. It may appear to be on Leo's terms, but actually Gemini's clever sense of humour, love of variety, and the detachment that goes with it, has the Lion by the tail at times. Overall, quite a subtle interaction for it engenders a tacit understanding based on Leo's power and Gemini's wit.

VIRGO annoyingly

THE JESTER AND THE ADVISOR - Both of you have a lot to say, but because each of you have different agendas or priorities a lot does not get understood. Virgo thinks practically, Gemini thinks for its own sake. And with all this thinking and talking there can be little room for any real emotional interplay. Still, you can learn a lot from one another, and have fun too.

GEMINI interacts with

LIBRA smartly

THE JESTER AND THE DIPLOMAT - You both have your own, yet compatible ways, of deftly manipulating things into appearing easier than they really are. And so you support one another in this to the extent of actually making things easier than they ought to be! As long as you are both happy to live and love so cerebrally, without profound emotions, all will be fine.

SCORPIO abrasively

THE JESTER AND THE SPY - Gemini makes light of things, while Scorpio makes heavy of them. A deal could be struck here, but the Twins lightness is seen by Scorpio as flippancy and emotional insincerity. Gemini regards Scorpio's depth as treacherous and hard work, so they wriggle even more. There can be a peculiar intrigue here, but not a bond to relax with.

SAGITTARIUS curiously

THE JESTER AND THE PRIEST - This is not such an unlikely combination as it appears. Gemini's streetwise wit can keep Sag from being pious and out of touch, while Sag can provide the Twins with an overall view or philosophy that can knit together their scattered thoughts. Failing this though, Sag could look down on Gemini, who then snaps at Sag's heels.

CAPRICORN condescendingly

THE JESTER AND THE PRESIDENT - On a material level, Cap is infinitely more astute and powerful than the Twins, whom they tolerate to keep them informed and amused. But Gemini may secretly regard Cap as a boring goat that they'll milk for what they've got and then be off. A mutual recognition of the real people would help, IF you both gave it the time.

AQUARIUS cerebrally

THE JESTER AND THE REFORMIST - You are both very much on the same wavelength, seeing life as a thing of the mind, spinning endless word plays and abstract concepts into a fabric which you agree on as being reality. The pattern you weave together makes sense and is fun, yet it may not be that fulfilling emotionally. But that is probably alright by both of you.

PISCES adaptively

THE JESTER AND THE MESSIAH - At some rarefied level you are akin, attuned, as you both are, to the truth that we reach the sublime through a blending of humour and humility. But unless you are spiritually disciplined, such can find you all froth and no substance. Something needs to keep you both down to earth - possibly the friends you delight, or a child.

CANCER interacts with

ARIES uncomfortably

THE MATRIARCH AND THE LEADER - Such classic extremes as Arian independence and Cancerian dependence can only find anything approaching harmony in a very traditional set-up where the Aries is male and wins the bread, and the Crab is female and keeps the home. Failing this, Arian selfishness and Cancerian neediness can only torment one another.

TAURUS comfortably

THE MATRIARCH AND THE BANKER - This is a bit like the farmer and his wife; a natural, traditional and productive arrangement of things. There will also be other timeworn elements as well though - like possessive and jealousy, and classic gender roles with their plusses and minuses. But these are as Nature's price for this wholesome combination.

GEMINI tentatively

THE MATRIARCH AND THE JESTER - Like fruit and blossom respectively, one must stay on the tree until ripe and the other must leave it. You are part of the same process but you do not gel at all easily. Gemini being off and about to bring home fresh ideas and people, while Cancer keeps the home, could work. But if Crab cling, Twins no come home at all.

CANCER caringly

TWO MATRIARCHS - Your instinctual need and sense of security, along with a warm and personal manner, ensures that you are Nature's veritable nest-builders and family-raisers. But as ever with same-Sign combinations, you get the best and the worst of them. In your case, beware of coddling you and yours to the point where your individual beings are lost sight of.

LEO dramatically

THE MATRIARCH AND THE MONARCH - Leo gives a sparkle to Cancer's security-oriented and possibly limited lifestyle; Cancer provides a sense of family and belonging. Unless this exchange is appreciated, Leo will soon feel suffocated by such 'familiarity', and the Crab can come to resent and feel threatened by the Lion's love of excitement.

VIRGO naturally

THE MATRIARCH AND THE ADVISOR - You are 'Mother Nature's own' in that together you create a comfortable, efficient and caring environment, be that in the home or wherever. The downside to this is that you can live in each other's pockets to the point of suffocation. The occasional outing would offset the 'risk of too much safety' in this excellent combination.

CANCER interacts with

LIBRA warily

THE MATRIARCH AND THE DIPLOMAT - Cancer needs security and Libra wants peace, which is a good foot to start out on. But whereas security is maintained by containing things, peace is sought by opening things up, being more gregarious - and this is where you can fail to understand one another. For harmony and comfort, respect your individual roles in this.

SCORPIO emotionally

THE MATRIARCH AND THE SPY - You can work very well together as long as you agree on emotional priorities, and avoid feeling that you should be everything to one another, an impression you initially give and receive. This should be sorted sooner rather than later, for being highly emotional, you could find yourselves with neither room nor mood to negotiate.

SAGITTARIUS inconveniently

THE MATRIARCH AND THE PRIEST - The home and the open road do not really ever meet, except perhaps in a caravan. Cancer clings to the safe and familiar, whereas Sag aspires to far-flung horizons. To Cancer, Sag is insecurity incarnate. To Sag, Cancer is like an open prison. Unless you can be more open or gypsy-like, your divergent values will separate you.

CAPRICORN complementarily

THE MATRIARCH AND THE PRESIDENT - Ideally you could make a quite 'complete' combination, with Cap looking after the worldly affairs and Cancer tending to the domestic ones, the ends being family and reputation. What clinches this is accepting that Cancer puts feelings first, and Cap practicalities - and to occasionally take a leaf from each other's book.

AQUARIUS adversely

THE MATRIARCH AND THE REFORMIST - As a rule, your values and goals are too different to make any kind of match. Cancer wants to maintain the status quo; Aquarius wants to change it. Cancer comes from the gut - Aquarius from the head. The fact that you are interacting at all indicates that you need to learn from one another - otherwise disaster!

PISCES sensitively

THE MATRIARCH AND THE MESSIAH - This combination is what the world needs more of! Your abilities to tune into and respect each other's feelings, dreams and fears is the mainstay here. What is more, you thrive on all this sympathy and compassion emanating out to family, friends and the world at large Be sure though, to allow each other to follow their own dream.

LEO interacts with

ARIES *heroically*

THE MONARCH AND THE LEADER - Much can be achieved and with plenty of fun and excitement too. But this can become a problem if the interaction turns into a competition to see who can dominate or win the most. When both of you are directing your prodigious energies towards a common goal, guided by similar principles, all goes well.

TAURUS *difficultly*

THE MONARCH AND THE BANKER - This is a solid and lasting combination, but it is unlikely to be without it storms. It is essential that you both appreciate what each is providing. Taurus could be seen as providing the 'stage' or steadiness, and Leo the 'drama' or excitement. Without such an agreement no amount of pleasure or wealth will compensate.

GEMINI *good-naturedly*

THE MONARCH AND THE JESTER - This is a playful interaction. It may appear to be on Leo's terms, but actually Gemini's clever sense of humour, love of variety, and the detachment that goes with it, has the Lion by the tail at times. Overall, quite a subtle interaction for it engenders a tacit understanding based on Leo's power and Gemini's wit.

CANCER *dramatically*

THE MONARCH AND THE MATRIARCH - Leo gives a sparkle to Cancer's security-oriented and possibly limited lifestyle; Cancer provides a sense of family and belonging. Unless this exchange is appreciated, Leo will soon feel suffocated by such 'familiarity', and the Crab can come to resent and feel threatened by the Lion's love of excitement.

LEO *respectfully*

TWO MONARCHS - That you interact 'respectfully' is mandatory rather than natural. Without determining your respectful areas of rulership, like who rules the home, finances, children, etc., then fierce competition for the spotlight will lead to tears and strife, or simply living in different 'kingdoms'. Get 'who rules what' right though, and bliss rules!

VIRGO *delicately*

THE MONARCH AND THE ADVISOR -This can work when Leo admits their need for one they can trust to keep them informed of what they should be aware of. In return, Leo gives Virgo much needed confidence, making them the power behind the throne. But if Virgo presumes upon this they could incur royal displeasure - be banished even - but Leo may regret it.

LEO interacts with

LIBRA graciously

THE MONARCH AND THE DIPLOMAT - This should be quite a graceful interaction because Libra defers to Leo's will, and Leo values Libra's social skills, especially those that iron out the bumps created by any royal gaffes. Libra loves the sense of being a part of something grand and dignified. But Libra beware of a sense of impotency, and Leo, of frustration.

SCORPIO dangerously

THE MONARCH AND THE SPY - These powerful Signs can be jealously at odds. To lessen the conflict, what Leo frowns upon as Scorpio's underhandedness best be seen as a psychological awareness in need of Leo's generosity of spirit, whereas what Scorpio scorns as Leo's highhandedness best be seen merely as naiveté in need of Scorpionic insight.

SAGITTARIUS magnanimously

THE MONARCH AND THE PRIEST - You both have your own 'affairs of state' to occupy you, and so your lives together can resemble a pageant with all the fun and colour that this engenders. Both are 'big' Signs, so a grand lifestyle can be enjoyed, but in order to prevent estrangement, care should be taken to observe 'small' things like tact and hidden insecurities.

CAPRICORN pragmatically

THE MONARCH AND THE PRESIDENT - You both like sticking to certain forms and social conventions, for this is what maintains the rule and order that you love. However trust and patience will be needed to relate to the sensitive soul in each of you that exists behind that power mask, and to wait for it to emerge. If not, relations can become decidedly frosty.

AQUARIUS reactively

THE MONARCH AND THE REFORMIST - This is the hardest of opposites to (re)unite, but also the most important. This is because it is the gulf between the privileged and the lowly that creates most of the world's ills. If the Heart of Leo can be noble and generous, and the Mind of Aquarius honest and truthful - then, and only then, will peace truly reign.

PISCES considerately

THE MONARCH AND THE MESSIAH - Fishes turning the other cheek can seem like they are giving the Lion carte blanche to rule as they please. After a while though, the Fishes are seen to have their own following which insidiously threatens Leo. Leo best see Pisces as an example of the power of humility, and Pisces regard Leo as a role model for how to face the music.

VIRGO interacts with

ARIES determinedly

THE ADVISOR AND THE LEADER - The problem for Virgo is that Aries will not listen and jumps in headfirst, and then, maybe, will listen when its too late. So Aries should learn to listen, weigh Virgo's advice carefully, and then act - or not. Virgo is learning to be more forceful, be more sure of their own counsel, and ultimately to act upon it themselves.

TAURUS agreeably

THE ADVISOR AND THE BANKER - This is a very harmonious combination. Taurus provides and Virgo maintains - and should Taurus get too bogged down in material things, Virgo coaxes them towards the finer things of life in the delicate manner they appreciate. The Bull's part is kindly to keep Virgo mindful of the wood when the trees get in their way.

GEMINI annoyingly

THE ADVISOR AND THE JESTER - Both of you have a lot to say, but because each of you have different agendas or priorities a lot does not get understood. Virgo thinks practically, Gemini thinks for its own sake. And with all this thinking and talking there can be little room for any real emotional interplay. Still, you can learn a lot from one another, and have fun too.

CANCER naturally

THE ADVISOR AND THE MATRIARCH - You are 'Mother Nature's own' in that together you create a comfortable, efficient and caring environment, be that in the home or wherever. The downside to this is that you can live in each other's pockets to the point of suffocation. The occasional outing would offset the 'risk of too much safety' in this excellent combination.

LEO delicately

THE ADVISOR AND THE MONARCH -This can work when Leo admits their need for one they can trust to keep them informed of what they should be aware of. In return, Leo gives Virgo much needed confidence, making them the power behind the throne. But if Virgo presumes upon this they could incur royal displeasure - be banished even - but Leo may regret it.

VIRGO critically

TWO ADVISORS - For a Sign that loves sanity, this combination can be preciousness gone mad! Everything is checked and scrutinised, fixed when it doesn't need fixing, to the point that life is all preparation and no living. An eternal dress rehearsal. However, if you can put up with this, such joint efficiency and precision will benefit someone else very much indeed.

VIRGO interacts with

LIBRA *pedantically*

THE ADVISOR AND THE DIPLOMAT - As you both have a definite sense of how things should be done, you can get along very well - at first. Eventually though, your lives can become so 'correct' that the more messy and untidy emotions that are the reality of a real relationship are banished to the closet. Regularly clearing that out together would help.

SCORPIO *exactingly*

THE ADVISOR AND THE SPY - Virgo's prudence can teach Scorpio the wisdom of leaving some stones unturned, whereas Scorpio's emotional insight can stop Virgo from being such a goody-two-shoes. But this inter-change will work only if you both consciously agree to this kind of 'deal'. Yet even if you do, such mutual cleansing and purging can exhaust you both.

SAGITTARIUS *disappointingly*

THE ADVISOR AND THE PRIEST - What starts out as Virgo's admiration for Sagittarian optimism and largesse, can develop into rank annoyance as their promises come to nothing. To all this, Sag just heaves a sigh and/or teases some more. For it to work, it must be recognised that Virgo's sense of detail and Sag's feel for the whole can complement one another.

CAPRICORN *efficiently*

THE ADVISOR AND THE PRESIDENT - This is a classic match - where would one be without the other?! Success depends ultimately on each person knowing their ground -something you both excel in. But as you categorise and compartmentalise, make time and room for some earthy fun and nonsense too - then you'll be in clover in more ways than one.

AQUARIUS *idiosyncratically*

THE ADVISOR AND THE REFORMIST - Both of you are highly individualistic, which can be your bane or your boon. Bane - if you think you should be the same type of individuals, a contradiction in terms giving rise to constant aggravation. Boon - if you give each other the space and time to find and be yourselves, to be two unique human beings more than a couple.

PISCES *humbly*

THE ADVISOR AND THE MESSIAH - The two of you can really help one another to enjoy sensitivity combined with order. The pitfall to avoid is Virgo's concern for detail missing the feel of a thing, and Pisces over-reacting to just that. You share the same concept of how good life should be - just appreciate that you see and approach this from opposing viewpoints.

LIBRA interacts with

ARIES confrontationally

THE DIPLOMAT AND THE LEADER - You can work as a team as long as Aries is allowed to forge ahead in their straightforward way, while Libra irons out the bumps caused by this. Also, Libra's pleasantness and Aries' forcefulness can temper one another. But without recognising how different you are, it can be felt as uncouthness and niceness grating horribly.

TAURUS indulgently

THE DIPLOMAT AND THE BANKER - Because you both like set procedures and ways of doing things, it would be a wonder if you ever gelled in a natural, emotional sense. Yours is more of an arrangement that has the pleasures of the flesh and society as a substitute for any-thing more profound. As far as this goes, you can enjoy this sedate and stable... arrangement.

GEMINI smartly

THE DIPLOMAT AND THE JESTER - You both have your own, but compatible ways, of deftly manipulating things into appearing easier than they really are. And so you support one another in this to the extent of actually making things easier than they ought to be! As long as you are both happy to live and love so cerebrally, without profound emotions, all will be fine.

CANCER warily

THE DIPLOMAT AND THE MATRIARCH - Cancer needs security and Libra wants peace, which is a good foot to start out on. But whereas security is maintained by containing things, peace is sought by opening things up, being more gregarious - and this is where you can fail to understand one another. For harmony and comfort, respect your individual roles in this.

LEO graciously

THE DIPLOMAT AND THE MONARCH - This should be quite a graceful interaction because Libra defers to Leo's will, and Leo values Libra's social skills, especially those that iron out the bumps created by any royal gaffes. Libra loves the sense of being a part of something grand and dignified. But Libra beware of a sense of impotency, and Leo, of frustration.

VIRGO pedantically

THE DIPLOMAT AND THE ADVISOR - As you both have a definite sense of how things should be done, you can get along very well - at first. Eventually though, your lives can become so 'correct' that the more messy and untidy emotions that are the reality of a real relationship are banished to the closet. Regularly clearing that out together would help.

LIBRA interacts with ♎︎♎︎

LIBRA deferentially

TWO DIPLOMATS - You are confronted with having to know how to respond, relate in awkward situations, and socially conduct yourselves in general. If you are good at this, you are either particularly gracious and naturally well-mannered, or, you are being superficial at the expense of emotional sincerity. Or somewhere between the two. The decision is yours!

SCORPIO demandingly

THE DIPLOMAT AND THE SPY - You are more than likely working at cross-purposes, with Libra wanting a fair and respectable match, but Scorpio desiring something of a deeper and darker hue. Libra's pleasant overtures are seen as superficial and trashed by Scorpio, who is then treated with kid-gloves, making them even more spiky. Be genuine - but just, too.

SAGITTARIUS reasonably

THE DIPLOMAT AND THE PRIEST - You are both adept at observing the ways of the society that you live in, and so you successfully conduct your relationship in accordance with its written and unwritten laws. Sometimes this means you are both coming from your heads rather than your hearts, which can diminish passion but that's the price you pay for order.

CAPRICORN formally

THE DIPLOMAT AND THE PRESIDENT - This is a very 'correct' pairing that does not allow much room for the highly passionate or free-and-easy. But just because of this conventional style you are able to build and fashion a respectable life together. But if there are any signs of dissatisfaction on either side, then it's time to be more emotionally aware and outspoken.

AQUARIUS thoughtfully

THE DIPLOMAT AND THE REFORMIST - If this could get off the ground then great things could be achieved and even some new social ground broken. You could be an example to others of how two people can harmonise as a pair yet still be individuals in their own right. But first you'd have to come out of your heads and into your bodies - from theory to reality.

PISCES kindly

THE DIPLOMAT AND THE MESSIAH - Libran indecisiveness and Piscean evasiveness can give the illusion of compatibility as you appear to fit in with each other, not wanting to face the dark or difficult bits. But if you do decide to really get down to the business of honest relating, you do so with fairness and sensitivity - otherwise it can interminably insubstantial.

SCORPIO interacts with

ARIES explosively

THE SPY AND THE LEADER - This is rather like fire and ice meeting up; a lot of passionate hissing and melting at first, but inevitably your elemental natures compromise one another, causing rage and resentment. Scorpio comes disdainfully to see Aries' straightforwardness as stupid, and Aries cannot abide Scorpio's covert behaviour. Gut-wrenching honesty is needed.

TAURUS powerfully

THE SPY AND THE BANKER - The Bull wants to keep things stable and as they are; the Scorpion wants to get down to the hidden emotional depths of why they are. The Earth and the Underworld are embedded together, yet they jealously guard their own realms. For this passionate involvement to work each must respect how different yet interdependent they are.

GEMINI abrasively

THE SPY AND THE JESTER - Scorpio makes heavy of things, while Gemini makes light of them. A deal could be struck here, but the Twins lightness is seen by Scorpio as flippancy and emotional insincerity. Gemini regards Scorpio's depth as treacherous and hard work, so they wriggle even more. There can be a peculiar intrigue here, but not a bond to relax with.

CANCER emotionally

THE SPY AND THE MATRIARCH - You can work very well together as long as you agree on emotional priorities, and avoid feeling that you should be everything to one another, an impression you initially give and receive. This should be sorted sooner rather than later, for being highly emotional, you could find yourselves with neither room nor mood to negotiate.

LEO dangerously

THE SPY AND THE MONARCH - These powerful Signs can be jealously at odds. To lessen the conflict, what Leo frowns upon as Scorpio's underhandedness best be seen as a psychological awareness in need of Leo's generosity of spirit, whereas what Scorpio scorns as Leo's highhandedness best be seen merely as naiveté in need of Scorpionic insight.

VIRGO exactingly

THE SPY AND THE ADVISOR - Virgo's prudence can teach Scorpio the wisdom of leaving some stones unturned, whereas Scorpio's emotional insight can stop Virgo from being such a goody-two-shoes. But this interchange will work only if you both consciously agree to this kind of 'deal'. Yet even if you do, such mutual cleansing and purging can exhaust you both.

SCORPIO interacts with

LIBRA demandingly

THE SPY AND THE DIPLOMAT - You are more than likely working at cross-purposes, with Libra wanting a fair and respectable match, but Scorpio desiring something of a deeper and darker hue. Libra's pleasant overtures are seen as superficial and trashed by Scorpio, who is then treated with kid-gloves, making them even more spiky. Be genuine - but just, too.

SCORPIO intensely

TWO SPIES - You understand each other because you both inhabit the same world of deep feelings and dark secrets. If you can steer your way around the spectre of betrayal that tries to threaten your essential trust, then you will have a lasting and unmistakable bond. It would be wise to check out/respect the chinks in each other's armour before they become liabilities.

SAGITTARIUS suspiciously

THE SPY AND THE PRIEST - You both love power, but whereas Sag expresses it openly, Scorpio uses it covertly. Your definitions of truth are very different. This makes it hard to read one another, so embarrassments and subterfuges are the awkward result. The reason your together is so Sag can learn some tact, and Scorpio some candour. If not, 'paranoia'.

CAPRICORN beneficially

THE SPY AND THE PRESIDENT - You can be very useful to one another. This does not sound very romantic, but then it wouldn't for you are a businesslike, no-nonsense pair. Yet it falls to Scorpio to remind Cap that they are an emotional being after all, while Cap teaches Scorp that they misuse their emotional wiles at their peril. A powerful pairing, for good or ill.

AQUARIUS frustratingly

THE SPY AND THE REFORMIST - Your agendas are so very different that you are liable to confound one another. Scorpio wants intrigue and emotional satisfaction; Aquarius is more intent upon exposing the 'truth' and things adding up mentally. Unless you can both recognise the validity of each other's requirements, you will both become exasperated.

PISCES intuitively

THE SPY AND THE MESSIAH - You have a strong bond but a strange one. There are deep and mysterious elements to your relationship that only reveal themselves in the fullness of time - and then maybe not at all. Being both intuitive and emotional, you are attuned to this submerged agenda and remain true to it and each other - barring the occasional reef, that is.

SAGITTARIUS interacts with

ARIES enterprisingly

THE PRIEST AND THE LEADER - This marries together a strong sense of being after something in life with the justification for getting it. Consequently, you have the wherewithal to go far and achieve a great deal. If this sounds more like an enterprise than a relationship, then you have spotted that a sense of personal intimacy could be amiss - but what matter?

TAURUS disagreeably

THE PRIEST AND THE BANKER - At first Sag looks like an exciting prospect to the Bull, but before too long they just don't deliver what Taurus thought they were promised. To Sag, Taurus initially seems to be the anchor they need, but they wind up feeling tethered by them. A healthy exchange could occur, if your different currencies or value systems would allow it.

GEMINI curiously

THE PRIEST AND THE JESTER - This is not such an unlikely combination as it appears. Gemini's streetwise wit can keep Sag from being pious and out of touch, while Sag can provide the Twins with a overall view or philosophy that can knit together their scattered thoughts. Failing this though, Sag could look down on Gemini, who then snaps at Sag's heels.

CANCER inconveniently

THE PRIEST AND THE MATRIARCH - The home and the open road do not really ever meet, except perhaps in a caravan. Cancer clings to the safe and familiar, whereas Sag aspires to far-flung horizons. To Cancer, Sag is insecurity incarnate. To Sag, Cancer is like an open prison. Unless you can be more open or gypsy-like, your divergent values will separate you.

LEO magnanimously

THE PRIEST AND THE MONARCH- You both have your own 'affairs of state' to occupy you, and so your lives together can resemble a pageant with all the fun and colour that this engenders. Both are 'big' Signs, so a grand lifestyle can be enjoyed, but in order to prevent estrangement, care should be taken to observe 'small' things like tact and hidden insecurities.

VIRGO disappointingly

THE PRIEST AND THE ADVISOR - What starts out as Virgo's admiration for Sagittarian optimism and largesse, can develop into rank annoyance as their promises come to nothing. To all this, Sag just heaves a sigh and/or teases some more. For it to work, it must be recognised that Virgo's sense of detail and Sag's feel for the whole can complement one another.

SAGITTARIUS interacts with

LIBRA reasonably

THE PRIEST AND THE DIPLOMAT - You are both adept at observing the ways of the society that you live in, and so you successfully conduct your relationship in accordance with its written and unwritten laws. Sometimes this means you are both coming from your heads rather than your hearts, which can diminish passion - but that's the price you pay for order.

SCORPIO suspiciously

THE PRIEST AND THE SPY - You both love power, but whereas Sag expresses it openly, Scorpio uses it covertly. Your definitions of truth are very different. This makes it hard to read one another, so embarrassments and subterfuges are the awkward result. The reason your together is so Sag can learn some tact, and Scorpio some candour. If not, 'paranoia'.

SAGITTARIUS idealistically

TWO PRIESTS - As long as you believe in something and each other, and respect each other's beliefs if they are different, then you can be a model relationship in that you are an example of two people progressing onwards and upwards together. This is like two hitched horses that keep looking ahead at their own paths, avoiding jealous or hypocritical sideward glances.

CAPRICORN competitively

THE PRIEST AND THE PRESIDENT - You think you grate upon one another because Cap sees Sag as over-optimistic and Sag regards Cap as a wet blanket. The real reason why you can fall out so easily though is because you both want to run the show. With Sag's vision and Cap's practicality you could team up and clean up. But nothing less than greed bars the way.

AQUARIUS liberally

THE PRIEST AND THE REFORMIST - As you both like the freedom to explore life and yourselves, this works well as you are likely to allow same to each other - hopefully avoiding bigotry. In the process though, your freedom to do your own thing can cause you to float apart and have only a pretend relationship. Until then, you can certainly hit some high spots.

PISCES deceptively

THE PRIEST AND THE MESSIAH - You are both into vision and belief as the mainstays of existence, and because of this, your faith, far-flung ideas and easy-goingness can take you, quite ecstatically, some way together. But unless something forces a truly honest showdown, then a mixture of vagueness, indulgence and impracticality can find you undoing one another.

CAPRICORN interacts with

ARIES conflictingly

THE PRESIDENT AND THE LEADER - Together you have the makings of success, but it is unfortunate and more likely that one of you feels superior to the other - usually Capricorn over Aries. So ultimately, as neither of you is one to be bested, rebellion or resistance, or locked horns, are a strong likelihood. A common goal, or enemy, might help to unite you.

TAURUS prosperously

THE PRESIDENT AND THE BANKER - You make a stable, industrious and eventually affluent couple, and enjoy together the pleasures of the flesh. Both of you have a style of living that is power-based, with Cap initiating projects and Taurus maintaining funds. As long as neither of you becomes greedy or philistine, you will last and last, happily and securely.

GEMINI easily

THE PRESIDENT AND THE JESTER - On a material level, Cap is infinitely more astute and powerful than the Twins, whom they tolerate to keep them informed and amused. But Gemini may secretly regard Cap as a boring goat who they'll milk for what they've got and then be off. A mutual recognition of the real people would help, IF you both gave it the time.

CANCER complementarily

THE PRESIDENT AND THE MATRIARCH - Ideally you could make a quite 'complete' combination, with Cap looking after the worldly affairs and Cancer tending to the domestic ones, the ends being family and reputation. What clinches this is accepting that Cancer puts feelings first, and Cap practicalities - and to occasionally take a leaf from each other's book.

LEO pragmatically

THE PRESIDENT AND THE MONARCH - You both like sticking to certain forms and social conventions, for this is what maintains the rule and order that you love. However trust and patience will be needed to relate to the sensitive soul in each of you that exists behind that power mask, and to wait for it to emerge. If not, relations can become decidedly frosty.

VIRGO efficiently

THE PRESIDENT AND THE ADVISOR - This is a classic match - where would one be without the other?! Success depends ultimately on each person knowing their ground -something you both excel in. But as you categorise and compartmentalise, make time and room for some earthy fun and nonsense too - then you'll be in clover in more ways than one.

CAPRICORN interacts with

LIBRA *formally*

THE PRESIDENT AND THE DIPLOMAT - This is a very 'correct' pairing that does not allow much room for the highly passionate or free-and-easy. But just because of this conventional style you are able to build and fashion a respectable life together. But if there are any signs of dissatisfaction on either side, then it's time to be more emotionally aware and outspoken.

SCORPIO *beneficially*

THE PRESIDENT AND THE SPY - You can be very useful to one another. This does not sound very romantic, but then it wouldn't for you are a businesslike, no-nonsense pair. Yet it falls to Scorpio to remind Cap that they are an emotional being after all, while Cap teaches Scorp that they misuse their emotional wiles at their peril. A powerful pairing, for good or ill.

SAGITTARIUS *competitively*

THE PRESIDENT AND THE PRIEST - You think you grate upon one another because Cap sees Sag as over-optimistic and Sag regards Cap as a wet blanket. The real reason why you can fall out so easily though is because you both want to run the show. With Sag's vision and Cap's practicality you could team up and clean up. But nothing less than greed bars the way.

CAPRICORN *undemonstratively*

TWO PRESIDENTS - Some would say that this is more of a corporate merger than a relationship, and it is true your quality of life together may get measured by joint status, or merely by how often you can fit one another into each of your schedules. It may take some kind of crunch, but when you discover the heart and soul of one another - success!

AQUARIUS *politically*

THE PRESIDENT AND THE REFORMIST - On the face of it, this is not a good mix - Cap's plans and pitch can be queered by Aquarian liberality, which in turn feels cramped by the Goat's conservatism. But the very fact that you are interacting at all points to the likelihood of Cap needing to update and loosen up, and of Aquarius having to get real and organised.

PISCES *auspiciously*

THE PRESIDENT AND THE MESSIAH - When Cap appreciates how much they need and profit from Piscean imagination and emotional sensitivity, and Pisces accepts the value of Cap's worldly hard-headedness, then this can be like Heaven and Earth happily meeting one another. So brook neither Piscean vagueness and evasiveness, nor Capricornian purblindness.

AQUARIUS interacts with

ARIES progressively

THE REFORMIST AND THE LEADER - This is a relationship that can really go places, change things, set new standards, etc.. You are both independent and freedom-loving, and so respect each other's space and wishes. There is a dark side to such undeniable brightness and lightness however: the little needy child hiding in one or both of you can get overlooked.

TAURUS unsuitably

THE REFORMIST AND THE BANKER - As Taurus effectively 'invests' in a relationship, they get extra-possessive when Aquarius shows signs of going out on a limb, as is their wont. Earth and Air co-exist rather than unite as seen in the differing priorities of Taurean physical needs and Aquarian mental abstractions. Both being stubborn, you persist - mostly in vain.

GEMINI cerebrally

THE REFORMIST AND THE JESTER - You are both very much on the same wavelength, seeing life as a thing of the mind, spinning endless word plays and abstract concepts into a fabric which you agree on as being reality. The pattern you weave together makes sense and is fun, yet it may not be that fulfilling emotionally. But that is probably alright by both of you.

CANCER adversely

THE REFORMIST AND THE MATRIARCH - As a rule, your values and goals are too different to make any kind of match. Cancer wants to maintain the status quo; Aquarius wants to change it. Cancer comes from the gut - Aquarius from the head. The fact that you are interacting at all indicates that you need to learn from one another - otherwise disaster!

LEO reactively

THE REFORMIST AND THE MONARCH - This is the hardest of opposites to (re)unite, but also the most important. This is because it is the gulf between the lowly and the privileged that creates most of the world's ills. If the Heart of Leo can be noble and generous, and the Mind of Aquarius honest and truthful - then, and only then, will peace truly reign.

VIRGO idiosyncratically

THE REFORMIST AND THE ADVISOR - - Both of you are highly individualistic, which can be your bane or your boon. Bane - if you think you should be the same type of individuals, a contradiction in terms, giving rise to constant aggravation. Boon - if you give each other the space and time to find and be yourselves, to be two unique human beings more than a couple.

AQUARIUS interacts with

LIBRA thoughtfully

THE REFORMIST AND THE DIPLOMAT - If this could get off the ground then great things could be achieved and even some new social ground broken. You could be an example to others of how two people can harmonise as a pair yet still be individuals in their own right. But first you'd have to come out of your heads and into your bodies - from theory to reality.

SCORPIO frustratingly

THE REFORMIST AND THE SPY - Your agendas are so very different that you are liable to confound one another. Scorpio wants intrigue and emotional satisfaction; Aquarius is more intent upon exposing the 'truth' and things adding up mentally. Unless you can both recognise the validity of each other's requirements, you will both become exasperated.

SAGITTARIUS liberally

THE REFORMIST AND THE PRIEST - As you both like the freedom to explore life and yourselves, this works well as you are likely to allow same to each other - hopefully avoiding bigotry. In the process though, your freedom to do your own thing can cause you to float apart and have only a pretend relationship. Until then, you can certainly hit some high spots.

CAPRICORN politically

THE REFORMIST AND THE PRESIDENT - On the face of it, this is not a good mix - Cap's plans and pitch can be queered by Aquarian liberality, which in turn feels cramped by the Goat's conservatism. But the very fact that you are interacting at all points to the likelihood of Cap needing to update and loosen up, and of Aquarius having to get real and organised.

AQUARIUS coolly

TWO REFORMISTS - You can work so well together because you are both living in your minds where awkward things like bodies and feelings do not intrude too much. The stuff of life is discussed and reviewed, with only an occasional dip into the physical or emotional. But this doesn't 'hold water' when there simply is no longer anything there to keep you together.

PISCES hopefully

THE REFORMIST AND THE MESSIAH - You can start out with similar idealistic intentions, but the very vagueness and airiness of such notions catches up on you later and you are no longer sure who or what you are to one another. Maybe one or both of you thought the other would change. Maybe you did in your own way. But it's never too late. Maybe.

PISCES interacts with

ARIES inappropriately

THE MESSIAH AND THE LEADER - Aries wants to win, Pisces is prepared to turn the other cheek. Aries takes direct action, Pisces uses passive resistance. It might initially seem that one of you is saving the other - but later it gets confusing as to who is saviour and who is victim. A case of tragically mistaken identities - unless you explode your respective myths.

TAURUS symbiotically

THE MESSIAH AND THE BANKER - This has all the joy and security of a fertile island set in a mysterious sea. You provide one other with what each needs: Fishes get something solid to contain and feed them; the Bull is kept alive to the wonders of life. Only your egoistic extremes of playing it too safe or of being too evasive could scotch this potentially fine match.

GEMINI adaptively

THE MESSIAH AND THE JESTER - At some rarefied level you are akin, attuned, as you both are, to the truth that we reach the sublime through a blending of humour and humility. But unless you are spiritually disciplined, such can find you all froth and no substance. Something needs to keep you both down to earth - possibly the friends you delight, or a child.

CANCER sensitively

THE MESSIAH AND THE MATRIARCH - This combination is what the world needs more of! Your abilities to tune into and respect each other's feelings, dreams and fears is the mainstay here. What is more, you thrive on all this sympathy and compassion emanating out to family, friends and the world at large. Be sure though, to allow each other to follow their own dream

LEO considerately

THE MESSIAH AND THE MONARCH - Fishes turning the other cheek can seem like they are giving the Lion carte blanche to rule as they please. After a while though, the Fishes are seen to have their own following which insidiously threatens Leo. Leo best see Pisces as an example of the power of humility, and Pisces regard Leo as a role model for how to face the music.

VIRGO humbly

THE MESSIAH AND THE ADVISOR - The two of you can really help one another to enjoy sensitivity combined with order. The pitfall to avoid is Virgo's concern for detail missing the feel of a thing, and Pisces over-reacting to just that. You share the same concept of how good life should be - just appreciate that you see and approach this from opposing viewpoints.

PISCES interacts with

LIBRA kindly

THE MESSIAH AND THE DIPLOMAT - Libran indecisiveness and Piscean evasiveness can give the illusion of compatibility as you appear to fit in with each other, not wanting to face the dark or difficult bits. But if you do decide to really get down to the business of honest relating, you do so with fairness and sensitivity - otherwise it can interminably insubstantial.

SCORPIO intuitively

THE MESSIAH AND THE SPY - You have a strong bond but a strange one. There are deep and mysterious elements to your relationship that only reveal themselves in the fullness of time - and then maybe not at all. Being both intuitive and emotional, you are attuned to this submerged agenda and remain true to it and each other - barring the occasional reef, that is.

SAGITTARIUS deceptively

THE MESSIAH AND THE PRIEST - You are both into vision and belief as the mainstays of existence, and because of this, your faith, far-flung ideas and easy-goingness can take you, quite ecstatically, some way together. But unless something forces a truly honest showdown, then a mixture of vagueness, indulgence and impracticality can find you undoing one another.

CAPRICORN auspiciously

THE MESSIAH AND THE PRESIDENT - When Cap appreciates how much they need and profit from Piscean imagination and emotional sensitivity, and Pisces accepts the value of Cap's worldly hard-headedness, then this can be like Heaven and Earth happily meeting one another. So brook neither Piscean vagueness and evasiveness, nor Capricornian purblindness.

AQUARIUS hopefully

THE MESSIAH AND THE REFORMIST - You can start out with similar idealistic intentions, but the very vagueness and airiness of such notions catches up on you later and you are no longer sure who or what you are to one another. Maybe one or both of you thought the other would change. Maybe you did in your own way. But it's never too late... Maybe.

PISCES dreamily

TWO MESSIAHS - This is more like two martyrs, unfortunately. And the 'cause' to which you sacrifice your lives can be alcohol, drugs, your 'dream', or to another who is even more of a victim than you both feel yourselves to be. Then again, you might just make it if you quit the self-pity or addictiveness, and really got down to realising that vision you first beheld.

4. PLANETARY CYCLES

Everything in life is subject to cycles: the life cycle of a frog or butterfly; the menstrual cycle; biorhythms; birth to death; migration, and many, many more - long and short. Astrology is the study of cycles too, but the cycles that are those of the Sun, Moon and Planets can be seen to be a measure of our personality's unfoldment throughout our lives. And like those more biological cycles, they too have their critical points. The Moon, by the way, could be said to figure in both these areas for it lies between our planet Earth and all the others, as well as the Sun. It is also useful to bear in mind that Planetary Cycles are simply cycles and not necessarily some weird 'influence' travelling all the way from say, Saturn, to your body here on Earth. The Planets in their courses are better seen as the hands of a gigantic clock - and as you know, clocks indicate the time, they do not actually make it.

Like any complex subject - which astrology certainly can be - there are simple expressions of it and more complicated ones. As far as Planetary Cycles are concerned, the more complicated ones are left to the attention of the professional or amateur astrologer for they involve difficult calculations or the informed use of computer software. Refer to the Resources at the back of the book if you wish to take your astrological enquiry further.

The Planetary Cycles given you in this book though, are easy to understand because all you have to know is your age. They are...

All you need to do is find the age of your interest and read on - but I do recommend that you read the relevant introduction first.

See pages 293-296, the Age Index, for an overall graphic view of all these Planetary Cycles as they occur over a whole lifetime.

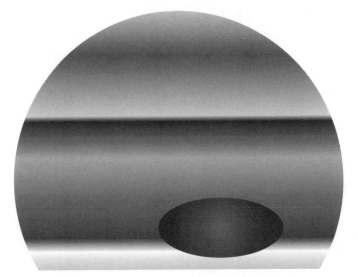

Your Jupiter Cycle
What Years are Lucky for What

Jupiter can be regarded as the Director of your life-play. As such, it knows your 'story' inside-out, what it means and where it's going. This is why Jupiter is the key to understanding what your life, and life in general, are about. It will also expand upon the original story, that is, your basic potential and fate. In fact, its prime aim is to make you 'more than you are or were' - this is why Jupiter is the Planet of Growth and Luck. Jupiter also teaches you how to be philosophical about life.

Jupiter takes approximately 12 years to go around the Sun - or around us from the Earth's point of view. So by taking each year of its twelve-year cycle and making it into a 'chapter' we can ascribe each year to the twelve Signs of the Zodiac. Each year of your life can then be understood in terms of developing according to the qualities of a particular Sign, through challenge, opportunity or sheer good fortune.

Actually the Luck of Jupiter is simply a result of being in the right place, and doing the right thing, at the right time. These Sign qualities of your Jupiterian process of Growth, Luck and Understanding can simply be called Growth Areas. But do not confuse them with Sun-Signs or Star-Signs (or with the Sign that Jupiter is actually placed in at birth or any other time) - which is why I place each Sign name in inverted commas.

However, you may well find that you come into your own during Jupiter years that are the same Sign as your Sun, Moon or Rising Sign (see my books 'Do It Yourself Astrology' or 'The Instant Astrologer' to discover what these are and mean). Also, by the same token, you will see that the meanings given in for each Sun-Sign in The Zodiacal Life-Stream on pages 33-36 are also applicable to your Jupiterian year 'Signs' - and you will be able to see each of those years in the context of the whole story or cycle. As it happens, there is an astronomical link between the Sun and Jupiter, for it is the only planet that generates more energy than it receives from the Sun itself. So in a way it is like a second Sun.

So, whatever Planetary influences are occurring at any particular age, look to your Jupiterian year or 'Sign' because its Growth Area will give you positive ways of looking at and developing through that time. The qualities of Jupiter's 'Sign' will also contribute to the various scenes and characters through which that year will be acted out. For example, you may well find that the Sign qualities (Sun-Sign, Moon-Sign or Rising Sign) of significant others correspond to the Jupiter year that you became involved with them or parted with them.

Following the table opposite are given the meanings of all the Jupiterian years as double-page spreads. The left-hand page is headed with the actual ages they occur and the 'Sign' name of those years, but don't expect each year to click on and off exactly on your birthday - give a week or so 'cusp' either way. Within each Jupiter Year interpretation that follow I give what are purely examples of what each individual age of that year could mean - but they are not the only possible manifestations for those ages. Then, on the right-hand page there is a 'Go-Zone' guide to fruitful areas of appreciation and understanding during those Jupiter Years. And, incidentally, Jupiter being Jupiter - that is, wisdom - Go-Zone information for any Year is useful at any time

Now you can just flip through the pages of this section and look for the age in which you're interested, or use this index if you wish to...

Age	'Sign' Year	Page	Age	'Sign' Year	Page	Age	'Sign' Year	Page
0	'Aries'	94	28	'Leo'	102	56	'Sagittarius'	110
1	'Taurus'	96	29	'Virgo'	104	57	'Capricorn'	112
2	'Gemini'	98	30	'Libra'	106	58	'Aquarius'	114
3	'Cancer'	100	31	'Scorpio'	108	59	'Pisces'	116
4	'Leo'	102	32	'Sagittarius'	110	60	'Aries'	94
5	'Virgo'	104	33	'Capricorn'	112	61	'Taurus'	96
6	'Libra'	106	34	'Aquarius'	114	62	'Gemini'	98
7	'Scorpio'	108	35	'Pisces'	116	63	'Cancer'	100
8	'Sagittarius'	110	36	'Aries'	94	64	'Leo'	102
9	'Capricorn'	112	37	'Taurus'	96	65	'Virgo'	104
10	'Aquarius'	114	38	'Gemini'	98	66	'Libra'	106
11	'Pisces'	116	39	'Cancer'	100	67	'Scorpio'	108
12	'Aries'	94	40	'Leo'	102	68	'Sagittarius'	110
13	'Taurus'	96	41	'Virgo'	104	69	'Capricorn'	112
14	'Gemini'	98	42	'Libra'	106	70	'Aquarius'	114
15	'Cancer'	100	43	'Scorpio'	108	71	'Pisces'	116
16	'Leo'	102	44	'Sagittarius'	110	72	'Aries'	94
17	'Virgo'	104	45	'Capricorn'	112	73	'Taurus'	96
18	'Libra'	106	46	'Aquarius'	114	74	'Gemini'	98
19	'Scorpio'	108	47	'Pisces'	116	75	'Cancer'	100
20	'Sagittarius	110	48	'Aries'	94	76	'Leo'	102
21	'Capricorn'	112	49	'Taurus'	96	77	'Virgo'	104
22	'Aquarius'	114	50	'Gemini'	98	78	'Libra'	106
23	'Pisces'	116	51	'Cancer'	100	79	'Scorpio'	108
24	'Aries'	94	52	'Leo'	102	80	'Sagittarius'	110
25	'Taurus'	96	53	'Virgo'	104	81	'Capricorn'	112
26	'Gemini'	98	54	'Libra'	106	82	'Aquarius'	114
27 '	'Cancer'	100	55	'Scorpio'	108	83	'Pisces'	116

AGES: 0, 12, 24, 36, 48, 60 and 72   'ARIES' YEARS

"GROWTH IN BUD" - These are the years when each twelve year long Jupiter Cycle of Growth begins, which is highly significant. The reason why the beginning of this, or any Planetary Cycle, is so significant is because it means that the nature and extent of the objective you have, and effort you put into setting out to achieve it, totally determine how successful you are going to be in attaining that objective. Such years are similar to Spring when the sap is rising and everything is bursting forth for a new cycle of growth. Like any good farmer or gardener, you plant your seeds now in order to maximise growth through utilising this important time. Included in all of this is what you have left over from the previous Jupiter Cycle (and particularly the last, 'Pisces' Year), because 'good seed' (ideas, experience and minimal claims upon you from the past) will obviously promise better 'fruit' during this cycle, whereas 'bad seed' (debts, preoccupations, doubt and little or no experience) will either not produce much, slow you down, or complicate matters.

For understanding the significance of year zero or birth, look to the circumstances surrounding your birth and you will find a microcosm of your whole life to come. At age twelve, some new departure is very likely (at school) which sets the scene for your (educational) progress for the remainder of this cycle, and possibly others too. Age twenty-four, along with all the other 'Aries' Years to come, offers you the chance to 'start again' or 'muster' yourself with respect to whatever you feel never got properly off the ground hitherto, or, to simply launch something brand new.

Looking back at the 'Aries' Years of your life so far, you are bound to find there the 'Spring' of something. You might find that you started something beforehand at half-cock, only to do so properly during an 'Aries' Year. I was forced to decide to become professional astrologer during an 'Aquarius' Year and 'Deciding Moon Phase' only to find that I hadn't really got my act together until the year after the next. I was not aware of Jupiter Years at that time, but when you are it makes a great deal of difference to the energy and focus you have available for the launch of a new project.

★ GO-ZONES
for your 'Aries' Jupiter Years

Areas of luck, encouragement, growth and wisdom - and how to make the most of them.

GO-ZONE	APPRECIATE & UNDERSTAND...
Action	That the time has come to walk your talk, rather than just keep things at the ideas or intention stage. That Action really does speak louder than words.
Initiative	How, as described above, these Years are times to launch any project, which would also include any private or secret undertakings.
Leadership	That if you wish to step out in front and take a leading position in the field of your choice, you will do so more effectively now than most other times.
Presentation	That you now have a natural sense of your own personal presence, at least relatively speaking, and so are more likely to make a good impression. This is 'selling yourself' time! Overdoing it could have the reverse effect though.
Self-Assertion	That this is a great time to improve your powers of assertion, either in the sense of making an important statement to a significant other in your life, or in the form of making an affirmation to yourself regarding some facet of your personality that you want to be more confident about.
Championing	If there is any cause or person that you want to uphold or win over then your are in the right time for it, but make sure you are in the right place too - that is, it is for the right reasons and not just you being gung-ho.

AGES: 1, 13, 25, 37, 49, 61, and 73   'TAURUS' YEARS

"GROWTH IN/THROUGH STABILITY" - Following 'Aries' Years as they do, these 'Taurus' Years see to it that whatever you then set in motion is now stable, in the sense of being physically productive, profitable or realisable at all. They basically make it clear what you have going for you - and depending on what that is, you are liable to attract something or someone of value to you. They can also be times when you become more than usually aware of your body's state and needs with regard to sustenance and/or sensuality. 'Taurus' Years are when ideally you are able to stand, four-square, on the earth - stand your ground, in fact. But making an effort in this respect is positive even if you did not manage to hold your position, or if you overdid it and found yourself stuck. Money is rather more essential to continued growth than at other times, and is either forthcoming or a lack of funds forces you to reconsider or cut-back. The Jupiterian point here is that you can improve your material position one way or the other, either through attracting funds/making a profit or learning how to adapt your 'product' to suit the 'market'. (see Self-Worth opposite).

At age one, your are discovering your body in a quite literal sense (walking, taste, etc.), and it could also be said that such an age used to be critical in terms of physical survival before modern healthcare. Age thirteen is classic in that it coincides biologically with the state of puberty and sexual interest - humans are now able to re-produce - and astrologically with the "Emotional Discovery" of your 'First Realising Moon Phase' (see page 154). So 'what you have going for you' comes into sharp focus at this time. Age twenty-five is also a time when some kind of sexual realisation can occur - be it having a baby or enjoying hitherto unknown pleasures of the flesh. In any event, in true 'Taurus' Year fashion you discover things by either having or not having. The other ages do not appear to have anything intrinsically significant about them - probably because money and physical pleasure are perennial issues for us all. It is just that they will find focus and a chance for advancement, or indulgence, during these 'Taurus' Years.

★

GO-ZONES
for your 'Taurus' Jupiter Years

Areas of luck, encouragement, growth and wisdom - and how to make the most of them.

GO-ZONE   APPRECIATE & UNDERSTAND...

Sensuality   That being in touch with your five senses can make you glad to be alive. Involvement with your own or another's body, or Nature herself, is 'go' now.

Steadiness   That now you are 'going steady' or, at least, there is a potential for steadiness with whatever or whomever you're involved. This is a time when it can be useful to maintain a 'steady as she goes' attitude, and not allow yourself to be fazed by the up/down or on/off nature of life. With Jupiter there is always the possibility of excess which, in this case, would amount to being 'too steady', that is, stuck in the mud of some safe but boring job or relationship or belief. Check out Self-Worth below for such is the issue behind you're being in a situation that is doing you no credit.

Self-Worth   That, like it or not, the most essential issue for anyone in today's world is that of what they are worth in terms of physical attractiveness, talent and earning power. Now is the time and opportunity to increase, enjoy or realise what you have going for you in any or all of these respects.

Productivity   Having something to show for yourself is what makes one feel worth something inside. Productivity can mean the obvious in terms of some saleable item you've made or helped to make, or a baby or piece of artwork, or in the sense of a fruitful relationship or activity.

AGES: 2, 14, 26, 38, 50, 62 and 74   'GEMINI' YEARS

"GROWTH IN/THROUGH COMMUNICATION" - These Jupiter Years are highly significant in that they are times when we reach out to our environment out of curiosity, eagerness for contact and response, or to simply feel the contrast between 'me' and 'not me'. This is the famous Geminian duality that is part of everyone's world, not just Geminis. This all begins at - surprise! surprise! - age two. In fact they are called the 'terrible twos' because this is when a child is mobile and into everything, verbal and asking everything. It then splits its reality further still by classifying reality into two parts: people and things who interact with it, on the one hand, and those that do not, on the other. This Geminian splitting occurs again at a more sophisticated level at age fourteen which coincides with the First Saturn Opposition, "Me Versus The Rest" (see page 208). We can see how adolescent awkwardness is characterised by his or her inclination to divide the world into 'us' and 'them' in order to create a sense of identity in the face of a million things that appear to oppose it. It can be seen that at both these stages of the Jupiterian Growth Process, the individual can take a step toward integration through interaction, or alienation through a lack of it.

Subsequent ages are also marked by the inclination to feel split within oneself, in the sense of being in two minds, or confronted equally by two external opposing forces that represent that split within one's own psyche. Apart from being caught in a 'valley of decision', there can also be the need to split off from whatever or whomever one is involved with. These 'schizophrenic' years do not seem very Jupiterian or advantageous. The reason for this is that Jupiter, the Planetary energy that likes to organise things and people into wholes, is not very at home in a Sign that wants to divide them all into two; (this is because Gemini is opposite to Sagittarius, the Sign Jupiter rules). The growth that takes place is, as the heading above states, one of Communication, because it is only through getting to know and intelligently interacting with one's opposite number that progress can be made. So whether it takes place between yourself and another, or between one part of yourself and another, or between your mind and some other source of intelligence, all such communication goes towards the growth of one's contacts and information banks.

★ GO-ZONES
for your 'Gemini' Jupiter Years

Areas of luck, encouragement, growth and wisdom - and how to make the most of them.

GO-ZONE	APPRECIATE & UNDERSTAND...
Levity	How a light touch works wonders now - while not taking things too lightly! That being too heavy or earnest definitely alienates and misses the point.
Humour	That a sense of humour is a sense of proportion; being able to see the funny side of things is actually a brand of wisdom for it diminishes self-importance, thereby allowing you and others to see things in a clearer and healthier light. 'Laugh and world laughs with you, weep and you weep alone' - though beware excessive irreverence and sarcasm that is mocking born of cynicism.
Eloquence	How the ability to make yourself clearly understood now attracts good fortune both socially and professionally, as distinct from gossiping and chattering, which if not avoided will find you being avoided.
Knowledge	That indeed, 'knowledge is power' - especially in the sense of knowing that there are two sides to everything and everyone. Being able now to see life 'stereoscopically' is very balancing and promotes healthy relationships. That an informed mind is better able to find work and a place in the world.

AGES: 3, 15, 27, 39, 51, 63 and 75   'CANCER' YEARS

"GROWTH IN/THROUGH NURTURING" - These are years when `you need to feather your nest and find a place and situation that is secure enough to create a root from which to grow. Sometimes however, such times can seem anything but secure while they are happening, for 'emotional development' could also describe these Jupiter Years. How you emerge from the 'terrible twos '('Gemini Year') and what happens at three years of age (also the 'First Striving Lunar Phase' - page 147) can set an 'emotional security tempo' for years to come. Likewise, the emotional tenuousness of fifteen is notorious, and not surprising considering the Saturn influences also prevailing then (see page 208). The 'Cancer' Year that is probably the most significant is twenty-seven when you also reach your First Lunar Return - so this is a very Lunar time (Cancer being the Sign ruled by the Moon). Issues concerning the past, home, family, mother, motherhood and emotional ties in general are therefore uppermost in your life at this time. Such issues can also come to the fore at thirty-nine or fifty-one, but at these times very possibly with regard to feeling trapped or compromised by them. And security and family concerns can take on a particularly poignant hue at sixty-three and seventy-five, or indeed at twenty-seven, thirty-nine or fifty-one.

Generally, these are years when you create a foundation upon which to build whatever you have in mind, or is going to unfold, throughout the remainder of the Jupiter Cycle (another eight years). So make such a foundation a priority, and do not get too distracted or dazzled by more ambitious or glamorous prospects or projects. As you do so, determine what elements in your life are more emotional habit or blackmail than security or nurturance. Jupiter's expansive and future-oriented energy can appear incongruous in safety- and past-oriented Cancer. This means to say that the 'emotional development' mentioned above can force you into emotionally upsetting situations in order that you grow emotionally, possibly pulling you away from past attachments, but with some difficulty. There is an image here of a plant being transplanted (therefore uprooted) into a soil that is more conducive to its future flowering and fruiting.

★ GO-ZONES
for your 'Cancer' Jupiter Years

GO-ZONE	APPRECIATE & UNDERSTAND...

Care That any field of endeavour that is concerned with the care or yourself, others or the natural environment is well-starred now.

Home That domestic improvements want to happen, which can mean anything from making a positive move (ultimately), to expanding/redecorating your living space, to possibly even living in a mobile home. Whatever the case, your home-life will figure strongly at this time.

Family That one or a number of aspects relating to your family, blood or otherwise, are in a process of development and/or increased awareness. This means that the 'life' of your family/mother is creating changes and realisations in you.

Dreams How by recording and researching your dreams during this time, there will be a vast improvement in your emotional well-being and understanding.

The Past How by looking into the past you can now discover many things that will aid you in the present, and eventually propel you into a more secure future. Going down 'memory lane' is a strong likelihood during these years, and this can give you a stronger sense of your life's continuum, that is, a sense that you came from somewhere and are therefore going somewhere.

AGES: 4, 16, 28, 40, 52, 64 and 76   'LEO' YEARS

"GROWTH IN/THROUGH CREATIVE SELF-EXPRESSION" - After hopefully securing yourself in the previous Cancer years, these are times when you grow in terms of making more of yourself. This can mean many things, from discovering that you have a personality all of your own at the age of 4, to discovering some unique talent at 16 that will serve you in your adult career. At 28 or 40 such self-expression could peak as creating children, art or music, or a better expression of yourself generally, while at 52 seeing your creative efforts more in spiritual terms such as what you are giving to society. Sixty-four, being possibly a time of, or prior to, retirement could mean finding some creative pastime to give meaning to a life after full-time work, and seventy-six would hopefully be the glow of a live lived to the full. Whatever the age, a Leo Jupiter Year is all about being celebrating the 'I' in you, that centre that creates its own reality, that is sovereign in its own realm.

Because Leo and Jupiter are both expansive by nature, such years as these can be a field day for simply enjoying life and creating or attracting a better lifestyle and class of people. However, the bias towards excess which is the nature of Jupiter can also make you overstep the mark and become undone by the very thing being used to further yourself, be it childish outburst or market speculation; snobbish, overblown ego-expression or passionate sexual involvement. Avoiding the pride, vanity or arrogance that comes before a fall is an elementary guideline here.

Having said all of this though, it is important not to check too much the natural flowering of personality that occurs during these years, for it is through such 'shows of self' that a feel for your life-force and creativity is discovered. Leo is the sign of gambling, and it is always a case of 'win some, lose some' when it comes to thrusting yourself into the field of play in a bid to succeed.

★ GO-ZONES
for your 'Leo' Jupiter Years
Areas of luck, encouragement, growth and wisdom - and how to make the most of them.

GO-ZONE	APPRECIATE & UNDERSTAND...
Play	Becoming as a little child is now the way to breathe freshness, spontaneity and vitality into your life. Playing is the art of living. The actor in you.
Romance	That 'love is in the air' in the romantic sense of there being opportunities to make yourself feel special because you find/have someone that thinks you are, and you think they are too. All the world loves a lover.
Creativity	It is the natural inclination of a human being to create. We have been created and therefore we must create - that is why we are called 'creatures'. The pursuit or promotion of any skill, especially an artistic one, is well-starred during such years. That (your)children are also (your)creations.
Enterprise	That you were born to make more of yourself, and that the key to this is having a sense that there is a spark within you that has its own significance, and that you owe it to yourself to kindle that spark into a glow, that you then fan into a flame. This is a time to shine and show who's boss.
Generosity	Giving of yourself - physically, emotionally, mentally or spiritually - is the surest way to feel worthwhile in yourself. That virtue is its own reward.
Recognition	The need to have recognised whatever worth you possess is a vital human requirement, without which self-worth problems will arise. You may first have to recognise this fact, then what it actually is in you that you want recognised. Whatever the case, make hay - for the Sun is now shining.

AGES: 5, 17, 29, 41, 53, 65 and 77   'VIRGO' YEARS

"GROWTH IN/THROUGH EFFICIENCY" - These are years when progress is difficult and painstaking. The attention that you have to give to myriad details and complications might give a feeling that you are getting nowhere fast. However, you should not let this get to you - try to see everything you are doing in the spirit of preparation for or service to something higher and better. 'Work' is the keynote now. A 'Virgo' year can be especially disheartening when compared to the high hopes and extravagant displays of the preceding 'Leo' year. But really Virgo follows Leo specifically in order to trim sails and cut the suit to fit the cloth - whether it's having to knuckle down to primary school at 5 years, exam or revision at 17, your Saturn Return at 29 (see page 213), Mid-Life Crisis at 41(see page 239), health issues at 53, retirement at 65, or the limitations imposed by old age at 77. And creative visions (Leo) are always followed by having to get down to the practical details (Virgo).

Generally, an issue that can arise now is one of health - probably from working too hard or of letting the slog get to you. Also a change of diet or some other health regimen may be imposed or called for, as well as finding a more efficient way of living that cuts down wear and tear. Try to get emotional issues into perspective so that they do not overwhelm you on the one hand or that you lose sight of them on the other. Much of this perspective will depend upon and be implemented by devising or discovering 'techniques for living'. Such techniques are methods one can use to deal with people and things in a way that is clever and effective. For example, a difficult person could be best handled by pre-empting whatever it is that makes them difficult. Like if they are indecisive, giving them too much choice would be asking for trouble.

All such efforts will bear fruit come your following 'Libra' year, but a 'Virgo' year just spent worrying and carping will breed very little. Now is the time for working and studying hard in order to improve yourself and the life you lead.

★ **GO-ZONES**
for your 'Virgo' Jupiter Years

Areas of luck, encouragement, growth and wisdom - and how to make the most of them.

GO-ZONE	APPRECIATE & UNDERSTAND...
Work	That work is the key to success. That 'the devil makes work for idle hands' in that being busy at anything is preferable to feeling slothful, useless, vacuous or pointless - or simply neurotic about what you think you 'should' be doing. Just get on with it and find out as you go.
Health	How to listen to, respect and care for your body and mind. How your psychological and physical well-being are absolutely dependent upon one another. How health is a priority and recipe for success in all areas of life.
Service	That being of help to others has a deeply satisfying effect upon your state of being, and also stops you from fretting too much over personal issues.
Analysis	How you and others tick as individuals. How to be clear in yourself by simplifying your life and prioritising your involvements, and vice versa.
Method	How much a job done in the right way is very satisfying, and that the right way must consist of a plan, preparation, order and the right tools and technique, or you'll just botch things and become frustrated.
Study / Retraining	How it will improve your mind and/or career prospects. How it will resolve financial problems, increase self-esteem.

AGES: 6, 18, 30, 42, 54, 66 and 78   'LIBRA' YEARS

"GROWTH IN/THROUGH RELATIONSHIP" - These are years when you grow towards becoming more of a 'member of society', depending on your age and social inclinations personally. At the youngest end, at six years of age one begins to become aware that there is something called 'Other'. Other is everything that you are not, be it an individual or a group, human or otherwise. At eighteen you are probably in the throes of taking relationship more seriously; at thirty, during or just after your Saturn Return (see page 213), you may well have made some lasting commitment to a relationship, such as marriage itself - or be at some kind of turning-point with regard to relationship. At forty-two your circumstances and experiences, being in the midst of certain mid-life crisis factors challenge you to relate in a far more sophisticated manner than ever before. At fifty-four, being the time of your Second Lunar Return (see page 186), apart from a new emotional focus coming into view, domestic/family relationships could well be a major issue. The last two ages for 'Libra' Years possibly involve the endings of some longstanding relationships, and of generally relating to others in the light of a wealth of experience.

All in all, 'Libra' Jupiter Years offer you the opportunity to be more socially aware and involved. How you go to meet such an offer is entirely up to you and your current relationship status, social life, and ability to relate. But it must be borne in mind that a 'Libra' Year is a highly important one in the Jupiter Cycle because it marks the point of culmination in your endeavours to establish yourself in the world of Other - which includes business and market relationships, and the public at large. In your adult years then, you stand to see the world as being far more available to you as it offers up its resources, agencies and avenues of expansion.

On a more psychological level, a 'Libra' Year, being that of Other, means that you can learn a great deal about why certain people are in your life through understanding that they are a projection of your own Self. In other words, through realising that everyone in your life is there for a good reason, and what that reason is, you then appreciate just what you are and have as an individual.

★ GO-ZONES
for your 'Libra' Jupiter Years

Areas of luck, encouragement, growth and wisdom - and how to make the most of them.

GO-ZONE	APPRECIATE & UNDERSTAND...
Relating	That whatever your relationship situation is, you stand to improve your skill in relating and thereby have a more rewarding love and social life.
Harmony	That the role of 'peacemaker' may well fall to you in that you are the one who brings accord and understanding to any situation that requires it. Any innate or learned skills regarding fields such as, counselling, diplomacy or public relations now come to the fore and enable you to make something of them. 'Libran' indecisiveness can and must be overcome now.
Attractiveness	How through being more socially and/or fashionably aware, in terms of skills and grooming, you become more in demand, personally and /or professionally.
Art & Aesthetics	That you are more than usually aware of what pleases the values and senses of yourself and others generally and can therefore become more successful materially and/or in terms of acclaim and self-esteem.
Justice & Balance	That you could be called to sue for justice in some respect. This will mean weighing the odds and coming to a just decision, sticking to your principles.

AGES: 7, 19, 31, 43, 55, 67 and 79   'SCORPIO' YEARS

"GROWTH IN/THROUGH INTIMACY" - This means that during these years intimate or sexual relationships, be they your own or belonging to someone close to you, play an important part in your growth process. It can also mean that any relationship of any weight or significance reaches critical mass and either breaks apart or breaks through to a new level. Alternatively, the unsatisfied need for intimacy can also reach critical mass and demand some sort of desperate release, which may not properly come until the following 'Sagittarius' Year. In any event, 'Scorpio' Jupiter Years can be quite cathartic as they force a piece of your soul to the surface - which is what intimacy is ultimately all about.

Because of the encountering of certain taboos, Scorpionic features such as obsession, manipulation, secretiveness, wrangling and intrigue can arise, creating grist for the mill of your emotional development. The biggest taboo of all, death, may also play a part in taking your life to a new level of involvement, but it is not something you should morbidly expect. At any rate, if a death does occur during a 'Scorpio' Year, you can be sure that it marks the end of an important chapter in your life, and the birth of an equally important new one, and again, act as a fillip to intimacy.

The individual 'Scorpio' Jupiter Years do not seem to coincide with conventional ages of any significance, other than perhaps age seven which could be regarded as a time when sexual interest first makes itself felt. Perhaps this is because such Scorpionic extremes as sex and death can rear their powerful heads at any time, with dynamically transformative effect. But if they do so during a 'Scorpio' Jupiter Year you can be sure of that such events are major turning points in your life's plot.

Another way of looking at a 'Scorpio' Year is seeing it as the intensification necessary to resolve any stalemate or deadlock created during the possibly too diplomatic or indecisive 'Libra' Year that preceded it. Shared resources or legacies could also be an area of good fortune or development.

★ ## GO-ZONES
for your 'Scorpio' Jupiter Years

Areas of luck, encouragement, growth and wisdom - and how to make the most of them.

GO-ZONE | APPRECIATE & UNDERSTAND...

Sex

What sex actually is and thereby take it to new levels of pleasure, health and general effectiveness in your world. That being or getting (more)sexually involved now is a strong possibility, and that this can either take you like a wave (mostly in the younger Scorpio Jupiter Years) or be something you consciously or ritually embark upon, like the practice of Tantra or Taoism.

Power

What power actually is in your life, and life generally, will be taken to a new level. Clue: through concentrating on what is most genuine within or about you, and not flinching from any challenge, you will empower yourself most assuredly. That if you see power as something that is outside or over you, then that is where it will remain, and possibly become an issue.

Dealing

That investing your time and energy in business and generally making a financial killing could be your Growth Area now. Taxation figures.

Delving

That you will be drawn (even more) into such fields as psychology and the occult as you seek to discover the hidden or root causes beneath outer phenomena. Growth in such inner knowledge is deeply influential.

Inevitability

That as one door closes, another one opens. An awareness such as this could now well be your most productive, informative or consoling truth.

AGES: 8, 20, 32, 44, 56, 68 and 80   'SAGITTARIUS' YEARS

"GROWTH IN ITSELF" - Because Sagittarius is the Sign that Jupiter 'rules' - meaning that they are both the same sort of energy - Jupiterian growth functions particularly well in the Sign of the Archer-Centaur. Consequently, 'Sagittarius' Jupiter Years are usually upbeat, expansive, advantageous or positive in some way. At the very least, they will be times when it is a case of it being 'an ill-wind that blows nobody any good'. In fact, the whole principle or philosophy of growth is something worth focussing upon at these times.

As the Archer, Sagittarius is growth in the sense of having a target to aim for, or simply letting loose an intention and following it, encountering whatever adventures you meet along the way as part and parcel of that growth process. So during these years, such enthusiasm for some goal or path is literally par for the course, along with the positive thinking that is integral to it.

As the Centaur, Sagittarian growth is greatly assisted by having the 'horse-power' and 'horse-sense' to get where you want to get to. So if you are going to make a lift-off, now is the time. The ground that you cover can be literal in the sense of travelling, cerebral in the sense of education towards some qualification that equips you and others even better for the journey ahead, or seeking in the sense of looking for a meaning to life, such as a philosophy or a set of beliefs or laws, or simply what you are after. The significant point here is that you have reached a significant point. Consequently, you are confident and eager about making a move, going for it, etc.. Time to think big.

So, furtherance is the byword now - into whatever field your aspirations or your loins lead you. The power of optimism and enthusiasm is what counts now, whether it your entertaining dreams at eight years old of what you are going to be when you grow up, university life at age twenty, a new path of learning at thirty-two or forty-four, or more religious or spiritual paths at fifty-six, sixty-eight or eighty. Indeed, at any age, but especially the later ones, being able to see the bigger picture is the important and encouraging thing.

★ **GO-ZONES**
for your 'Sagittarius' Jupiter Years

Areas of luck, encouragement, growth and wisdom - and how to make the most of them.

GO-ZONE	APPRECIATE & UNDERSTAND...
Sport	How now your physical body is able to prove itself, whatever your 'Sagittarian' Jupiter Year, notwithstanding your age and condition. Some form of physical culture is now in the offing or is a path to further success.
Travel	That travel and foreign issues not only broaden the mind but can be a lot of fun too, and they gives you a sense of the adventure that life essentially is.
Friction	How through engaging with whatever it is that opposes, threatens or frightens you, that you will make your greatest advances. Anything or anyone that now confronts you is probably a great teacher for you.
Higher Mind	How a sense and awareness that there is some higher reason for life will now transport you to a new level of social and/or professional involvement. Such could entail your pursuit of any subject that is never-ending in its content, like law, philosophy, religion, astrology, etc..
Higher Education	That at any one of these stages of your life you stand to advance through improving your mind or (working towards) winning educational honours, be it in a formal or informal way.

AGES: 9, 21, 33, 45, 57, 69 and 81   CAPRICORN' YEARS

"GROWTH IN/THROUGH AUTHORITY" - After the expansiveness and opportunity of a 'Sagittarius' Year, the Growth Principle of Jupiter is limited or conditioned in 'Capricorn'. This is because anything that goes through Capricorn has to pass its tests of practicality and authority. So at nine years of age there is the possibility of hitting some sort of crisis with respect to those who have or had authority over you, like teachers and parents. In other words, this is a critical time because it determines how you're measuring up in the eyes of those authority figures and the systems that they set up and control. Consequently, if you pass their tests you go up a step, but if you fail you go back one, or 'miss a turn'. Similar circumstances force themselves upon you at twenty-one, when you 'come of age', particularly considering your First Saturn Waning Square (page 212) occurs then too. (Saturn has a similar influence to Capricorn because it rules it, that is the Planet and the Sign have the same energies). Thirty-three can be critical because you may go up the career ladder then, or conversely have to knuckle down to the real world (again), or at worst, find yourself out of favour with those in authority. Interestingly, from a Christian viewpoint, Jesus was crucified at this age, and one could say that at that time he ran foul of the existing authorities, but the authority he gained in being nailed to the cross (a Saturnian symbol, by the way) was inestimable. Age forty-five follows your Second Saturn Opposition (page 224), so this can be very telling with respect to status and authority, whereas fifty-seven should be an age when you really do know where you stand. With regard to the two eldest ages, it should be borne in mind that Capricorn and Saturn both rule old age, and so the plusses and minuses that go with this are strongly in evidence at these times.

★
GO-ZONES
for your 'Capricorn' Jupiter Years

Areas of luck, encouragement, growth and wisdom - and how to make the most of them.

GO-ZONE   APPRECIATE & UNDERSTAND...

Status   That your professional and/or social position will now be increased in proportion to the efforts you have made previously.

Discipline   That through adhering to some course or regimen you will build for your future and create an inner sense of stability as you do so. This would have to include making certain sacrifices, hopefully in the sure awareness of necessity.

Authority   What you think authority is for you. Is it something which is created by the status quo and the powers that be, or something more of your own making or on a higher, spiritual, level? Such years are times when you can, or rather must, find out. Then you will have to do whatever you have to in order to measure up to what that authority is demanding of you. On a more personal level, you can now build a sense of authority that dispels an unnecessary need for approval from certain figures in your emotional life.

Objectivity   That you now have the ability or opportunity to see things as they really are. From looking hard at what is going on in your life as dispassionately and fairly as possible, you then know what is, and what is not, required of you. Knowing where you stand is the big advantage now.

Organisation   These are times to create structure, functionality and order in your life, both businesswise and personally. This is when you create systems or are beaten by them. If you are stuck in a system, then now you should organise yourself either out of it as a 'system' in your own right (ready for the 'Aquarian' Year that follows), or into a better position within it.

AGES: 10, 22, 34, 46, 58, 70 and 82   'AQUARIUS' YEARS

"GROWTH IN/THROUGH PRINCIPLES" - If the 'Capricorn' Year was about status and ambitions as the means and object of growth, then the 'Aquarius' Year sees ideals and aspirations as what need to be expanded and expounded. All this means that some kind of reform, rebellion, splintering or breaking away is what has to happen in order to make way for new growth. As ever with Aquarius, there is the danger of 'throwing the baby out with the bath-water' in the sense that the structures and associates you have previously acquired become ditched or affronted as you make your Aquarian bid for freedom. Ideally, you should aim for a happy medium, but not sacrifice your principles in the process.

At age ten, the Aquarian drive to not be 'one of the many' is largely unconscious, and so any signs of rebelliousness then should be interpreted as the child connecting with some deeply installed program to be true to themselves rather than to the system in which they find themselves. Age twenty-two can be a time of groups and friends splintering as you determine what your true course and company are. For many people, thirty-four and forty-six can be times of being 'settled' and as such the Aquarian Growth in/through Principles may just manifest as boredom with existing involvements. For the more individualistic type though, new horizons beckon or are sought. Age fifty-eight is a contradictory one because it occurs on or near the Second Saturn Return (page 230), an influence which inclines to conforming in some way. So, 'Be what you are, my friend!' is the definite convention for this, or any Jupiter year. Seventy, being the allotted three score years and ten, must have some unique significance for the individual human being. At eighty-two, you would be sliding into your Uranus Return, a highly Aquarian 'moment of truth' as Uranus governs (is of the same energy as) that Sign.

★ **GO-ZONES**
for your 'Aquarius' Jupiter Years

Areas of luck, encouragement, growth and wisdom - and how to make the most of them.

GO-ZONE	APPRECIATE & UNDERSTAND...
Friends	Friends are an integral part of your growth process now. New friends will be particularly instrumental in affecting your life course and development as an individual. Old friends and associates may need to be given a shot in the arm - or be left behind as being no longer suitable to your evolution.
Idealism	That your growth and furtherance as a unique individual has everything to do with being true to your ideals or vision, which would necessitate knowing what they are. The clearer your sense of 'dharma' or individual purpose, then the clearer will be your path ahead. What is unusual about you.
Humanity	An increase in your awareness of what actually being human is will now greatly encourage you and simplify your life too. That human is what you are but may never have really been shown how to be so, and that through being more or merely human you discover who you are as a one-off that has never occurred before or ever will exist again. All this could lead you to help others discover their humanness, and uphold their right to be so.
Revolution	The Chinese symbol for Revolution is an old skin being shed, which means that these 'Aquarius' Years are times of 'moulting' for you. You could find yourself out of sorts at these times because you could feel you are neither one thing or the other - the old you hasn't gone and the new you has not yet grown to replace it. But that is what moulting is, a new skin (life or persona) growing beneath and sloughing off the old one.

AGES: 11, 23, 35, 47, 59, 71 and 83   'PISCES' YEARS

"GROWTH IN/THROUGH ACCEPTANCE" - Through simply allowing things to happen during these times, you find that, eventually, you move forward and on. And considering that this is the last stage of a Jupiter Cycle, things 'happening' can mean that something ceases to happen, often in the sense of 'fading away'. A 'Pisces' Jupiter Year could therefore be regarded as a time of dissolution or disillusionment, or both, depending upon your emotional state or philosophy of life.

By the same token, such a year can be best used as an opportunity to relinquish anything that is proving too difficult or damaging or draining to keep up. Such a thing could be a relationship, a style of living, a job, an appearance, or a habit. Then again, you may not have any choice in the matter as whatever it is just seems to slip from your grasp. But it is at just such a time that this relinquishing must take place, for otherwise you could end up like someone who is about to embark on a new journey (in the following 'Aries' Year), but is still carrying the baggage from the last one. This would be particularly true of emotional baggage in the form of unresolved relationship issues.

At age eleven you have to leave behind your childhood as you go to 'big' school with its more serious curriculum; there may too be other moves away in that period. At twenty-three an adolescent hangover or some feckless lifestyle may have to shaken off in order to move forward, or then again you could find yourself in some backwater as you attempt to retreat from life's harsher realities. Age thirty-five or forty-seven could also be times when the pressures of life tempt you to find a way out, say into alcohol or some other distraction, or to find a transcendental path through some spiritual discipline. Age fifty-nine coincides with your Second Saturn Return (see page 230), making this time a major watershed in your life, with the necessary bill of acceptance of the way things are. Age seventy-one and/or eighty-three should hopefully see 'Growth through Acceptance' in the light of some kind of submission to one's mortality and any thoughts on an afterlife, as well as a realisation that compassion is the ultimate response to the human condition. In typical Piscean fashion, none of the above suggestions should be strictly ascribed to each age, for such endings and submissions as a passport to the next round are common to them all. 'Pisces' Years are essentially times of coming to an understanding of what (your) karma is, and endeavouring to clear it.

★ **GO-ZONES**
for your 'Pisces' Jupiter Years

Areas of luck, encouragement, growth and wisdom - and how to make the most of them.

GO-ZONE	APPRECIATE & UNDERSTAND...
Mystery	That now you can accept the way things are and learn to just go with the flow This means that basically we know nothing in the face of the mystery that is life, and that the best and only way forward is to trust and succumb to one's fate and the beautiful and sublime feelings that characterise such a mystery. Mysticism and mythology could also show you the way through and ahead now. The power of sacrifice.
Devotion	That some task or ministry to which you can give yourself body and soul would be a wonderfully appropriate way of showing your acceptance that there is some greater cause to serve. Devotion may also be to some commitment that is to your own salvation. Making amends is advantageous.
Sensitivity	Any higher or psychic sense or ability that you have and attune it to relieving or enlightening others. The healing arts now call.
Imagination	That art and music can be the channels for the expression of the visions and finer feelings that you currently experience, taking you and/or others to new heights, in preparation for the next stage of growth.

Your Moon Cycle
The Tides of Your Emotional Life

I Must Go
Down by the River
Down to the Sea
See if The Fishes
Agree with Me
I'm Born of Water
Born of Water
I Must Flow

In the end there is no better single word to sum up the complex significance of the Moon than SOUL. Your Soul is the feeling deep within you, a longing for home and security, to be where you belong - and the instinct for what is safe or familiar, or, dangerous or alien. The Soul is also the emotions that bubble up from the well-spring of your being when enraptured by love or art; that dwell still, sometimes stagnant and fearful, within you; that course consistently through your life and being, or at times rage like a torrent. You can see from this kind of imagery that the Soul and the Moon are decidedly Watery - and indeed the great majority of our physical make-up is water (around 70%), and the tides of the waters that comprise most of the surface of our home planet Earth are governed by the Moon. And so your body, and the thoughts and feelings that it experiences, are also subject to 'tides', the nature of which are what your Moon Cycle describes. One way or another, such thoughts and feelings can then seek to be given form or take place as events.

The Moon is our own satellite, and as such it is our 'governor' (that which regulates flow) in that it gives us that monthly cycle and rhythm that is short enough to be familiar, and long enough to digest or regulate the experience of something, or in the case of a woman, to produce a new egg and shed it if not fertilised, along with the old lining of her womb. And this last vital point tells us that this 'governor' is really the Mother, doing her rounds looking after her children, or creating or making ready for them. So Mother is arguably a word as valid for summing up the Moon as Soul - be it your biological mother, a mother-like figure or institution, a Moon Goddess, or anything or anyone that protects or nurtures. The connection between Mother and Soul is as close as the words 'Nature and Nurture', or 'Chicken and Egg'.

By the same token, you can never have a Mother without there being a Child, a third contender for the Moon Keyword title! And no matter how old you are, there is always that Child within you, with its need for security, its longing for a 'welcome in the hillsides', and its yearning to express and give form to its feelings and memories. Most importantly, that child - which we could call your Receptivity - is in need of protection or it can drown in a sea of emotional input, or conversely, can dry up through denying or being denied that emotionality. In this light, we can regard the passage of the Moon through the skies around our planetary home as, like a shepherdess to her flock, gathering and guiding us towards that 'home', be it far or near. She is the measure of our emotional development and experience. As such her cycle is more of a continuous flow or succession of waves than a number of significant points like the cycles of the planets, like Saturn.

Consequently, we look at the cycle of the Moon in terms of a number of 'Phases' that flow in and out of one another, although there still are 'significant points' at the times when any 'Phase' actually begins. And I put the word 'Phase' in inverted commas because they are not the actual phases of the Moon which we see in the sky through the month - they are but symbolic of them. This is because the Moon that we use to see the Cycles of our Emotional Life is the Progressed Moon. The Progressed Moon takes the lunar month of an average of approximately twenty-seven and a third days, and projects it onto a wider screen of approximately twenty-seven and a third years - that is, twenty seven years and four months. This period is then divided up into eight 'Phases' of our emotional life and development, as depicted in the illustration overleaf. These 'Phases' are using the same principle of waxing and waning, flowing and ebbing, as the actual lunar phases we see, but they are not exactly the same because the actual lunar phases are produced by the Moon's angle of relationship to the Sun. Such phases are used in astrology as something called the 'progressed soli-lunar cycle', but it is far too complex and technical to include in this book!

Beginning on page 125 I give descriptions of the general meanings of each of these 'Phases', and then from page 143 specific meanings as they occur at the different times through your life, both in the context of where you are according to your age and of other Planetary Cycles that are active at the same time. Generally speaking, the influence of each 'Phase' is at its strongest at the time it begins, lasting for about nine months. Its influence then fades until it gives way to the onset of the next 'Phase'. This 'hit and fade' process is graphically depicted in the graduated shading of each 'Phase' as seen by their headings. Do not, however, take the depicted fading too literally, as in some cases the initial strength of a 'Phase' can persist. Your Moon Cycle is hereby seen as a succession of eight waves, four 'flowing in' or 'waxing' for the first half of the cycle, four 'ebbing out' or 'waning' for the second. The Waxing half of the cycle is the 'sowing' time when we bring something to Realisation, whereas the Waning half is when we 'reap' or harvest what we have sown.

All of this serves to show how our life unfolds, like a prewritten tale that

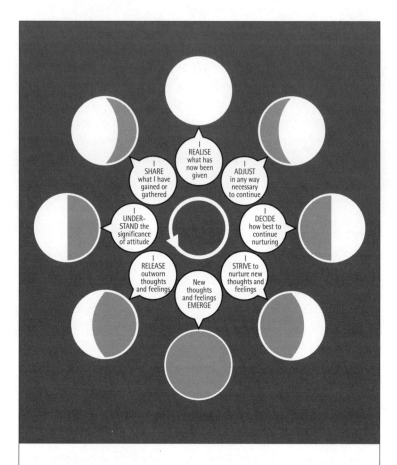

Each Cycle, which lasts twenty-seven years and four months, begins with the 'Emerging Phase', at the bottom of the picture, with the 'Phases' unfolding in an anti-clockwise direction. The NAME and a Keyphrase or Affirmation for each 'Phase', which lasts three years and five months, are given in the bubbles, the diameter of which also denotes the actual beginning and end of that 'Phase'.

Note that 'thoughts and feelings' can take form as products or events. Also observe how the right Waxing half of the picture/cycle mirrors the left 'Waning' half.

we can also edit as it does so. And the Progressed Moon's Cycle is marvellously revealing in this respect. However, you may sometimes see that major changes or moves (often with regard to home and emotional relationships) happen up to a year before or after they are 'supposed' to at the time a particular 'Phase' begins. Apart from there being another Planetary Cycle prevailing at that time which would account for it, there seems to be either an inclination to pre-empt a change by jumping before it jumps on you, or that delays are due to the time it takes for it to sink in that the change is unavoidable, or to the time in takes, say, for a house sale to go through. Also, the notion springs to mind of Moon-ruled gestation, in that an event occurs nine months after it was conceived. Even so, be careful not to force an event to 'fit' the astrological influence. Concentrate upon what really happened or is happening at the time and you will see what it really meant and is telling you - and this would include your Birth and the period prior to it (see 'First Emerging Phase' on pages 125 & 144). For example, an elderly client of mine made a major move a year after the start of her 'Second Emerging Phase'(page 164), but where she stayed for a short time whilst it was actually occurring is where she regularly visited all her life from then on, and where eventually she returned to live and has remained for the last twenty-five years.

Possibly more than any other astrological influence, the Moon can show you where you are coming from and where you are going to - and more importantly, give you a definite sense that your life has emotional meaning, direction and purpose. So it is worth taking the time and making the effort to remember and ponder the events and feelings that comprise the course and the flow of that River of Your Life. It can also help to see each cycle of eight 'phases' as a kind of 'gestation process' through which you are formed as you were in your mother's womb, to be born again at each 'Emerging Phase' every 27⅓ years.

A FILTER FOR EXPERIENCE

As the Moon is what gives form to things rather than what actually creates them - which is the role of the Sun - the 'Phases' are not actually making events or experiences happen but informing you of the way in which you should naturally emotionally respond to those events and experiences. So for instance, during an 'Emerging Phase' you are emotionally in tune with that time when you are living it in the spirit of something Emerging or New in your life. The Moon being the Realm of the Unconscious and a case of 'chicken and egg' means that something may indeed Emerge before you even think about it, but being consciously attuned to whatever 'Phase' it might be ensures that you are feeling as positive as possible about whatever is happening.

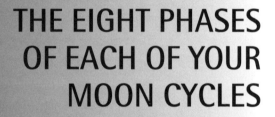

THE EIGHT PHASES OF EACH OF YOUR MOON CYCLES

1. A general overview of the meaning of each Moon 'Phase' – beginning on page 125

2. The meaning of each of the Moon 'Phases' as they occur throughout your life- beginning on page 143

EMERGING 'Phases'

BIRTH to 3y 5m (p 144)
27y 4m to 30y 9m(p 164)
54y 8m to 58y 1m(p 186)
82y 0m to 85y 5m (p 198)

This 'Phase' we could see as the symbolic equivalent to the New Moon, the start of a new emotional cycle of twenty-seven and a third years, and also the end of the previous one. In fact, it is the previous cycle, and particularly the last 'Releasing Phase' (see page 140), that bear greatly upon what you make of the birth of this new cycle, and of the cycle as a whole. If the previous cycle ended with certain emotional or family issues still unresolved, then the new cycle could be hampered or confused by this. Then again, the whole nature of the new cycle, and beyond even, could have the express purpose of sorting out that 'unfinished business' - whatever it may be. Furthermore, that previous cycle has probably provided you with the experience and insight to forge ahead with the new one. But whether or not you are 'clear' of the undertow of previous encumbrances or actually well-equipped because of them, the beginnings of any new cycle are always somewhat indistinct - just like the image of the New Moon itself (see above).

But the main point is that it is the start of a new cycle of emotional experience and development, a bit like getting seven new letters in a game of Scrabble with which to a make a brand new word, except one usually has some odd letters left over from the previous go! The clues as to what this new cycle is going to be about are essentially written into the 'set and setting' of the time during which it begins. This means that the emotional and mental attitude that you have now, along with the physical and relationship circumstances in which you find yourself, have everything to do with what that new cycle is going to be concerned with - and again with what could be influencing it from the previous cycle and 'Phase', for good or ill.

So whether it a past or present situation that you are investigating here, look closely at the circumstances of that time (and what immediately preceded it) and you will find some wonderful clues as to where the River of Your Life is wanting to go. These instances, because the Moon is what it is, can be very personal, so it is hard to find examples of this amongst public figures - so I will give my own experience of the Second Emerging Phase which begins at around twenty-seven and third years of age. About four months prior to this point in time, the woman with whom I had a longstanding relationship that had been winding down over the few years previously (very much in accord with the 'Releasing Phase' that was occurring then) was reading my 'horoscope' from a magazine. At the time I had no interest in astrology or knowledge of it other than my Sun-Sign, and so as the forecast for the coming year said I was going to leave my current job, find a new home, and, unless a miracle happened, come to the end of a relationship, I could be forgiven for raising an eyebrow or two! But yes it all happened - even though 'horoscope' columns cannot take into account anyone's 'Lunar Return' as the 'Emerging Phase' is also called. This so impressed me that I began my study of astrology.

Apart from this being the rebirth of my professional and personal life, and the main theme of the whole 27⅓ year cycle to come, the point is that the reality of this was not that evident to me as it was happening - I was still busy trying to become a successful songwriter. I did not actual decide to go for it as a profession until the 'Deciding Phase' almost seven years later, encouraged, believe it or not, by my then meeting the author of that 'horoscope', the late Patric Walker!

All of this personal anecdote indicates how at 'Emerging Phases' we have this strong sense of something 'sprouting' or 'germinating'. As such, at this time you have to be quite self-possessed, and not consider too much the opinions or even feelings of others. This does not mean to say that you should be insensitive, but that the little sprouting seed of your Emerging self should not wonder and tarry too much because of what someone else says or does that disagrees with it. It cannot afford to be otherwise.

DURING ANY 'EMERGING PHASE' YOU CAN MANAGE, LEARN AND BENEFIT FROM IT BY ALLOWING AND NURTURING WHATEVER IS WANTING TO EMERGE.

STRIVING 'Phases'

3y 5m to 6y 10m (p 147)
30y 9m to 34y 2m (p 168)
58y 1m to 61y 6m (p 189)

This 'Phase' we could see as the symbolic equivalent to the Crescent Moon, which literally means 'growing one'. Whatever has been set in motion at or since the start of the cycle at the preceding 'Emerging Phase' you can now see signs of what is to come. The trouble is, so can everyone else, and that means that whatever the world thinks, or whatever you feel the world thinks, of what you are developing at this stage is taken on board very personally by you. And again, like with all other 'Phases', the sense of what has gone before is also highly influential but particularly the previous 'Emerging Phase'. In effect, you are now having to make an effort to establish a trend, that can be maintained for some years to come, in the face of the competition, conditions and opinions that you feel are put forward by the outside world on the one hand, and any inner doubts or need to withdraw or tread water on the other. It is during this 'Phase' that something can occur that challenges our progress or confuses it. Such could be an external event or an internal feeling, or a combination of the two. If the 'Emerging Phase' was akin to being a 'seed', the Striving 'Phase' is like a 'seedling' in that it suggests what is trying to grow or take shape. And just because of this 'tenuous visibility' we can be easily put off by such outer or inner influences. However, all being well, one can usually feel more confident, or is made to be so, around half way through this 'Phase'.

But when all is said and done, it is called the 'Striving Phase' with good reason. You have to Strive against any possible active or passive discouragement from that outer or inner world, and Strive to discern what really is trying to grow, and Strive to nurture it in whatever way you can. By way of example, allow me to continue with the events and experiences in my own life that begun with the onset of my 'Second Emerging

Phase'(see page 164) when I moved from city to country and began my study of astrology, but with the initial intent of becoming a professional songwriter. With the 'Striving Phase' I moved back into the city, which initially meant having to leave behind the peace and quiet amidst which I had been able to write songs. So effectively, my Striving was firstly to leave behind that life and the ambition to be successful in the music field. My Striving was also greatly involved with having to make my way in the city again, which actually included coping with the difficulties and distractions that I had originally left the city because of. But all the time I was Striving to learn more and more about astrology, and now, because there was a larger and more varied social input, I was able to be far more practical in terms of helping others through astrology, as well as getting a lot more feedback. And all this was having to be done when I had time free from my day-job and normal social engagements.

During a 'Striving Phase' then, the vital issue is to detect what is trying to take form, and to nourish it in whatever way you can. At the same time, be wary of inclinations to revert to the 'devil you know' in the form of old habits and haunts, attitudes and activities. Whatever that 'growing one' is, it will then assuredly GROW even more.

DURING ANY 'STRIVING PHASE' YOU CAN MANAGE, LEARN AND BENEFIT FROM IT BY STRIVING WITH AND THROUGH WHATEVER IS HAPPENING.

DECIDING 'Phases'

6y 10m to 10y 3m (p 149)
34y 2m to 37y 7m (p 171)
61y 6m to 64y11m (p 191)

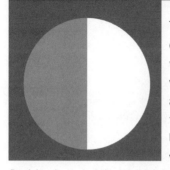

This 'Phase' we could see as the symbolic equivalent to the Waxing Half Moon, which can be viewed as a critical point in your emotional life in that whatever you are involved in is now demanding some form of Decision. Alternatively, it could be a case of a Decision being made for you. In the first case, making a crucial Decision is one of the hardest things to do if you are having to deal with an emotional issue where the rights and wrongs are not so clearly defined. Yet the 'tide' is coming in fast now and you cannot afford to dither or procrastinate - the time for action has come. Otherwise you could be become overwhelmed by whatever the existing situation is. So this is a kind of 'publish and be damned' or 'the fat's in the fire' situation. The important point is to set something definite in motion, one way or the other. You can 'fake it 'til you make it' and make any necessary alterations come the ensuing 'Adjusting Phase'. But if you sit on the fence you could get torn in two or feel compromised for a long time to come. Everything depends ultimately upon you having the courage of your convictions - and thereupon having convictions in the first place. What is really helpful is gaining a sense of where your fate, where that River of Your Life, actually wants you to go at this time. To do this you will probably have to distinguish between essentials and non-essentials, and accept the course that your life wishes to take.

In the second case, your Decision may be made for you. To continue with my own case, during my 'Second Deciding Phase' I was made redundant from the job I had with a publishers. It was Decided for me that I was not supposed to be going where that job and everything it involved was taking me. But then I had to Decide what to do as this was closed to me - and I Decided to go professional as an astrologer.

For many people, there are Decisions like this that are made by someone or something in their lives who is more 'powerful' than them. Although this is probably par for the course at the 'First Deciding Phase' when you are a child, later on such situations may point to the necessity of Deciding to be your own power in your life. It is then that it can be discovered why people are in power - they're good at making Decisions! They are also prepared to take the flak if what they Decided was wrong - or they ought to be.

It has been said that it is not making Decisions that is so difficult - it is keeping to them. This implies that we can think some course of action is a good idea until it gets hard to maintain, and then we look for reasons to get out of it - like dieting, for instance. In order to keep to a decision we need to have a very firm sense that that is the way we must go, can go, and want to go. If you don't get an honest 'yes' to all three - I must, I can and I want to - then the chances are that your Decision will come to naught.

DURING ANY 'DECIDING PHASE' YOU CAN MANAGE, LEARN AND BENEFIT FROM IT BY BEING DECISIVE ABOUT WHATEVER IS HAPPENING.

ADJUSTING 'Phases'

10y 3m to 13y 8m (p 151)
37y 7m to 41y 0m (p 173)
64y 11m to 68y 4m (p192)

This 'Phase' we could see as the symbolic equivalent to the strangely named 'Gibbous' Moon which is the phase before the Full Moon. So during this 'Phase' we are between the decision that was made in the previous 'Deciding Phase' and the form of what was set in motion reaching fruition at the 'Realising Phase'. The word 'Gibbous' literally means 'hump-backed', so this 'Phase' is like a hump-backed bridge you have to cross in order to attain that peak of 'Realisation'. So this indicates that we have to Adjust our speed and trajectory to negotiate this bridge from the one 'Phase' to the other. It is human nature to feel that once you are past a crucial stage such as the previous 'Deciding Phase' you can relax and free-wheel a bit. But the fact is that this Adjustment has to be made carefully, otherwise, if you are unable or unwilling to do so, you could well 'get the hump' - and as any driver knows, 'free-wheeling' gives you the least control over your vehicle, especially when that is just what's required.

In terms of the events that can characterise the 'Adjusting Phase' we are mainly confronted with a change or changes that demand some kind of acclimatisation. Such a change can be quite subtle, and not necessarily externally obvious. Remember that the Moon symbolises our subjective experience of things; what can come and go without hardly being noticed by one person can have a major emotional effect upon another person. And again, like with the 'Deciding Phase', an Adjustment may be made for you, and have long-lasting repercussions. Personally, during my 'First Adjusting Phase', I was made a prefect at school, only to be demoted a few months later for 'behaviour unbecoming someone in authority'. For many years after this, in order to fit in or make any impression on the world around me, I was forever having to Adjust my radical 'outsider' stance to the demands of the status quo and the authorities that control it - in fact I still have to!

So what equips you for handling this 'Phase' successfully is firstly, as ever, an awareness and acceptance of there being this necessity to make Adjustments. Following upon this, flexibility and a sense of accommodation are the vital qualities - but avoid overdoing this and becoming a yes-person. Conversely, obstinacy or a know-it-all attitude can be fatal - or at least, have you finding that your principles are a lonely place to stand by. During these 'Phases' one can expect to experience any contrast between what we essentially are and the nature of the environment in which we find ourselves. Such a contrast can be interpreted as a useful sense of getting the measure of our own character, or as an indictment against it. As a rule, this is not a time to dig your heels in, but paradoxically it is a time to persevere. The difference between the two being that the former can be arrogant rigidity asking for a rocky ride, while the latter is sure enough of its long-term goals to bend enough in order to negotiate that hump.

DURING ANY 'ADJUSTING PHASE' YOU CAN MANAGE, LEARN AND BENEFIT FROM IT BY ADJUSTING TO WHATEVER IS HAPPENING.

REALIZING 'Phases'

13y 8m to 17y 1m (p 154)
41y 0m to 44y 5m (p 175)
68y 4m to 71y 9m (p 194)

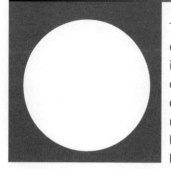

This 'Phase' we could see as the symbolic equivalent to the Full Moon, which in itself is symbolic of the maximum energising and illumination of the emotional state of things, and a revelation of what the foregoing period has amounted to. So it is the 'Realising Phase' both in the sense of becoming aware of something, and of something being made real or coming to a point of fruition.

This 'Phase' is highly significant because, if we look, we can now get a far clearer idea of what is going on, what we're really up to, and how we're doing. It has to be said that we can be reluctant to look because we fear that what we see might tell us something we did not want to know. But to this I can only say that astrology is not a subject for ostriches!

Furthermore, if you do see something at the time of one of these 'Phases' that disturbs you, then hold your gaze a little longer and you will then have revealed to you something very valuable that will better equip you for the future. Admittedly, this is a bit like going for a medical scan - but what you don't know not only can, but will, hurt you. If there is anything festering in your unconscious or out of sight somewhere, now is your chance to spot and eradicate it.

Positively speaking, it becomes plain now if you are doing well with whatever your endeavour might be, giving rise to confidence and further success. In any event though, your 'Realising Phase' should not be regarded as a judgement any more than the Sun itself could be seen as judging any darkness it is dispelling. Apart from this, it is through owning your darker side that you make your brightness shine - or as that poet of

133

ancient days, Danté, said "Take away my Demons and you take away my Angels".

It has to be remembered that the Moon is essentially about your emotional and private life, so do not expect such Realisations always to be material ones, although they can coincide with such events brought about by other planetary influences. Anyway, it is through keeping track of and in touch with our feelings that outer success is made more possible. After all, it is our emotions that motivate us, not ambitions as is commonly believed, for ambitions are the externalisation of our emotional needs. My own 'Second Realising Phase' saw a time when it was made evident to me that the confident image I presented to the world gave the lie to the insecure emotional being behind that image. Most of this came about with the help of a male friend, through a new sexual involvement, and as the result of a belated and vain attempt at bonding with my mother. None of this was easy but it was a vital Realisation for me in terms of making me infinitely more aware of my inner state, and consequently far more strongly motivated from within regarding my career and social relationships. Interestingly, that 'confident image' of mine is down to having 'Leo Rising', and the male friend, the lover, and my mother, are all Leos!

So, although a 'Realising Phase' can be rather exposing - a kind of emotional 'outing' - it does have the advantage of finding out what's in your 'basement'. In there, maybe all you can see at first is the rubbish, but clear some of it away and you can then see and lay claim to something valuable you forgot existed. It also means that you no longer have to hide behind some mask that is possibly suffocating you. In fact, the 'Realising Phase' is so useful and clarifying that personally I sometimes wish I had it on tap!

DURING ANY 'REALISING PHASE' YOU CAN MANAGE, LEARN AND BENEFIT FROM IT BY REALISING WHAT IS OR SHOULD BE HAPPENING.

SHARING 'Phases'

17y 1m to 20y 6m (p 157)
44y 5m to 47y10m (p178)
71y 9m to 75y 2m (p 195)

This 'Phase' we could see as the symbolic equivalent to the 'Disseminating' Moon phase, which is all about letting others know and experience what you have accomplished, learnt, and become interested in so far - but especially what came into flower or focus during the preceding 'Realising Phase'. So this is called the 'Sharing Phase' because it is about imparting to others something which is felt to be worth having or knowing, or of giving away that which is deemed as not being exclusively your property, and the circulation of which is regarded as being mutually beneficial.

Furthermore, it is through Sharing in this way that we become more sure of whatever it is that we are feeling, demonstrating or communicating - all of which contributes to a better 'Understanding', the 'Phase' following this one. It is as if we are sometimes 'road-testing' what we have emotionally and mentally assimilated previously, seeing if it needs tweaking this way or that in order to make it more effective and cohesive. It can be seen from the picture of this 'Phase' that it is the mirror image of the 'Adjusting Phase'. This time however, you are adjusting what has already taken shape, rather than adjusting what is on the way to 'Realisation'. This is rather like the actor who 'wears in' or edits his part of the script so as to appeal more to his audience, as distinct from the playwright who edits and fine-tunes his script as a whole into the finished article before it is actually performed. So the 'Sharing Phase' poses the necessity of shaping your personality and its expressions so that they appeal to others rather than just one's own pet ideas. It is quite possible that you do not feel able to Share yourself with others at this time, or that what's inside of you should 'cook' for a while longer. But this is not a good idea because it is through this 'wearing in' or 'weathering' that you substantiate your personality and become clearer about its nature. Letting things fester inside can give rise to emotional and mental problems later on.

By way of example, I will Share my own experiences of this 'Phase'. My 'First Sharing Phase' was marked by making the harsh transition from an English public school to working in a job on a factory floor where I had desperately to 'edit my script' to fit in with people who had prejudices about people of my social and educational background - even though the very reason I was working there was because I did not have the social or financial privileges of that background. But in retrospect I can see that this was my initial basic training in becoming able to reach the 'man in the street' through being merely one human being amongst others, free of any socio-cultural sub-typing. Come my 'Second Sharing Phase twenty-seven years later I had my first book published, Sharing what I had learnt from astrology and life.

Like all the other 'Phases', the meaning of this one can be expressed passively rather than actively - people Sharing their thoughts and feelings with you as well as, or instead of, you doing so. This may take the form of some significant emotional exchange, being a sympathetic listener, or simply being taught something academically. If you are of a passive disposition this is far more likely to be the case, yet at the same time you could also interpret Sharing as a physical or bodily act. After all, the way we sensually or sexually express ourselves is as much a Sharing of ourselves as demonstrating what we think and feel in other ways. In fact, it is probably doing do so at a far more fundamental level.

Then again, the Sharing could be more in the usual sense of Sharing what is yours with someone else - willingly and gladly, or maybe not. Consciously and genuinely Sharing in this way can be profound or spiritual in the sense of being quintessentially human -'What's mine is yours' kind of thing. Inasmuch as there is no sense of 'property' then there is no sense of loss either.

DURING ANY 'SHARING PHASE' YOU CAN MANAGE, LEARN AND BENEFIT FROM IT BY SHARING WHAT IS HAPPENING OR HAS HAPPENED.

UNDERSTANDING 'Phases'

20y 6m to 23y 11m (p 160)
47y 10m to 51y 3m (p 181)
75y 2m to 78y 7m (p 196)

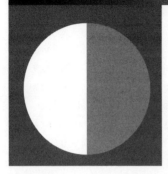

This 'Phase' is the symbolic equivalent to the Waning Half Moon, which we could see as representing a period requiring re-orientation as involvements and certain attitudes of mind that are no longer necessary to our life must fall away, like the husk of a fruit. Seeing that the Waning part of the Moon Cycle is like a Harvest-time, at this, the critical point in it, we have to separate the wheat from the chaff - that is, retain the 'good seed' and let go of what is useless. But the main issue here is that we 'Understand' why this letting go must happen, otherwise we are inclined to hang on to that attitude which we do not need. What is basically demanded from us now is an Understanding of the simple truth that cycles are all about renewal, and that we only hang on to the unnecessary out of the mistaken sense that life only deals you one hand. It does not. The Player remains what he or she essentially is, but the scripts and new parts keep coming round - be they good, bad or mediocre.

This 'Phase' is a critical one because although at the time there may be some great or small crisis occurring, we are not easily inclined to Understand what it means. All we can focus upon is what or who has departed from our life, or is threatening to do so. Again this harks back to that ignorance of the fact that our lives are cycles within cycles. Nature has Her purpose. Like the Lord, She giveth and taketh away - and giveth again, and so on and so on. But what is really critical now is the attitude that we have to whatever is happening now, and to life in general, because "as you think, so shall it be". To put it another way, whatever difficulties you are experiencing emotionally now, they are there because of an attitude or philosophy that is no longer appropriate. It is as if your attitude is like the combination that unlocks the door to the next chapter of your life - and it is different to the one you have been using. If you still hang on to some role or outlook that you have grown too attached to, then your mind is closed to whatever life is trying to present you with, and whatever that is simply becomes unavailable to you - and possibly you'd never know what it was.

If you look at the above picture of the 'Understanding Phase' you will notice that it is the mirror image of the 'Deciding Phase' on page 129. This says that this too is a time of decision, but now it is a decision of how to view what is happening, not necessarily a decision of what to do or how to act. You have to know what you are looking at before you can do anything effective to, with, or about it. When you do know, you then have the new combination, and the way ahead becomes clear.

In terms of what kind of events can characterise this 'Phase' and its need to reform your attitude, they are bound to have one thing in common - the old departing to make way for the new. This could be a mother giving birth to her first child at the start of World War Two, the end of a relationship that frees you up for a fresher and better one, the death of a parent forcing you to become someone in your own right or reappraise your feelings, the end of a personal era of life that ultimately ushers in a whole new chapter, a new relationship or form of relationship, or the loss or demise of a job that forces you to look at what you are doing with your mind and hands. Whatever it might be, the point is that you must Understand it in this light of the old dying and the new being made room for and conceived, and ultimately born. The timing of this can be quite straightforward, or decidedly subtle, or a combination of both. Moreover, it may not be fully appreciated or Understood until viewed in retrospect from the next Cycle - and as ever, its meaning could be extremely personal to you. In my own case, during my 'First Understanding Phase' I let go of a whole group of people who were previously my whole life; retreated even more from them during the following 'Releasing Phase', and was positively reborn when I left for a new life somewhere else come the beginning of the next Moon Cycle. But to emphasise the point once more, at the time I was not aware of quite what I was doing or where I was going - I was only aware of what could not or should not be in my life, not what was going to take their place. In the light of this awareness, my attitude to what was happening, or rather ceasing to happen, was what changed.

A new attitude to life not only paves the way for the future, but actually heralds it in. What that is could arrive at any time if you've adopted the right attitude, but in terms of this, your Moon Cycle, it is 'scheduled' to come at or during your next 'Emerging Phase'.

DURING ANY 'UNDERSTANDING PHASE' YOU CAN MANAGE, LEARN AND BENEFIT FROM IT THROUGH ENDEAVOURING TO UNDERSTAND WHAT IS HAPPENING AND THEREBY ADOPTING THE RIGHT ATTITUDE TOWARDS IT.

RELEASING 'Phases'

23y 11m to 27y 4m (p 161)
51y 3m to 54y 8m (p 183)
78y 7m to 82y 0m (p 197)

This 'Phase' is the final phase of the twenty-seven and a third year cycle. Being the symbolic equivalent to the Waning Crescent or 'Balsamic' Moon, it is a time of healing in the sense of letting go as much as possible of the very last of anything that could impede or compromise you during the next cycle, especially at its beginning. As well as having to do with healing, Balsam is also an oily substance that can smooth the way if properly applied.

Ideally then, this is a time when we can empty ourselves of feelings, memories, attachments and habits that are inappropriate to our current circumstances, and in so doing oil the way for the future. But in reality, we can still feel that if we give something up, even that which we find uncomfortable, there won't be anything left or coming to replace it, or that something untoward will happen. In Western culture at least, we are conditioned to avoid feeling empty. This is because we are achievement orientated, which is more to do with the Waxing Crescent or 'Striving Phase'. If you look at the picture of this 'Phase' above, you will see that it is the mirror opposite of the 'Striving Phase' on page 127. And the opposite to 'Striving' is 'Releasing' or letting go, going with the flow. We can also 'Release' ourselves from pressures and conflicts with certain others by not reacting to them, but simply 'letting it go'. So a 'Releasing Phase' could be regarded as being in aid of making room for what is arriving with the 'Emerging Phase' and New Moon Cycle that follow it. The less you give up or let go of stale or redundant thoughts, feelings and reactions - or any involvement that goes with them - then the less room there will be for the new. Hanging on to the outworn in this way could amount to a self-fulfilling prophecy because you might lose someone or something through doing so, and mistakenly think that you should have hung on more rather than let go.

So consciously or unconsciously, deliberately or involuntarily, at this time we 'Release' from ourselves anything that is 'imprisoning' us. And remember we are talking about internal things, like thoughts, feelings, attitudes and habits - not necessarily external things like relationships, jobs, domestic set-ups, etc.. Nonetheless, 'Releasing' such internal things can, and does, prepare the way for a 'Release' from any external ones that have passed their 'sell-by date'. All this can mean a surrendering to whatever forces are prevailing - and to be more precise, we also encounter the need for making some kind of sacrifice for the good of the whole. Indeed, the 'good of the whole' is in many ways the essence of the 'Releasing Phase'. This is because the 'emptying' that takes place during this 'Phase' is rather like a river emptying into the sea. This means that individual feelings are having to be sacrificed for the good of the feelings of the group - be it a large group or a group of two, or for the good of the whole of the rest of your life. You may well experience a feeling of being lost or 'at sea' during one or more of these 'Phases', and this would be a sign that you are trying to hang on to your sense of separateness and self-containment, rather than surrendering to the 'outgoing tide'. Any such egotism, for that is what it is, could be regarded as the enemy now - although the exception to this could be the 'First Releasing Phase' (see page 161).

And so, the kinds of events that one could experience during this time are ones where it can appear that you are losing out, or that life is passing you by. To complete the example of my own experiences through the Moon Cycle, during my 'First Releasing Phase', after having accepted quite a few endings in the previous 'Understanding Phase', I then seemed to lose everything I had had going for me formerly in terms of profession and social life. From being a record producer in London during the Swinging Sixties I went to vegetating in a boring office job, and living a very uneventful private life. Amazingly, this period of surrendering to my rather unprepossessing fate lasted three years and five months, the exact length of this 'Phase'. Then, having emptied myself completely, the New Cycle began with absolutely everything changing.

From reading the above, you may have felt that this 'Phase' is quite similar to the foregoing 'Understanding Phase' in that they are both to do with letting go of what it is in your life and personality that is no longer appropriate. But while the 'Understanding Phase' is akin to the stage where a vessel goes from being half-empty to a quarter empty, the 'Releasing Phase' is when it goes from there to being totally empty. Apart from anything else, this means that whatever thoughts, feelings and attitudes that were past their sell-by date and had not yet been revised or eliminated during the previous 'Phase' are rotten and must be rooted out during this one. In fact, considering that 'Balsamic' viscous quality, this 'Phase' is perfectly analogous to an 'oil change'. You cannot fill the tank with fresh oil until it has been emptied, and when it is being drained you cannot go anywhere. But once it has been filled again you are refreshed and can go on your way, travelling smoothly again, ready for the next compete Moon Cycle. None of this means to say that during the whole of this 'Phase' you are going to be 'off the road'. This is because, firstly, this would be labouring the metaphor (we still carry on living), and secondly, that notorious thing, the human ego, can ignore all these psychological traffic-lights and needs for emotional servicing, and steam on regardless - only to grind to a halt somewhat further down the road.

DURING ANY 'RELEASING PHASE' YOU CAN MANAGE, LEARN AND BENEFIT FROM IT BY RELEASING YOURSELF AND OTHERS FROM WHATEVER IS HAPPENING OR HAS HAPPENED.

Each of the Moon 'Phases' as they occur throughout your Life

You can just flip through the pages of this section and look for the ages in which you're interested, but here is an Index if you wish to use it. Simply find the age you're looking for (index starts at Birth, top left, the start of the First Cycle) and the 'Phase' that is occurring then is shown beneath it along with the page to find it described on. But first of all read - if you haven't already - the General Interpretation of that 'Phase', given next to the actual picture of it in the previous section (see below 'Overview of All Cycles' for exact page).

FIRST CYCLE

FIRST EMERGING 'PHASE' BIRTH – 3y 5m	FIRST STRIVING 'PHASE' 3y 5m – 6y 10m	FIRST DECIDING 'PHASE' 6y 10m – 10y 3m	FIRST ADJUSTING 'PHASE' 10y 3m – 13y 8m	FIRST REALISING 'PHASE' 13y 8m – 17y 1m	FIRST SHARING 'PHASE' 17y 1m – 20y 6m	FIRST UNDER-STANDING 'PHASE' 20y 6m – 23y 11m	FIRST RELEASING 'PHASE' 23y 11m – 27y 4m
(page 144	(page147)	(page 149)	(page 151)	(page 154)	(page 157)	(page 160)	(page 161)

SECOND CYCLE

SECOND EMERGING 'PHASE' 27y 4m – 30y 9m	SECOND STRIVING 'PHASE' 30y 9m – 34y 2m	SECOND DECIDING 'PHASE' 34y 2m – 37y 7m	SECOND ADJUSTING 'PHASE' 37y 7m – 41y 0m	SECOND REALISING 'PHASE' 41y 0m – 44y 5m	SECOND SHARING 'PHASE' 44y 5m – 47y 10m	SECOND UNDER-STANDING 'PHASE' 47y 10m – 51y 3m	SECOND RELEASING 'PHASE' 51y 3m – 54y 8m
(page 164)	(page 168)	(page 171)	(page 173)	(page 175)	(page 178)	(page 181)	(page 183)

THIRD CYCLE

THIRD EMERGING 'PHASE' 54y 8m – 58y 1m	THIRD STRIVING 'PHASE' 58y 1m – 61y 6m	THIRD DECIDING 'PHASE' 61y 6m – 64y 11m	THIRD ADJUSTING 'PHASE' 64y 11m – 68y 4m	THIRD REALISING 'PHASE' 68y 4m – 71y 9m	THIRD SHARING 'PHASE' 71y 9m – 75y 2m	THIRD UNDER-STANDING 'PHASE' 75y 2m – 78y 7m	THIRD RELEASING 'PHASE' 78y 7m – 82y 0m
(page 186)	(page 189)	(page 191)	(page192)	(page 194)	(page 195)	(page 196)	(page 197)

OVERVIEW OF ALL CYCLES

EMERGING 'PHASES'	STRIVING 'PHASES'	DECIDING 'PHASES'	ADJUSTING 'PHASES'	REALISING 'PHASES'	SHARING 'PHASES'	UNDER-STANDING 'PHASES'	RELEASING 'PHASES'
(page 125)	(page 127)	(page 129)	(page 131)	(page 133)	(page 135)	(page 137	(page 140)

1st EMERGING   BIRTH to 3y 5m

"YOUR BIRTHING" - It cannot be stressed enough as to how important and significant this 'Phase' is, for the nature of your birth - and also your time in your mother's womb - fundamentally affects your personality and life to come. Events and experiences during that time were 'in at the basement', not just the 'ground floor'. This means that such influences got to you before you had any means of vetting them whatsoever, and that they remain entirely unconscious until you are somehow made aware of them or take steps to familiarise yourself with them. And even when you have found out or been told what your birth and womb-time was like, it often does not sink in as to what it actually felt like or indicated. The truth is that whatever it did feel like has coloured and determined your most basic emotional responses and patterns of behaviour. So ask your mother, father or anyone around during your time in the womb and at birth, what was going on. Then allow yourself to remember what that felt like. As you do so you will then see how much such experiences have, and probably still are, affecting you. There are an infinite number of possible experiences, but a common one is that the unborn child is so supersensitive to its mother's state of being that it will pick up on her hopes or fears for her child to be. After all, her state is described as 'expecting'. Often I have had clients who have found out that their mother was expecting or hoping for a child of the opposite sex to what they turned out to be. This sows a seed of confusion, rejection or disappointment as an opening act - what I call 'bombing at birth'. Another common one is the mother's fear of giving birth, possibly owing to a previously difficult one or miscarriage. A common result here is that the child is born anxious with a sense of dread. Yet another is a premature birth with the baby not being expected to survive. This confers upon the infant a feeling that their existence makes no difference, that whatever they do is going to be ineffectual - all giving rise to a rather victimlike personality. When a 'Second or Third Emerging Phase' comes round though - or preferably before - they should tell themselves that they are still alive and that they have made a difference.

On the positive side, good influences at this time are probably taken for granted - which is possibly because that was how Mother Nature originally intended pregnancy and birth to be. Even so, if you find positive experiences around that time for you, then it would be wise to draw upon them to offset your current cares, or to encourage and care for others with the feelings those positive experiences have bestowed upon you.

Sooner or later, we cannot really consider this subject of pre-birth experience without taking reincarnation into consideration. Whether you believe in it or not, the fact is that more people in the world believe in it than do not. Suffice to say, that purely from a cause and effect standpoint, whatever happened previous to birth has an enormous bearing upon it and the one being born. The whole concept of reincarnation can get extremely complex, and seeing that there are many complete books written on the subject I won't expand upon it here. However there is one astrological idea, amongst many, which has always appealed to me, perhaps because it is so simple. Whatever Moon-Sign you were born with is what your Sun-Sign was in your last life. (To determine your Moon-Sign, if you do not already know it, see my books 'Do It Yourself Astrology' or 'The Instant Astrologer'). So if, like me, you were born with your Moon in Aries then you were an Arian in your previous incarnation. This means that your immediate memory(Moon) is Arian in nature, in that your last life would have been concerned with issues of war, soldiering, fighting for a cause, self-assertion, pioneering, etc - what I call 'battle karma'. And so your main predisposition(Moon) in this life would centre around these things, either literally or metaphorically. Furthermore, your 'Emerging Phase' would tend to be coloured by whatever your Moon-Sign is.

Whatever your birth and pre-birth scenario, the remainder of the 'First Emerging Phase' is also going to strongly affect your behaviour and sense of what life is like because you learn and experience some very elementary functions during this time: walking, talking, potty-training and breast-feeding. How well we do with these things, and any problems we encounter, form our basic attitude and patterns of behaviour. Walking initiates our sense of how to get on in life; did we streak ahead then or have a bad fall? Talking - how easily did we learn, was anyone listening and responding, etc? Potty-training symbolises our ability to process our experiences and not hold on to them and poison our system - how did that go? Breast-feeding - our sense of supply in terms of quality and quantity got firmly established in accord with this experience - from having little or no breast-feeding to being fed that way until around or beyond the end of this 'Phase'. Society's current preoccupation with breast-size probably has something to do with all this in that the Child in many men needs 'feeding' and the 'mother' in many women wants to oblige. Sex, in the usual sense of the word, has little real bearing on it, but merely distracts the attention away from the embarrassing truth of the matter.

Many of us cannot remember this 'Phase' of our lives hardly at all, particularly the birth and pre-birth parts, and wonder why we are sometimes so much at the mercy of uncontrollable feelings. This 'Phase' really does set the scene - so looking into it, remembering it, and reliving it (possibly through some therapy such as Hypnosis or Rebirthing), is rather like at last seeing the picture on the box of the jigsaw puzzle of your life. It may not be the picture you expected or wanted, and what you'd pieced together so far may resemble it somewhat or just be a work of fantasy, but at last you'll know and feel what you truly set out as. The fact is, we do start out as we mean to carry on - but that does not mean responding forever to natal rejection with feelings of guilt or apology, or to natal disappointment with self-defeating behaviour, or, by way of compensation to pretend everything is alright until we find that we are getting nowhere with a relationship or our career because we are not being true to ourselves. The idea is to regard the experiences and impressions of the 'First Emerging Phase' and immediately before as a challenge to overcome the negative feelings that they engendered. If you start out feeling rejected then you may have to keep 're-rooting' yourself (changing homes and relationships) until you find somewhere you feel you truly belong and leave behind the 'no room at the inn' feeling you encountered at birth and/or before. Additionally, you would have to superimpose a positive belief about yourself (through affirmations and refusing to accept bad treatment from others, for instance).

This description of this 'Emerging Phase' would not be complete without stressing how important it is for parents to be aware of what is actually going on in their child's life, or children's lives, at this time.

Through being keenly, and empathetically, aware of your infant's state with respect to all the above, you will give them a start in life that is as powerfully positive as it is patently subtle. The phrase 'the soul of sensitivity' suggests itself here in a slightly different light. The 'soul' is the child is 'sensitivity' is what is being conveyed here. A baby that knows that it is known at this deep level will eventually better know itself as youth and adult, and therefore be more confident, happy and successful. As one child I know said of a sleeping baby "Look, it's dreaming of its past lives".

 JUPITER GROWTH MODES - 'ARIES-TAURUS-GEMINI-CANCER'
(see pages 94-100)

1ˢᵗ STRIVING Phase   3y 5m to 6y 10m

During this 'Striving Phase' the most strikingly significant event that occurs for everyone in the civilised world is that of going to school for the first time. The 'seed' that was originally planted and germinated in 'Mother Earth' before and during the 'First Emerging Phase' is now that 'seedling self' which has to contend with the elements that lie beyond hearth and home. Events may occur now that destabilise in terms of changes to the security system that the infant has just come to accept as permanent. For instance, apart from the well-known rigours of early schooldays, home moves at this time can be a common cause of later feelings of being unsettled or of a need to keep moving. There can be other events, such as younger siblings being born or a much older brother or sister going away to college. Such events are not bound to happen, by any means, and those that do are significant because of one's subjective experience of them - subjectivity ever being the case with the Moon.

The point to grasp is that if there are changes that destabilise, then it indicates that the child's fate has somehow called for it. The need to Strive has logged itself on early on. And this can go one of two basic ways: it can make the child grow up as, or into, a real tryer, or, the child feels a 'leaf in the wind' with not much point in trying because it believes there is bound to be something else to come along and render such effort useless.

Psychologically this has to do with the first type having what is called an 'internal locus of control' and the second type an 'external locus of control'. It doesn't take too much imagination to see what a difference falling into one category or the other makes to a person's life as a whole. Tracking back to what happened for you, and how it affected you, can be enlightening and ultimately healing in this respect. This applies mainly to the second type, because such can hamper one's progress through life. However, people with a strong internal locus of control can suffer the more subtle complaint of not being able to understand how others tick, with subsequent relationship problems. As ever, that Lunar riddle of 'Nature or Nurture' arises here. The answer is both, because people are born with either an internal or external locus of control, and it 'registers' itself during this 'Phase'. But if as a parent you are aware of it at the time, then you can take steps to make sure that your child is not unduly disturbed by any unavoidable changes between the ages of 3 years 5 months and 6 years 10 months.

If you are viewing all this in retrospect, then endeavour to 'recast the past' by putting yourself back in that subjective state and viewing it with the objectivity of an adult, seeing what alterations and rationalisations you could have made in order to see how it was 'good', or at least 'right', for you! You can also try to rectify it now.

JUPITER GROWTH MODES - 'CANCER-LEO-VIRGO-Libra"

(see pages 100-106)

1ˢᵗ DECIDING Phase   6y 10m to 10y 3m

"THE DIE IS CAST" - This really is a 'Decider' because any Decisive event occurring now strongly affects the course your life takes for a large part of it - if not all of it. This is stressed by the concurrence of your First Waxing Square of Saturn between six and seven(see page 205), the time when this 'Phase' kicks in. All this echoes the saying 'Give me the first seven years of a child's life and I'll show you the adult'. Essentially though, the crucial Decision or Decisions being made now are more or less bound to be ones made by someone other than yourself. And so this implies that it is purely your fate in action, not some conscious choice on your part. It could be argued that a ten year old can make Decisions of their own, but it is even more arguable that they are totally responsible for them. The extremely prickly case of young offenders, especially of serious crimes like murder, raises this issue. Did they make utterly their own choice, or were they some unconscious expression of the questionable moral standards of the society in which they grew up, and in which they are still growing up? And then there is the further Decision as to what their fate should be by the judge who sentences them.

But apart from such dire cases, your life is bound to take a Decisive turn now. Because of this, it pays to focus upon this time in your life, or that of a child with whom you are involved as a parent, relative, carer, etc.. Look very closely at whatever crops up or arises, or did so, during this period, for it sets a trend that triggers certain personality traits, and therefore life patterns, that have hitherto been dormant. Such events may be quite internal in the sense that they are on a feeling level and are not that evident to others. A client of mine's mother began an affair with another man at this time. This eroded the family structure generally, and relegated the father to some kind of loser status. But the effect upon my client was that she then began to harbour feelings of deep rejection and insecurity, for her mother had made a priority of her time spent with her lover, and left her youngest daughter to suffer in silence. It was only during her Second Emerging Phase at twenty-seven years of age that she had a chance to begin to leave behind that pattern of rejection that had been Decided at that earlier time and get out of a relationship where she was tied to someone who had kept her where he wanted her (that is, like her father, not rejecting him) through her own fear of being rejected.

From the above it should be apparent just how much events at this time affect us, and, how it is not that easy to spot what those influential events were. My client had always glamorised her mother in an attempt to deny the unacceptable fact that her mother's sexual desires were more important than she was. It could also be said that her mother probably felt rejected by her husband and looked for love and acceptance in her lover. But this just further emphasises the vital importance of identifying such events at this time in one's own life and the lives of others, coming to terms with them, and ultimately healing whatever damage they inflicted, or actually pre-empting any damage occurring at all . In this way the rot, the so-called 'sins of our fathers' (and mothers), is Decidedly stopped.

In endeavouring to discover how one may have been affected at this time, especially around six to seven years old, it does help to bear in mind that the Moon is mainly to do with 'Mother'. My own mother saw her mother for the last time at this age - giving rise to emotional complexities and denials that boggle the mind - hers in particular, and mine by referral.

That other Lunar issue, 'Home', can also be a main player with regard to how the emotional course of one's life's can be set during your 'First Deciding Phase'. For example, a move at this time to a better house and neighbourhood would give a general sense of uplift and progression to a child which would stay with him or her through life, perhaps in the feeling that changes are positive. On the other hand, a downward move of this kind could infect the child with a sense of negative trend overall.

Fortunately, when the First Waxing Trine of Saturn (see page 207) occurs between nine and ten years of age, there can be an upswing in our fate. This can either ameliorate any misfortune that happened earlier, or lead to a far more stable life trend. Making an important friend or having a good teacher at school could be the case here.

Once again, if it is your own child you are looking at concerning this time in their life, I must stress how sensitive they are to what is happening to them and around them. And to not merely interpret things from their outward behaviour if it appears okay, but to check how they are feeling inside. Then again, just looking at what is going on in your child's life could be the simple but Decisive action now that forestalls any possibility of an emotionally afflicted life.

JUPITER GROWTH MODES - 'LIBRA - SCORPIO - Sagittarius - Capricorn - Aquarius' (see pages 106-114)

1st ADJUSTING Phase   10y 3m to 13y 8m

Apart from having to Adjust to any Decisions made for you or by you during the previous 'Phase', there are two obvious Adjustments that have to be made during this 'Phase'. The first one is biological/hormonal - puberty. Whole books have been written about this subject so I won't expand upon it too much here. Suffice to say that we go from being children to being capable of producing them during this period, and that discovering sexual urges and body hair and emissions, not to mention such visible signs as breasts and spots and puppy fat, can be exciting to some and intimidating to others. At one extreme, if you feel vibrant and attractive at this time then Adjusting to things will be relatively easy, and probably persist as an underlying sexual self-assurance throughout life. At the other extreme, feeling awkward, suppressed or unattractive now can cast one big shadow over your sexual development and experiences for years to come. So check out your experience of puberty and discover that what went down then was the prototype of the kind of sexual being you are now. If you are bringing up or relating to kids of this age, then again refer to your own experience if you wish to understand them better - that is unless you were one of the chosen few that encountered no problems at all then! A common problem can be that as you are attempting to Adjust to increased hormonal activity and all that it poses, one or both parents are busy trying to keep you where you are, thereby making relating a lot harder now and in the future.

The other obvious Adjustment that has to be made, especially at the significant beginning of this 'Phase', at least in the civilised world, is the result of changing from junior to senior school, from a educational establishment that treats you as a child to one that regards you as an adult in the making. In some educational systems, owing to place or time, there may not be an actual change of school at this time (as in my case, where I went to English preparatory school at age nine - see general description above). However, whatever the case, some kind of change or shift of emphasis at this time creates some need to Adjust your 'natural' inclinations to the set-up in which you find yourself. As ever with the Moon, quite what is meant by 'natural' inclinations is open to question, because whatever they are, you are now faced with a 'when in Rome do as the Romans do' type of situation. On the face of it, because you also have your First Saturn Waxing Trine happening at this time which assists fitting in with the status quo (see page 207), this should not present too much of a problem. However, the strength of your individuality is going to be one of two major contributing factors now - something which is further emphasised by having an individuality-provoking 'Aquarian' Jupiter Year (see page 114) happening at the start of this 'Phase'. How the other individuals that you are currently in the midst of respond to your individualism is going to be the other major contributing factor.

Looking through my client files, I am made to recall an Aquarian female whose experience at this time was to be bullied in class by some of the other pupils(because she looked unusual), and to be ridiculed by a school set-up frighteningly different from her previous one, and to be subjected to an experimental educational technique which was eventually scrapped because it did not work. Basically then, she could not Adjust to all this and simply found herself wanting, installing a long-lasting inferiority complex, not to mention resentment. One is inclined to think that it is the system that should have Adjusted to the individual here! But the Moon is showing us the Soul's course, that River of Your Life, and as such, the reality it encounters at every step or 'Phase' is there to form and conduct its course - just like how the banks of a river contain it. And at this stage the 'river' is very young, a mere trickle, and so the reality of the 'earth' it encounters verily dictates where it has to go. The trickle has to Adjust to the lie of the land. Years later, during her 'Second Emerging Phase' and the start of a whole new lunar cycle, she began to see the significance of these experiences, and to turn the resentment into a justifiable sense of injustice, which in turn fuelled a pledge to help others thus afflicted. And incidentally, she made her greatest friend and 'protector' at school at this time, thanks to that 'Aquarian' Jupiter Year (matching her Sun-Sign) and the stabilising assistance of her First Saturn Waxing Trine.

Quite often the need for Adjusting can be 'serial' in its effect. Another, this time elderly, client was first fostered out to another family at ten years, then they had to move to a 'not so good' neighbourhood owing to the father of the house going to jail. Then come the third year of this 'Phase' the father returned and made good, moving them upwards again. However, he started drinking and my client had to cut a very low profile - something against her Leonine nature. Not surprisingly, this woman has been 'Adjusting' all her life because these experiences triggered an innate inclination of hers to fit in with the circumstances, yet all the while her suppressed need to be her own person kept bubbling under and awkwardly asserting itself, as she forever felt put upon.

Yet another case, which is rather relevant to our current obsession with physical looks and to the sexual aspect of the 'Phase', was a male who at this time was teased for being plump at a new school. Needless to say, he could hardly Adjust himself by suddenly not being overweight, and grew up feeling very self-conscious, especially with the opposite sex. He is now of 'normal' weight and size, but the ongoing feeling of not fitting in persists, even though (or possibly because) he is an extremely nice guy.

Finally, a famous example of how critical this 'Adjusting Phase' can be is Elizabeth Taylor. As a child star of eleven years of age she not only had to

Adjust to fame at this tender age (like many other child stars), but she also injured her back filming 'National Velvet' which created a lifelong need to Adjust herself to the ongoing pain of this injury. This example also shows how Moon 'Phases' can show how we deal with things emotionally in accordance with whatever that 'Phase' is. In turn, how we dealt with them then can persist for years, as in her case, for her continual ill-health is still a call for help that is not really being heard. In typical Piscean fashion she is too good at adjusting as opposed to contacting and expressing her pain more directly (see also pages 167 and 219 regarding Liz).

It can be seen that the 'First Adjusting Phase', as with all the 'Phases' of the First Lunar Cycle, is subtle and profound in its effect upon the growing child, and therefore upon the adult. If only parents, carers and teachers were more aware of the potential trials and perils of Adjustment being imposed at this time, perhaps they'd take time out to help them Adjust with the benefit of their adult experience and objectivity. In the first case, the Aquarian female, for example, if her parents or teachers had enquired into what was going on perhaps some allowance and provision could have been made, and/or her own self image reinforced.

 GROWTH MODES - 'AQUARIUS-Pisces-Aries-Taurus'
(see pages 114, 116, 94&96

1st REALISING Phase   13y 8m to 17y 1m

"EMOTIONAL DISCOVERY" - Now we are right in the thick of adolescence, so 'Realising' here can be somewhat of a rude awakening. The essential Realisation here is that life is now polarised into Self and Other, you and somebody or something else, what you feel yourself to be against what others want you to be - peers versus parents, for instance. Perhaps in order to simplify matters at this time, we are inclined to see things in black and white, along with the brittle confidence that is common to adolescents. So it is not that your environment is necessarily divided - it is just that you insist on seeing it that way in order to establish a sense of your own identity. If there is a 'them' there has to be a 'me'. This 'splitting off' is particularly noticeable at age fourteen as it is a 'Gemini' Jupiter Year (see page 98).

Because hormones are still raging around your system, your sexual state is especially aware of polarities - male/female being the main one. However, the inputs received from each of your parents also gets processed now. This means that if they don't get on that well, then unconsciously you will pick partners you cannot have or make out with, or you avoid getting involved at all, thus setting a future pattern. Conversely, a stable parental relationship would mean that you enter a similarly 'normal' relationship, or feel secure enough to take your time, and be choosy. Any latent homosexuality, which may have been triggered by a dominant mother or father, now comes to the fore - either confidently or as a confusing contrast between what you are supposed to feel and what you actually feel. However, through being aware of these processes you can diminish, if not wholly overcome, their effects.

Another 'sexual scenario' that can arise now is that of one parent or the other seeing you either as sexual competition or temptation, or as being sexually significant in some other way. For example, a mother can focus upon her son as being a man now, and as more malleable than her husband who she has given up trying to 'reform'. And so a boy can get sexually 'manipulated' into the image of what his mother thinks her ideal male to be - which is probably in sharp distinction to what he is actually like. So what he is Realising here is the contrast between the two versions of himself. But the astrologically significant fact here is that such a 'split' or identity confusion would have been latent at birth - it is just that the 'Realising Phase' now makes it real. A female client of mine, whose parents had previously split up, had her father making a love object out of her, but never touching her. So at this time was Realised her innate desire to be looked at and admired but not actually touched or got close to.

It should be pointed out that such 'heavy Realisations' as described in the previous paragraph usually only take place during the First Saturn Opposition between fourteen and fifteen years of age (see page 208). But whatever the case, we can view our experiences at this time as creating a 'role model' for the way we relate to others, especially sexually. Anything that is said or done, or not said or not done, to us at this time has a dynamic and lasting effect upon our ability to relate and the type of relationships we attract - or do not attract. So if you are at this stage, then be aware of what you are choosing to be in relation to others - for it'll carry through into the future. Are you reacting or interacting? Are you developing your relating skills with a person or with a computer? Now is the time to express yourself openly and receive back a sharp impression of how that other experiences you. You are interacting now in order to find something out - not to prove anything other than that you are a person in your own right. And interaction leads to a stable personality and relationship, whereas reaction lead to alienation.

In retrospect, whether your life was full and active at this time, or unavoidably awkward or barren -the Realisation was that whatever was going on then was a 'read-out' of who or what you started out as. If your 'seed' is that of a 'daisy' it shows itself as such during this 'Realising Phase', not as a 'rose' or whatever. What is more, we get an 'ego flash' now which creates a model that persists until you are able, being armed with an awareness of this model, to refashion it somehow. One client's father said to her at this time 'I don't like clever girls'. She was and still is most definitely clever - and such has been both the bane and the boon of her life for she still attracts men who like but do not like her mental superiority.

And talking of mental ability, this 'Phase' is also a time when we Realise what we are made of at school during and leading up to examination time. Generally speaking, at this time we get some kind of feedback as to what kind of person we are in the making - be it good, bad or indifferent.

Not surprisingly during this 'Phase', differences and conflicts can flare up. These can show like skin disease - literally. Acne, that notorious affliction of adolescence, can be interpreted as the eruption of differences or poisonous feelings between, say, father and son.

The classic 'splitting' at this time is literally a case of leaving home or running away from school. This could be interpreted as a straightforward way of discovering who you are by putting yourself outside of the set of people that think they know you, and putting yourself in the midst of one that definitely does not know you. Then again, it might set a trend for running away from difficult or confining relationships. Whatever the case, you can be sure that this 'Realising Phase' may be viewed as preview of how you relate and see relationships.

JUPITER GROWTH MODES - 'TAURUS - GEMINI - Cancer - Leo - Virgo' (see pages 98-104)

1ˢᵗ SHARING Phase   17y 1m to 20y 6m

Now at last we reach this period which could be regarded as late adolescence, with the accent upon showing others how 'in the know' you are with regard to whatever it is your peer-group regards as worth knowing. If you're maybe a bit of a wallflower and find yourself mainly on the receiving end of this 'Sharing', then there has to be something that has happened (or not happened) previously that has made you shy of Sharing yourself. Because of this, or maybe it's innate, you feel that there is something about you that you'd rather not Share. This is particularly likely at seventeen when going through a self-critical 'Virgo' Jupiter Year(see page 104). But this is rather like what I call the 'Venous Blood Syndrome' which is analogous to the process whereby deoxygenated blood in your body is returned to the lungs for re-oxygenation - and it is a dirty purple colour. People are often surprised to discover this, saying that they have never bled any purple blood - and certainly not the dirty sort. This is because if you cut a vein, the blood immediately hits the air and is re-oxygenated, turning bright red.

The metaphor here is that what we regard as negative in ourselves (the deoxygenated blood in need of regeneration) we are inclined to keep to ourselves until we are attacked, wounded or get angry (see red). If we consciously and deliberately let it, the 'blood', out, it changes into something (more) positive because we have 'aired' it. At a 'Sharing Phase' - especially this one - do not wait to be wounded, let it out anyway and you will be amazed at the transformation. If anyone is shocked or repelled to see what you're made of, then that is their problem - i.e. you're reminding them of the 'dirty purple blood' they themselves are holding inside.

Between nineteen and twenty years of age your First Saturn Waning Trine kicks in (see page 211), which should somehow give you a greater sense of being in tune with the world around you, or that someone in authority approves of you - or that the time has come when you cannot keep it in any longer. Either way, this is a good time to 'let it bleed'. The feeling now of having found someone you can connect with can be so strong that you should be careful not to overreact - a tendency if you are of an insecure disposition and think this could be your last chance. Remember to get the measure of any significant other's Sharing of themselves. If it seems more like a self-advertisement, or a lack of any self-disclosure, rather than an honest emotional expression or exchange, then be cautious, and do not Share too much of yourself with them. There are far too many cases on my books of clients now marrying in haste and repenting at leisure. With the Saturn Waning Trine particularly, you have time on your side, so don't be pushed. Generally speaking, Sharing one's thoughts and feelings with other, or rather one other in particular, can set the trend for being emotionally open or closed later on in life - depending on what kind of empathy or abuse such disclosures encounter now.

Sometimes, the 'Sharing' can be of the more obvious kind - like Sharing resources and living space, intentionally or otherwise. Several clients of mine have had late siblings born at this time, or had a parent remarrying, meaning that they feel they now have to Share their mother's and/or father's attention and resources. This can even give rise to a reluctance to Share emotionally and mentally as an adult, with negative consequences. Then again, such experiences can teach you as a youth just how to Share, with positive consequences. As ever, neither the Moon or any planet creates a situation, but simply activates what is already there within the individual. Sharing of this kind can also be strongly imposed if you should become a parent now - needless to say. And as for the Sharing of living space - this is the most common and elementary experience of Sharing that most people have upon moving away from the family home - or possibly the Sharing with one's family home becomes an issue. But Sharing is still the keyword.

Another event that can now be peculiarly influential is the death or serious illness of someone close. If you are not able or allowed to Share your feelings and grief with someone it can inhibit a Sharing of your deeper self later - especially on a sexual level. Having said this, sexual Sharing to excess during this Phase can desensitise you later. Note that such issues as Sex and Death are more likely to arise during your 'Scorpio' Jupiter Year at nineteen. One client of mine tragically lost her mother at this time, but the only way she could Share the intensity of her emotions was through sex, which led to further complications that she still could not Share.

So if you have not got the message by now, the priority during this 'Phase' is to find someone with whom you can be and Share yourself. If you cannot find a person, keep a journal where you freely allow your thoughts and feelings on to paper - or talk to a pet, or a tree. But Share you must!

JUPITER GROWTH MODES - 'VIRGO - LIBRA - Scorpio - Sagittarius' (see pages 104-110)

1ˢᵗ UNDERSTANDING   20y 6m to23y 11m

After the roller-coaster of the three 'Phases' of your adolescence, upon entering your twenties, you begin to formulate your own code for living - that 'new combination' mentioned above in the general introduction to this 'Phase' (see page 137). But it would seem pretty unavoidable that confusion will arise as your old attitude to life conflicts with the new one that is trying to take shape. Whatever the content of your confusion though, it will have a key bearing upon the direction your life wants to go, emotionally and attitudinally speaking. For example, during this time one client of mine was obsessed with the fear of catching AIDS (with no good reason other than a brief infidelity with someone of virtually non-existent risk) and could only find one person to confide in. To cut a long story short, the fear of AIDS passed but then she felt hostage to this friend's continuing confidentiality. Such an attitude of mind, that she had the threat of exposure hanging over her, was an emotional blackmail scenario that had been haunting her since she was very young. The poetic reason for this was that from the age of seven she had to keep her mother's extramarital affair secret from her father. In her seven-year old head she believed that if she did not keep the secret, her mother would run off with her lover. Now this pattern was trying to come to an end, but true to the nature of this 'Phase', some form of crisis had to arise to force the issue. The Moon, that is her unconscious, was saying to her 'this paranoid belief that you have a guilty secret is driving you into a very tight corner'.

Now my client did not Understand what was actually happening to her at the time, and her only change in attitude was to tread even more carefully and consequently intensify her paranoia. But one of the beauties of your Moon Cycle is that though back-tracking in this way, we can then 'recast the past', which is a bit like editing the videotape of your life. My client managed to do this during the following Releasing Phase when she 'Released' all this material to me. Then come her Second Emerging Stage when she was able to put these shadows of the past behind her as she moved away from the area and changed to a partner with whom she could be open.

All of this hopefully conveys how both critical and subtle the Understanding Phase can be - especially during your early twenties when you are having to devise your own moral standards. Such pressures to alter your attitude are most likely to occur during your First Waning Square of Saturn (see page 212) between twenty-one and twenty-two years of age. This was when my poor paranoid client divulged her dark secret to her new-found friend (note that twenty-two is an 'Aquarius' Jupiter Year, the Sign which governs friendships).

Such inner conflicts created by this Understanding 'Phase' are common to people in their early twenties. Often all the individual can feel is depression because they cannot begin actually to look at what comprises the conflict. This is probably because, by its very nature, it involves a lack of self-awareness. During such a difficult time, possibly the key lies in that 'Aquarius' Jupiter Year mentioned above. To unburden yourself to a friend, or a professional therapist, is to lend some vital objectivity to what can be a horribly subjective state. And incidentally, my client's friend (an Aquarian, to boot!) never did break her confidence - but that's another story.

JUPITER GROWTH MODES - 'SAGITTARIUS - CAPRICORN - Aquarius - Pisces' (see pages 110-116)

Also occurring during this time...

FIRST SATURN WANING TRINE (see page 211)
This influence should come to help you to whatever Understanding is needed in a relatively controlled and stable fashion. Such help is quite likely to come from someone older or more experienced, who you respect or like.

1ˢᵗ RELEASING Phase   23y 11m to 27y 4m

The surrendering or sacrificing quality of this 'Phase' is not so likely to take place voluntarily or consciously. This is because at this age you are still in the process of building and developing a life and career, and such passive and selfless responses to whatever is happening to you or around you could be regarded as inappropriate and ineffectual. But this is precisely what makes the 'First Releasing Phase' a potentially difficult one. Having said all this though, statistically there is the great likelihood of having one or more children at this time, and that is probably the most sacrifice-demanding thing that a human being can experience. I daresay that if one looked into the figures, one would find that this is precisely the event that characterises this 'Phase' for most people. It could also be said that for a pregnant woman, the experience of at last giving birth is a classic form of 'Release'!

Even if you don't experience early parenthood, it is at this time that you really have to 'put away childish things'. Such 'things' can be girlish or laddish behaviour, or any pursuit that was really just an extension of adolescent fun and experimentation. This does not mean to say that having a good time and trying things new should come to an end - far from it, for such letting off steam is a Releasing in itself - but it does mean that there now has to be some consideration of how you fit into the greater scheme of things. Although the Moon does not have anything directly to do with socialisation, the 'Releasing Phase' does have this quality of making you feel one among the many. But as I say, during your twenties you are quite likely to be still looking out for number one. Yet it all depends upon what that entails. One client of mine was at this time working hard to make it as a professional healer, but the fact of the matter was that she did not have enough sense or experience of people, or of being one of the people, to get very far, despite winning the academic qualifications.

Another client came to see me during this 'Phase' bearing all the trademarks of a sad social misfit. His 'Releasing' took the form of unloading all the peculiarities of his personality and life experience so far. This was very intensive, involving his strange thoughts, feelings and activities that no-one on Earth knew about, let alone his alcoholic parents with whom he still lived. After numerous appointments spreading over three years he came to see me for the last time. He said that he did not need to come anymore because he at last felt that one person now knew him. He went down my drive looking almost ethereal. He died in his sleep a few weeks later, at the very end of his First Moon Cycle - (see more of what I call 'Once around the bay' lifetimes under 'Second Emerging Phase' on page 164).

Now don't go thinking that you too are likely to come to a premature end at the close of this 'Phase' and Cycle. True astrology is not so much in aid of predicting events as understanding what those events mean when they happen or happened, or preparing yourself for certain possibilities. This is particularly the case with Emerging Moon 'Phases'.

Then there was this the young mother who during this 'Phase' did not so much feel 'at sea', until her husband went away to sea! I also have a few clients who actually lost or aborted children during this 'Phase', giving rise to not just intense feelings of loss, but also of being lost, and that the 'Release' was unnatural or premature. Also, being newly married during this period and then feeling totally cut off can be a problem, possibly because you do not feel ready yet to make that kind of sacrifice of your individuality - but for the time being that is what your unconscious is saying you must try to do.

A final and famous example of this 'Phase' - and how during it one can appear to be losing out when in truth it is just that there is a bigger issue at stake - is Muhammad Ali. At this time he had his World Heavyweight boxing title stripped from him as a result of being convicted for refusing induction into the U.S. Army(owing to his own religious convictions). It was not until his Saturn Return (page 213) that this conviction was reversed, and he could eventually go on to regain his title. (See also page 169 concerning Ali's life).

All in all, you can see that the experiencing of the 'Releasing Phase' of your mid to late twenties is a apparently contradictory set-up. But in Nature's terms, the Moon's domain, it probably all makes sense - it is just that we have departed from Nature to a significant degree.

JUPITER GROWTH MODES - 'PISCES - ARIES -Taurus - Gemini - Cancer' (see pages 116 & 94-100)

2ⁿᵈ EMERGING Phase   27y 4m to 30y 9m
1ˢᵗ LUNAR RETURN

"YOUR FIRST EMOTIONAL ROUND-UP" - The first nine months to a year of this 'Phase' is one of the most significant points in anyone's life, and it is highly unlikely for there not to be some important change or milestone marking it. The reason for this is that the 'Second Emerging Phase' is like a form of rebirth. This is akin to the transformation from caterpillar to butterfly in that your 'caterpillar stage', the first Lunar Cycle of twenty-seven and a third years, is you going through a range of emotional experiences that serves to make you aware of your life's potential and possibilities. And so during this 'Phase' you are moved towards whatever events, places and relationships - along with the opportunities and experiences they engender - to develop whatever you have discovered as most valid about your personality so far. This discovery may or may not be conscious. Remember that the Moon is symbolic of the unconscious, so it usually moves you for reasons you do not recognise first of all, that is unless you are particularly in touch with your emotions. Then again, you may think you know where you are going but discover later that your unconscious mind had something else in store for you - or you might get it partly right. But you'll only know for sure what the case is in retrospect, because it could take several further 'Phases' of this, your Second Lunar Cycle, to notice what is now trying to take shape in your life, or as your life. Having said this, come the equally important First Saturn Return at around twenty-nine years of age (see page 213), there could a more definite sign of what that shape is supposed to be - or not supposed to be.

Added to all this, at twenty-eight you enter your Second of The Three Ages (see page 279), where you move from being more or less entirely, and necessarily selfishly, concerned with the development of your 'basic self' to becoming a 'social being'. The 'basic self' is what we develop in order to function in the world in a fundamental way - rather like taking a foundation course before deciding exactly what 'subjects' you wish to specialise in. Some people are well on their way career-wise at this time, but the Moon has more to do with how you feel on the inside than what you are doing on the outside.

However - and it's a big however - unlike the natural world where creatures grow and develop according to a ruthlessly efficient and unbending schedule, we as human beings do not. This all has something to do with how we have been reared, for human mothers and fathers vary in efficiency in a way that birds and beasts do not. And so at this time our level of security in the world becomes very evident. Personal and family life are therefore most likely to be the focus of concern. Any children born at this time usually have some significance over and above what is usual. In fact, issues around birth and babies are common now, but they are emotionally unique for each mother or father. However again, just like in the natural world, it would seem that many people have children at this time when they are only just 'grown' themselves. It is therefore not surprising that children born during this time in a parent's life turn out to be a greater than usual responsibility because they are somehow an extension of what still needs nurturing in that parent. It is as if we produce in a child that which is the child in ourself. This is not unnatural or neurotic, but quite the reverse. Nature uses subtle means to achieve Her ends - any half-decent natural history TV program will show you that. So, returning to the 'caterpillar to butterfly' metaphor, there is also a 'pupation' period when we may not be sure what we are. This period would occur during the preceding 'First Releasing Phase'(see page 161) when we have to succumb to the close of the First Cycle.

The 'chrysalis' that we live in can be quite comforting or isolating, until we Emerge from it - or someone Emerges from us - during this 'Second Emerging Phase'. Certain people, for some reason close to their own Soul, choose not to Emerge from that 'chrysalis' at all. Rather than shuffle 'it' off, they shuffle off the mortal coil altogether.

Famous examples of this are rock icons Brian Jones, Jimi Hendrix, Jim Morrison and Janis Joplin- all dying within six months of the start of their 'Second Emerging Phase' (Brian was dead on time, so to speak, at 27½years). I call these 'Once around the bay' lifetimes, for it seems that this single emotional circuit was sufficient for them to make their point, either to the world or themselves. And yet it would appear from contemporary reports that Brian, Jimi, Jim and Janis were rather lost and in between prior to their deaths (like motherless children), and to a lesser extent such an emotional state can characterise this time for any of us. Someone else who made a monumental mark at this point in his life, but then kind of shrivelled up and died not long after, was Russian cosmonaut Yuri Gagarin. He didn't so much go 'once around the bay' at twenty-seven and a half, but was the first man to go once around the Earth - just like the Moon! He literally couldn't follow that, being killed in an air-crash seven years later. I also give an uncelebrated example for this kind of lifetime as part of the description of the 'First Releasing Phase' on page 161. This concerned one of my clients who informed me that he had 'got what he had come for' and then left.

Here are a four more celebrated examples of the 'Second Emerging Phase' - who all just happen to be male and definite fighters for certain causes. South African president, Nelson Mandela, was appointed as National Secretary of the African National Congress, which led through the events at and between his Second and Third 'Realising Phases' (see pages 175 and 194) up to becoming his country's first black president at the start of his 'Third Understanding Phase' (see page 196).

Palestinian leader, Yasir Arafat, co-founded the Al Fatah movement, which was his first step towards becoming Chairman of the Palestine Liberation Organisation during his following 'Realising Phase'(see page 175). See also page 230 concerning his renunciation of terrorism and recognition of Israel.

Civil rights leader, Martin Luther King, in his first high profile act concerning civil rights, led a 381 day boycott of Montgomery city buses at the very start of his 'Second Emerging Phase', during which he soon after founded a national vehicle for civil rights reform, the S.C.L.C. See also page 245 regarding the assassination of Martin.

John Lennon married Yoko Ono (very much the mother figure to him) and then the Beatles split up - all at the beginning of his 'Second Emerging Phase'. See also pages 219, 245 and 249 concerning John's life and death.

Now here are three women whose lives took a significant turn right at the very beginning of their 'Second Emerging Phase'. In fact, for the first two their respective events took place a few months before the twenty seven years and four months mark, which indicates that they were a little 'premature', something that happens quite often with Emerging Phases because they somewhat like a birth.

Queen Elizabeth II of England was crowned on June 2nd 1953. As the Moon governs womanhood, Elizabeth becoming the country's 'leading lady' and Mother of the Church of England at this time was very much 'on time'. Furthermore, her Moon-Sign is Leo, the Sign of royalty. See also pages 193 and 213 with regard to this sovereign.

Another, this time theatrical, leading lady, Elizabeth Taylor converted to Judaism at the start of this 'Phase'. This little known fact demonstrates how private and personal the Moon's influence can be, even for someone so much in the public eye. Having lost her third husband Mike Todd in a plane crash the previous year, she felt in dire need some inner support, and this was her predilection. (See also pages 154 and 219).

Marilyn Monroe married Joe DiMaggio in January 1954. This is sadly significant because, in a way, she had 'come home' in marrying him because he was reputed to be the one male in her life who truly cared about her. He could have given her the lunar protection that she so sorely needed - but glamour and a confused sense of independence tempted her away, and she divorced and left him after being, as it happened, nine months in the womb of his care. More about Marilyn on pages 172, 219 and 221.

So the 'Second Emerging Phase' is very much a 'birth and death' kind of time - but obviously the event of a literal death is quite rare. All the same, that caterpillar, that old skin or pupal stage, is what has to die, for hanging on to it would be suffocating (which is what Marilyn, ironically, was feeling in her marriage to Joe). It is all part of the process of 'putting away childish things' - and significantly, the word 'pupa' means 'doll'. It is also an emotional landmark, with home-, nest- and family-building, not to mention marriage, being high on the list of life priorities - but as such it could eventually affect your outer or work life as well. Moreover, it can be helpful to refer back to your emotional orientation at this time to get a bearing on your life at a later date. This highly important 'Phase' could also be dubbed 'Bringing It All Back Home'.

 GROWTH MODES - 'CANCER(very appropriately!) - Leo - Virgo -Libra' (see pages 100-106)

2ⁿᵈ STRIVING Phase   30y 9m to 34y 2m

Considering that this 'Phase' follows upon the most powerful and important points of two Planetary Cycles, your First Lunar Return (or 'Second Emerging Phase') and First Saturn Return, then it is not surprising that this, the 'Second Striving Phase' lives up to its middle name. Whatever changes, pressures or events were experienced between twenty-seven and thirty years of age, you now more than likely dealing with the aftermath, backlash or consequences of them. Remembering that a 'Striving Phase' is all about nurturing the growth of something that has just begun to take shape, your particular effort could relate to any number of things. However, whatever it might be is very likely traceable or connected to whatever happened back then, particularly when you were twenty-seven.

Looking through my client files, two things I note is that relationships or bodies can start to creak now. As a result of this, affairs and illnesses are in evidence. If yours happens to be the first case, I suggest that an affair is possibly a symptom of trying to find something you believe you have lost. The fact is that you have probably lost track of whatever was trying to spring forth while you were in your 'Second Emerging Phase', and either you gave up on that or did not even notice what it was. If this raises a frown, then go back and read it on page 164 and the general description of 'Striving' on page 127. Anyway, looking for what you have not discovered in yourself is not going to be found in someone else - at least, not directly speaking. By this I mean that your cage might need rattling to bring home the fact that you've placed yourself in one, that you settled for a seemingly secure life with someone only to find that it cost you the freedom to pursue your journey of self-discovery. So until you retrace and resurrect that 'seedling' of future growth, you are in danger of chasing your own tail, or of going from the frying-pan into the fire. Apart from all this however, bear in mind that Striving to make your relationship(s) work now is very much on the cards - so do not let one 'go to seed' for lack of attention.

On the other hand, you may well have discovered, clearly or vaguely, what you want to make something of in your life —and this 'Striving Phase' demands that you put your money where your mouth is, that you walk your talk. A couple of famous examples of this are Muhammad Ali and Fidel Castro. Ali Strove to regain his world heavyweight boxing title at this time, ultimately doing so with a knock-out punch, while Castro defeated the CIA-backed invasion of the Bay of Pigs - see pages 163 and 219 for more concerning Ali's astrological life, and page 171 for Castro's. Going back to my files, another thing I notice are clients who are Striving to build some kind of professional practice at this time - often having to prove their independence at the same time. But as ever, the secret is to not lose sight of that 'seedling' which is trying to grow into a healthy plant. As any gardener knows, seedlings have to survive spells of bad weather, being trodden on, or even trying to grow too quickly. They also have to be fed and watered regularly. If this metaphor fails to penetrate, this means that any infant project will be challenged by market forces, encounter attacks from others, or take on too much too soon. And you have to have encouragement, information and experience. Most of all, keep in touch with whatever spurred you to start that project in the first place - for that will be the seed itself.

Talking of infants and growth, children being born or raised at this time can prove more demanding than usual. Again, as I have pointed out elsewhere, this would have everything to do with something that needed nurturing or healing in yourself re-presenting itself to you in the form of your 'offspring' - something that sprung from you. Everything is natural and meant to be as far as the Moon is concerned, it is just that so often we have been driven off-course by a society divorced from Nature. Remember that a child is saying 'I am more yours than anything apart from your own body, mind and soul'. A child is also a symbol and a messenger, telling you something about you as parent and parents, as a couple, as a human being. And like the literal meaning of the word 'crescent', the shape of this 'Phase', a child is also literally a 'growing one'.

Health. This is not to say that this is a time when you are more than usually likely to get sick, but Striving can be a strain on the system. A good way to cut down wear and tear is to draw up a list of essentials and non-essentials, on either side of a page. For instance, an 'essential' could be to make sure that you reach a goal you have set yourself, whereas a 'non-essential' would be to entertain doubts of ever getting there. Then again, another 'essential' could be to entertain enough doubts to make sure you organise yourself well and do not drop any stitches. You will find that by drawing up such a list your 'natural intelligence' is able to access these essential and non-essentials quite easily. This is because within you is a wealth of answers - you just have to ask the right questions. Having sorted this out, stresses and strains are marvellously diminished. However, you may still have to Strive to root out the cause of any serious complaint, should there be one. In fact if there is one, it is there expressly to get you to track down why. One paradox here is the possibility of the complaint being caused by Striving too much or in the wrong way or wrong direction. In fact, the correct kind of Striving is the essential 'essential'.

JUPITER GROWTH MODES - 'LIBRA - SCORPIO - Sagittarius - Capricorn - Aquarius' (see pages 106-114)

2ⁿᵈ DECIDING Phase   34y 2m to 37y 7m

After the Striving of the last 'Phase', whatever happens during this period has to have a Decisive effect on the direction your life now takes. You may regard events now as not that significant or just plain hard, but the truth of the matter is that something is trying to push your life into a new chapter that had its beginnings during your 'Second Emerging Phase' (see page 164) - even though you may not have recognised it. So if you are not aware of these significant events and how they are connected, then take time out to become so. Stresses and strains in your life are simply 'growing pains', not just bad luck or there merely to depress you. The crisis now can be small or great, but whatever the case, it is intensifying feelings to the point of forcing you to take radical steps to pull away from negative or fearful feelings about where you are, what you are doing, and who you are with - or not, with respect to any or all of these three cases.

Anything negative or unpleasant in your life at this time is rearing its head because it is telling you that you must act in order to resolve the difficulty you perceive to be experiencing. Occurrences such as physical complaints, new involvements or children are messages from your unconscious which are saying 'What does this mean, because it represents a call to Decisive action', something which may simply mean saying your piece. A famous example of this was Fidel Castro who, having Striven to defeat the invasion at the Bay of Pigs (see page 169, Decided to mobilise his Cuban forces in the Soviet Missile Crisis, which apart from strengthening his own power base effectively led to the Soviet Union Deciding to make him a Hero of that nation.

A crisis of Decision could also take the form of the loss of someone or something in your life. During this 'Deciding Phase' such a loss is making a Decision for you, and forcing you to be more Decisive in yourself. The heavier the crisis or loss, the greater the need must be for you to take the reins of your life. The chances are that if you have been stronger on the inner or emotional side of life, then the decision is probably one that has to take place on a more practical and material level. Conversely, if you have been more capable in the outer world, then it means you must now Decide to be more emotionally aware, committed and involved.

Between thirty-six and thirty-seven years of age your Second Saturn Waxing Square kicks in (see page 220), and this will add further weight to the above described imperatives. If all this sounds rather grim - or it actually is - it is having to be so because this time could be described as the run-up to your 'Mid-life Crisis' which in astrological terms is mainly your Uranus Opposition (see page 239). The Planetary Cycles appear to be quite concerted and adamant about your late thirties to early forties being a major shift in your life's direction and/or meaning. And this, your 'Second Deciding Phase' is setting you up for it - or rather, it is forcing you to prepare yourself for it. Such preparation is essentially about your life becoming more consciously constructive. This means that it is no longer appropriate to adhere to any conditioning you have which promotes the notion that life is merely about toeing the line, responding to immediate needs, conforming to what you think everyone else does, or just getting from A to B unscathed. 'Deciding Phases' - and particularly this one - are expressly about getting you to appreciate that life is a challenge, and that it(you) therefore has a unique and definite purpose. It may have to jolt you - out of any complacency or just living automatically and going along with crowd - into an awareness of this. To put this all another way, the more of a leaf in the wind you are, the harder will be the Decision forced upon you. On the other hand, the more self-actualising you are then the more you will view all this as healthy grist to the mill, and eventually achieve something.

The classic and tragic example of how badly a 'leaf in the wind' can fare during this 'Phase' is the death of Marilyn Monroe. Or it could be said, considering some theories, that her fate was Decided for her. Whatever the case, Monroe was no more.

Notwithstanding this 'leaf in the wind' syndrome, during this 'Phase' you stand to become a stronger, more effective person. Someone who is in the driving seat of their own vehicle.

JUPITER GROWTH MODES - 'AQUARIUS - Pisces - Aries - Taurus'
(see pages 114,115,84 and 96)

2ⁿᵈ ADJUSTING Phase   37y 7m to 41y 0m

Whether your Second Moon Cycle has so far made you a lot more mature, confident or experienced, or only a little, this 'Phase' still demands that you bend with the wind, whether you're in pursuit of something or someone, or even if you're not doing much in particular. Although this 'Phase' starts off with a change-resistant 'Taurus' Jupiter Year (which is just as well for you won't bend too readily), when you reach your 'Gemini' Years at thirty-eight, being in two minds about something will make being firm and unequivocal decidedly elusive. What is now in need of 'Adjusting' is whatever it is in your current situation that is getting in the way, whereas more technically speaking it will be something you begun at your 'Second Emerging Phase' (see page 164). Or the 'Adjusting' may simply take the form of putting things on hold or carrying on in the face of circumstances that are far from ideal. Fortunately, between thirty-eight and thirty-nine, your Second Saturn Waxing Trine arrives to assist you (see page 223), providing you with a steadying influence or opportunity.

Having said all of this though, the very nature of Adjusting at this time of your life implies several things. Firstly, by now you probably have a number of things going on in your life - like family, a busy work and/or social schedule, ageing parents, etc.. - so the chances are that you have not got that much room to manoeuvre. Secondly, there is also the possibility that you are beginning to think you can settle into a comfortable rhythm of life, that you have and know your priorities, that you have a degree of control or authority in your life - so why should you have to Adjust?! The short answer is that this is the way Nature intended it - that human beings should not get too set in their ways just because they've reached the halfway mark. Our culture's idea of life's progression can very often be at odds with the greater scheme of things.

This 'scheduled' need to Adjust can be prompted by more or less anything, some self-induced, others apparently beyond one's control. Having an affair can be one method of stirring up your life, to shatter any complacency or emotional inertia that may have crept in. Because this need to Adjust is the agenda, be very careful in how you assess your feelings. Maybe the real Adjustment was needed in your marriage or ongoing relationship, and an affair is just a red herring or a lesson. You find you have to Adjust, whatever the case - so allow yourself to go through the process of doing so, and learn what you need to know as you go, without making any hard and fast decisions until you reach or are some way into your 'Second Realising Phase'(see page 175).

Then again you may be having to Adjust to a divorce or the demise of a relationship, or your partner having an affair. But the same 'lunar logic' would apply - keep Adjusting, bending with that wind of change, finding out that you are far more flexible than you thought - or paradoxically, that your Adjustment is one of not being so flexible. The 'Second Adjusting Phase' can be very demanding, but it will only seem impossible if you will not Adjust to the basic fact that you are able to Adjust! Thinking that your life should be free of the need to make Adjustments is what would be asking for the most trouble. 'Bend or break' is the call of the day. Trust your unconscious mind, for it is throwing things at you which will force you into becoming a stronger, better and more capable and aware person. Impress yourself with that famous human aptitude for adapting to circumstances.

Some other classic events that are Nature's way of getting you to Adjust are: having children at this age; reaching a crisis of confidence because your beliefs are not suited to the reality you live in; losing your job and having to retrain, rethink or go freelance; having to live on less money; experiencing changes in your domestic set-up; health issues; or any curve ball that Fate chooses to pitch you. They are all in aid of getting you to Adjust, and it won't last forever - unless you *refuse* to Adjust.

 **JUPITER** GROWTH MODES - 'TAURUS - GEMINI - Cancer - Leo'
(see pages 96-102)

Also occurring during this time...

SECOND SATURN WAXING SQUARE (see page 220)

This influence emphasises the need for maturity described above. What needs Adjusting should be plain to see - if not that easy.

Also possibly occurring during this time...

URANUS OPPOSITION (see page 239)

First check out when this occurs for you on page 00. This is the classic astrological indicator of your 'Mid-Life Crisis' and having it occur during this 'Phase' could be regarded as very appropriate because both influences are demanding that you change and Adjust, Adjust and change. Events or involvements that call for Adjustment are liable to be more dramatic and obvious - as too is the inclination to overreact. So Adjust your speed and intensity of reaction as well.

2ⁿᵈ REALIZING Phase   41y 0m to 44y 5m

"EMOTIONAL AWARENESS" - Having got to this time, certain emotional truths that are relative to your overall state of emotional awareness are shown to you, or at least are begun to be. Such truths can bear upon your life history as a whole, or stem particularly from whatever was happening or you set out to achieve during your 'Second Emerging Phase' between twenty-seven and thirty (page 164).

How this 'awareness' comes upon you is usually the result of one or usually more emotional confrontations - or even showdowns. As ever, the scenarios that can bring these about are as varied as experience itself, but emotional relationships are the prime ones. It is as if the significant other in your life now shows themselves to you 'full frontal', as it were. Consequently, the mirror to your own emotional state is now directly opposite you, not at some more oblique angle.

In the purest psychological terms, such 'confrontations and reflections' are an excellent opportunity to gain a far clearer idea of where you are coming from emotionally, to see your patterns of behaviour and how they either serve you or do you in. However, in most people's realities there is quite a degree of need and desire involved, so seeing the emotional score for what it actually is can be distorted by those ever present fears and wishes. So although this is a 'Realising Phase', the Realising is in strict proportion to how much you are able or willing to do so. Because of this, the content of such Realisation is probably going to unfold over several, even many, years to come. And this will happen despite whether the relationship that begun or is going on at this time still exists. In fact, in retrospect this time can be viewed as a kind of emotional landmark, a registering of one's most basic and essential emotional make-up. At its most extreme, it is rather like some deep and complex subject which is a lifetime's work and study. In any event, it is probably a good idea to view it this way, for thinking that whatever goes on now is of passing significance could be classed as flippancy at best, or grave emotional denial at worst.

Other areas of focus for such emotional revelation, apart from one-to-one relationships, can be those involving one's parents - especially your mother. Becoming considerably more aware of her influence upon you is what can take place now. Again, what you can draw, learn and benefit from this is entirely up to you. Although this is by no means a stock expression of this 'Phase', losing a parent (or anyone close) can obviously act as a powerful emotional awakening.

A more straightforward, and therefore advisable, way of experiencing your 'Second Realising Phase' is through some form of therapy, counselling or group-work. If you are intentionally looking for increased emotional and self-awareness, then now is the time to get it.

Although all Moon 'Phases' are most powerful during their first year, this one can end as it begun because your Second Saturn Opposition occurs at that time (see page 224). This period also makes it clear that there is ultimately no side-stepping or rationalising away what is emotionally on the cards. If there is any music to face, then this is the time you are forced to do so. This may entail the 'real world' of external authority or material conditions, or as some health condition.

This, possibly one of the most difficult 'Phases', is basically about 'contrast' - between what you want and what you have, between what you feel and what you think, between reality and the dream, between yourself and someone or something else. Although he never reached this age, the poet John Keats lived his life according to the principle of contrast because he found that in such a way he became as acutely aware of existence as it is possible to be. This gave rise to some of the most moving and profound poetry ever written, and reading it is recommended to anyone suffering the extremes of emotional life, at this or any other time.

Finally, a famous example of someone who experienced an ugly but highly significant contrast and Realisation at this time in their life was Nelson Mandela, who was arrested and imprisoned at the very end his Second Realising Phase' and spent a few months over an entire Moon Cycle of 27⅓ years in jail, coming out at the very end of his 'Third Realising Phase'. It was as if he needed that whole cycle to go from one Realisation to another, and come to a complete Realisation. When he became South Africa's first black president in May 1994 his government immediately established the Truth and Reconciliation Commission to investigate and come to terms with the country's violent and apartheid past, such being a perfect and positive expression of his then current 'Third Understanding Phase' (see page 196).

JUPITER GROWTH MODES - 'VIRGO - LIBRA - SCORPIO - SAGITTARIUS' (see pages 104-110)

Also possibly occurring during this time...

URANUS OPPOSITION (see page 239)

First check out when this occurs for you on pages 252-254. This is the classic astrological indicator of your 'Mid-Life Crisis' and having it occur during this 'Phase' is doubly exposing and revealing. The contrast between what you think life to be and what it actually is can be particularly acute. The more you have a fondness for the unadulterated truth (or can cultivate such) the more likely you are to progress as a result of this time of truth - for that is what it is. Nelson Mandela, cited above, was experiencing this when he was arrested in 1962 for sabotage and terrorism, which are ruled by freedom- and rights-seeking Uranus.

2ⁿᵈ SHARING Phase   44y 5m to 47y 10m

As this 'Phase' kicks off with your Second Saturn Opposition (see page 00), it is quite likely that there is a reluctance to Share or exchange your thoughts and feelings with someone. This is because Saturn's influence can emphasise our inhibitions, and/or find us in the midst of what we regard as an emotionally unsympathetic environment. Yet looked at another way, Saturn could be regarded as forcing us to look at our weaknesses by Sharing them with someone else. In so doing, you would loosen up blocked feelings and generally clarify your emotional situation. Furthermore, such Sharing would lead to the Understanding necessary for the next 'Phase'. As ever, in order to Share just when it is most difficult to do so would require courage - and as Cyril Connolly wrote "Courage is not merely one of the virtues, but the form every virtue takes at its testing point".

Looked at in yet another way, as Saturn governs the objective or professional world, a Sharing of yourself with someone on that level - like a counsellor, therapist or impartial friend - is very advisable. Whatever happens though, you are going to be finding yourself Sharing in some way or other, consciously or unconsciously, willingly or unwillingly. As our lives at this time are usually quite full or busy with the accumulated commitments that come with middle age, Sharing can take on a number of meanings, depending, as all Planetary influences do, on the context of experience in which they take place.

If in the midst of a separation or divorce at this time, the issue of Sharing can be one of having no-one to Share with any more, or having (had) to Share your partner with someone else. In either case the importance of Sharing is driven home. This poses further issues, or rather questions you might need to ask yourself: Have I been receptive, open or honest enough for Other to Share with me? Have I been a good or bad example of Sharing? Have I been too possessive - or not possessive enough? Have I Shared myself too much in that I leave no mystery? Answering any of these questions may entail Sharing what you think are the answers with someone else. This is because Sharing is ultimately involves being emotionally very honest, something which few people are to that great an extent - so a 'mirror' in the form of someone else is necessary. I am made mindful of how powerfully influential self-honesty, and the lack of it, is, by a client of mine who had kept his feelings close to his chest all his life. Following the death of his father during the preceding 'Realisation Phase', during the beginning of this Sharing 'Phase' he got so much 'off his chest' that he ceased to suffer from the asthma which he had had all his life.

This brings us to another important experience that would bear upon the importance of Sharing - grief. Apart from the more obvious, but no less important, aspect of grief which is that of simply missing someone very deeply, there is also the case where resentments and other negative feelings towards the deceased can give rise to very complicated and confusing states of being. Without Sharing such convoluted feelings of guilt and grief, all manner of quite dangerous emotional and ultimately physical complaints can ensue. After the 'Full Moon' of the preceding 'Realising Phase', we are supposed to 'empty' ourselves more and more through the Waning half of the Moon's Cycle. Without doing so, such thoughts and feelings can fester like the contents of an old storage jar. So now is the time to begin to unload negative feelings, leading to eventually 'making your peace'. (see 'The Venous Blood Syndrome' described under the 'First Sharing Phase' on page 157).

New relationships that begin during this time should, apart from other things, be viewed as being an opportunity to Share like you have never Shared before. If it doesn't work out, the chances are that it was down to not seeing this writing on the wall, or that it was simply a part of your Sharing process. Within existing relationships, difficulties in Sharing can take the form of going from one form of Sharing to another, as in the case of physical sex being no longer (so) available or possible, posing that a new level of Sharing must be attained that either replaces your sex life or that revitalises it.

Other likely scenarios of Sharing may include having children at this relatively late stage, or being witness to forms of Sharing that you never knew before (like being in an Asian, Oriental or Third World culture), or making breakthroughs in work or creative life by Sharing what you might have previously kept to yourself, or getting blocked or stuck because of a reluctance to Share your ideas.

JUPITER GROWTH MODES - 'SAGITTARIUS - Capricorn - Aquarius - Pisces' (see pages 110-116)

Also possibly occurring during this time...

URANUS OPPOSITION (see page 239)

First check out when this occurs for you on pages 252-254. This is the classic astrological indicator of your 'Mid-Life Crisis' and having it occur during this 'Phase' is doubly exposing and revealing. The contrast between what you think life to be and what it actually is can be particularly acute. The more you have a fondness for the unadulterated truth (or can cultivate such) the more likely you are to progress as a result of this time of truth - for that is what it is. Nelson Mandela, cited above, was experiencing this when he was arrested in 1962 for sabotage and terrorism, which are ruled by freedom- and rights-seeking Uranus.

2ⁿᵈ UNDERSTANDING Phase   47y 10m to 51y 3m

Now this 'Phase' is all about putting together an attitude of mind that allows you to manage and relate to the world in a way that could be regarded as 'mature' and in keeping with what should be expected of someone of your age and experience. One reality could be that you experience situations that demand this, and how well you fare has everything to do with the current state of your individual personality. The chances are that the part of your life and/or character that finds itself in the frame will be what is in need of being brought up to par. Then again, you may have arrived at a point where your emotional Understanding has developed to a degree where some new level of living and relating comes about in the form of a new or renewed relationship, job or lifestyle. Seeing that this 'Phase' gets under way at forty-eight during an 'Aries' Jupiter year and a Saturn Waning Trine (see page 227), the odds are that some definite forward push is there to get you moving, or at least, give you some sense of being in control of your life and its direction. Taken together, these two possibilities pose circumstances that are both encouraging and demanding. This could be a career move that is upward but more stressful, or a love interest that both delights and confuses you, complements and compromises you. But it is still all down to attitude, that is, the way you are looking at it and consequently, the way you are presenting yourself to it.

If you look at whatever is demanding your attention in a fashion that is inappropriate, then it will demand even more of your attention. For example, I had a client who was newly involved with someone and she was wanting more from him than he felt he could afford. But this attitude was the very thing at fault, for in putting his usual limit upon emotional commitment his new partner put even more pressure upon him, eventually compromising his professional position. He failed to Understand that in giving a little more quality time and attention to her than was his usual 'quota', he would satisfy her needs and diminish the pressure. Instead, by sticking to his old but unintentional attitude of 'treat'em mean and keep'em keen' he was making the situation into the very one he feared - of feeling emotionally put upon. At a deeper level, he had to Understand why he felt that he could not give enough emotionally, and why he felt so easily crowded. Giving her a loving look rather than a dismissive one took exactly the same amount of time, but his faulty attitude had him believe that a loving look would incur some kind of unwelcome complication or obligation, while a dismissive one would dispel it. Not surprisingly, such an attitude got formed earlier on in his love-life at the time of his 'First Sharing Phase' during his late teens when he was rejected by a girlfriend after having shown his feelings.

All this very much bears witness to the esoteric dictum that 'Energy follows thought', that how you are thinking determines what will happen to you. After all, everything in the world that did not begin with a seed began with a feeling or idea. This is particularly applicable to cases where you could be giving yourself a hard time over some issue, particularly a relationship. Either with some concentrated introspection, or preferably with the help of a good friend, counsellor or therapist, you will find that what you thought was a problem was not a problem - but just the way you were looking at it. This is analogous to getting headaches when all that is required is a (new) pair of spectacles.

Apart from your attitude changing the circumstances, most circumstances occurring during the 'Phase' are there to change your attitude. Resisting this simple formula can make a hard time harder - and last longer. This is especially the case if an inappropriate attitude that the difficult situation is reflecting has been around for a long time. Simply facing the truth is often the first step to a solution, whereas arguing the toss is asking for the 'lawsuit' to persist, perhaps for years.

Considering that this is a critical 'Phase' and that it occurs at a time in your life when one is 'supposed to know better', it is not too surprising that it has a kick in its tail. This is the Second Saturn Waning Square at the very end of it (see page 228). This is saying "If you haven't got the message - take that!". In other words, the pressure increases as reality impinges upon that unsuitable attitude, compounded by the inclination to cling on created by the concurrent 'Cancer' Jupiter Year. However, that same pressure can lift instantaneously when you at last look at the situation in the right way. It may help if you cast your mind back to your 'Second Realising Phase' (page 175) and determine what you learnt or what became clear then. Whatever it was - and it should have been something - it contains the key to your correct Understanding now.

JUPITER GROWTH MODES - 'PISCES - ARIES - Taurus - Gemini - Cancer' (see pages 116 and 94-100)

2ⁿᵈ RELEASING Phase   51y 3m to 54y 8m

This time in your life can either be experienced as the beginning of the (bitter) end, or as a surrender to a life lived in a more spiritually or psychologically aware fashion. In reality, it could well prove to be an oscillating mixture between these two extremes. Everything depends upon whether you experience Fate in general, and your own fate in particular, as something you feel offended by or trapped in, or as something that you should trust as knowing best. On the face of it, it would appear that the latter choice of surrendering to your fate (and possibly another's) is far more desirable. The trouble is that the ego always likes to think that its life-style should live up to its romantic, glamorous, self-indulgent, comfortable or vain idea of itself. Consequently, seeing that your situation during this 'Phase' has the in-built necessity of making some kind of sacrifice, your life-style is going to appear wanting from the ego's point of view. Such an 'inadequate life-style' may include a restricted or even non-existent social or love life, a materially or emotionally unrewarding job, or any situation that seems to be out of your control or beyond your influence.

Returning to our River of Your Life metaphor, this stretch is the estuary where the river inexorably empties into the sea - especially as the tide is now ebbing (this is the last 'Phase' of the Waning or second half of the Moon cycle, remember). This symbolises that time and place where your individual path has to succumb to universal, collective or karmic forces - Fate in other words. And unlike your 'First Releasing Phase' which was a more unconscious mingling with the masses during your mid-twenties, this one means having to live for others. This engenders a most practical definition of that much misused word 'spiritual': meeting a collective need. This can be anything from looking after and abiding an ailing parent to helping someone close to you and getting little (or worse) in return; from swallowing your pride and doing what has to be done, to surrendering what seems most precious to you personally for the good of the whole. Unless you are consciously committed to and involved with some form of healing process or spiritual discipline (the best expression of this 'Phase'), the trouble is that the ego regards all these courses as a surrender of control or what it wants, and therefore possibly inviting chaos (the word 'estuary' means commotion, by the way). But the truth of the matter is that if the ego tries to get its way then there will be commotion - not least of all inside of you. This could be physical (health problems), emotional (relationship problems) or mental (work problems). And the reason for any commotion would be that you were trying to control the situation in the face of uncontrollable forces. This is why this 'Phase' is termed Releasing, for you need to Release physical, emotional and mental blockages - or rather what is creating them. Such can be very old issues. I had a client who was experiencing all manner of skin and hair problems as something was trying to break out and Release itself through the only channels being allowed it. Astrologically, I was able to locate a point in her early life that contained a trauma about which she had told nobody. It was a great relief to her there and then to at last Release this matter, but I emphasised that it would be highly compressed after more than forty years, and encouraged her to Release it more and more, whenever, however and to whomever she could. Whether or nor my client continued to empty her old hurt, I do not yet know - but truth will out as surely as the river finds the sea. If one accepts and lives through the 'commotion' of the struggle between one's fate and one's ego, peace and resolution are Released into your life.

In my own case, I had a 'message' from my motor car, that wonderful symbol of one's own physical-emotional-mental vehicle (the personality). For the first time ever I ran out of petrol - and on my way to seeing my doctor. This was symbolic of an unconscious need to empty myself of whatever I regarded as essential to my ego's idea of progress, something which was interfering with my physical health. I also had to surrender to the need to be helped out by someone or something else. However, I did not get this message at the time - my radiator had to blow up a month later and empty out all the water and coolant!

This 'Releasing Phase' could be described as one of 'enforced selflessness' as you are obliged to live up to something higher or more inclusive than an egocentric sense of life. A symptom of this is that of feeling more sensitive than usual. This is owing to sensing the whole more keenly, with a view to attuning yourself to your role in it. Such increased sensitivity can express as irritability and feeling 'drowned' by others or circumstances. As well as letting go of your ego barriers in the way that is being suggested here, it is also a good idea to protect yourself because there is not too much point in being incapacitated. One exercise given there that can be particularly useful with regard to allowing inside what's on the outside is what I call 'Listening to the World'. This is a simple meditation in which you sit somewhere where you are not going to be disturbed (preferably outside) and listen in an intent but relaxed way to whatever sounds are going on around you. Do not try to analyse or identify the noises, just aurally acknowledge them. After a short while you will hear sounds that you were not even aware of, until eventually you have a sense of 'listening to the world'.

This is quite integrating, and automatically instils a trust in the great 'out there'.

Seeing that this 'Phase' kicks off during your Second Saturn Waning Square (see page 228), you can be forgiven for initially wrestling with and balking at whatever assails you from without. But this should be regarded as just a sensible stance to adopt as you assess the situation, with a view to seeing what or who it is in your life that you are possibly going to have to meet more than halfway. This 'Phase' is a time to go with the flow - not for maintaining a stiff upper lip or being rigidly non-compliant, for this would sink you.

 JUPITER GROWTH MODES - 'CANCER - Leo -Virgo -Libra'

(see pages 100-106)

3rd EMERGING Phase   54y 8m to 58y 1m
2nd LUNAR RETURN

"YOUR SECOND EMOTIONAL ROUND-UP" - This can be quite a extraordinary time for you, but a great deal depends upon where your preceding 'Second Releasing Phase' has left you. If you fought against the tide that was trying to get you to let go, which was what that previous 'Phase' was in aid of, and hung on to certain attitudes and feelings because they were the devil you know, then the 'extraordinary' is not going to enter your life. An 'Emerging Phase' is quite simply the tide turning, coming in again. But if you are caught on the reef of some old attachment then it will be to no avail, and you could eventually drown in whatever comprises that attachment. Hopefully though, you have shaken off the cobwebs of your last Moon Cycle and are primed to set sail for new horizons. If my voluminous client files are anything to go by, new departures are more the norm than getting stuck in the mud - or on that reef.

True to the Moon, home moves are a common expression of breathing some fresh air into your emotional lungs. And such home moves are not, or should not be, merely a change of address. Most moves at this time involve a shift in career emphasis or life-style too. One possibility is moving into a larger house which can be used as a guest house or for functions of some kind. Conversely, sizing down to make life simpler or less expensive, and leaving more time for one's inner life could be the desirable route. Apart from these contingencies, a home move could be forced by some occurrence such as the death of a parent or loved one, illness or divorce/separation. Then again, changes in domestic set-up could be on the cards, as distinct from actually moving.

The important thing now is to be alive to the fact that Nature herself does not regard human beings as over the hill just because they have reached their mid to late fifties. On the contrary, most who have had the responsibility of parenthood, or elderly parents, are free from it now. If they are not, then their 'Second Emerging Phase' is presenting them with a new beginning with respect to such responsibilities. A son or daughter who still needs parental support, or conversely, the parent who needs the (continued)support of one or more of their children, are also possibilities now. It all depends on what the Moon deems fit for you with regard to caring or being cared for.

If the previous 'Second Releasing Phase' found or left you somewhat confused with regard to what you are doing with your life then this 'Phase' could present you with the breakthrough you need - but that would still depend upon not being attached to some habitual attitude and the situation that goes with it. A classic example of this is the person who for some time has had a partner outside of a stale marriage but for some reason just cannot seem to make the break. Come this 'Phase' they can Emerge from out of that marriage, like a stranded boat being floated free by the incoming tide. However, if they still stay in that old marriage, then their extra-marital partner should be careful not to also consign themselves to Davy Jones' Locker because they would then be hoping against hope. But the reverse could be the case, where one could be the person being cuckolded.

With the Moon being the Moon, another strong possibility now is that of going, or being taken, to some new level of caring. This could entail embarking upon some course of healing - for oneself or others, or both. An illness at this time can shift one's priorities or emotional orientation quite dramatically, causing one to review one's old ways and attempt to be more open and tolerant with both oneself and others. In fact, any such illness or complaint at this time could well be ascribed to either a lack of self-care or the insufficient care of others. Any longstanding imbalances in one's system (caused by life-style or habits) really have to be addressed now because the body or mind can no longer take such strain. Returning to our nautical analogy, this is a bit like a vessel that lists heavily to one side being capsized by a bigger wave than usual and/or because its structure is no longer quite as sound or elastic. Celebrated examples of such capsizing are Peter Sellers who died of a heart attack brought on by drug abuse at 54 years 10 months; Humphrey Bogart who died of cancer at fifty-seven afters years of heavy drinking and smoking; Adolf Hitler killed himself at fifty-six after it finally struck him that he really had got it a bit wrong; and Andy Warhol who also died at fifty-six following a gall-bladder operation after what could be described as a rather unnatural and impure mode of living (that part of the body deals with purifying it).

Unlike Peter, Bogie, Adolf and Andy, here are two examples of characters who reckoned they were doing rather well at this time of their lives, but in fact such dynamic events actually set them up for their future demise: Benito Mussolini led his country Italy into war at fifty-six with great hopes of becoming a world-class leader and country, only to be shot dead by partisans five years later, four days before his abovementioned partner-in-crime Hitler committed suicide; and Richard Nixon became the 37th U.S.president at fifty-five but resigned in disgrace six years later. It is interesting to note that both 'Il Duce' and 'Tricky Dickie' came a cropper during the first few months of their 'Third Deciding Phase' when indeed their fate was Decided (see page 192).

At the very close of this 'Phase' you experience an equally important planetary influence in the form of your Second Saturn Return(see page

230). Probably then, this will affect the transition from this 'Phase' to the next, your 'Third Striving Phase'. This implies that whatever was changed or produced during your 'Third Emerging Phase' will then be tested for its 'roadworthiness', or rather whether or not it holds water. According to what the result is, you will have to Strive to make things work, or you will be happily Striving while thriving. But see page 230 for a more thorough description of that highly significant Second Saturn Return. One famous person who is a good example of the connection between these two important influences is Boris Yeltsin. At fifty-four, at the very start of his 'Third Emerging Phase', he was appointed to the Politburo of the then U.S.S.R. by Mikhail Gorbachev. Come his Second Saturn Return however, and following the intervening demise of the Soviet Union, he resigned from the Communist Party at fifty-nine, and was elected president of the Russian Republic the following year (see more about Boris on pages 218 and 230).

Staying in the political premier vein, Margaret, took off as Prime Minister of Great Britain just prior to her 'Second Emerging Phase' (she couldn't wait!), and came out fighting during it by declaring war on Argentina following its invasion of the Falklands Islands. She did this with the ferocity and zeal of a lioness protecting one of her cubs - not surprising considering she was born with her Moon in Leo! More about Maggie on pages 193, 213 and 233.
Finally, with regard to four of the above example personalities, note how their lunar experiences had to do with their Home- or Motherland, which are ruled by the Moon.

 JUPITER GROWTH MODES - 'LIBRA - SCORPIO - Sagittarius - Capricorn - Aquarius" (see pages 106-114)

3ʳᵈ STRIVING Phase   58y 1m to 61y 6m

This 'Phase' takes on great significance because it coincides with one of the most important of all planetary influences, your Second Saturn Return (see page 230). Basically, Saturn's effect at this time emphasises the difference between, on the one hand, a life that has reached a state of maturity bordering on the wise, and on the other, a life-style that has grown so rigid and resistant to any change, either externally or internally, that circumstances and prospects appear bleak and lonely. Its effects can also range between these two extremes.

And so the Striving at this time is one of making the effort to see life from a more spiritual standpoint and to avoid going to seed by being weighed down by seeing life from a solely material viewpoint. The words 'wise' and 'spiritual' are linked here because they both pose a response to life and others that is strongly coloured by the sense that everything and everyone are here for a purpose - and a higher purpose, at that. As a consequence of this, one's Striving is in aid of somehow teaching others from one's experience rather than boring them with it; or simply carrying on learning rather than believing that you can't teach an old dog new tricks. Seeing and living life in this way can mean that it is better seen from the perspective of being a spiritual entity having material experiences rather than that of being a material entity having occasional spiritual experiences.

For many this is a time of possible retirement, but in astrological symbolism such a thing does not really exist for the Planetary Cycles persist from birth and before, up to and beyond one's physical death. And so so-called retirement at this time is really just emphasising the transition from one style of life and outlook to another as a result of leaving behind the material world of career and day-to-day labour.

Alternatively, this could be a time when your Striving could be academic in the sense that it is the Striving you have exercised down through the years that is now at last appreciated, rather than just come to an end with 'retirement'. Or this could be a time when what has been so long in the growing through your efforts now needs that last push to take it that vital stage further, perhaps to that final vital stage. It is also quite possible that your creative efforts of the past are appreciated by those born a generation before you.

Whatever the case, this all stresses the significance of Striving to make some kind of positive mark in life - or as the Vikings saw it, to not leave this world without being remembered well for your time here. The emphasis is upon what you have created, or are creating in life, rather than how long it took or takes to do so.

JUPITER GROWTH MODES - 'AQUARIUS - Pisces - Aries - Taurus"
(see pages 114-116, 94 and 96)

3ʳᵈ DECIDING Phase   61y 6m to 64y 11m

Like the 'Third Striving Phase' that came before it, this 'Phase' may precede or coincide with retirement from regular employment or your profession. One could simply say that this was the Decision made for you or by you at this time, but the real Decision is what to do now that there is not that daily routine to give form and meaning to your life. As this is an utterly personal issue which I myself have not yet experienced, I cannot do anything other than give a general astrological point of view or guidance for this point in human life...

In addition to what I said regarding retirement under your 'Third Striving Phase' on page 189, it can be helpful to look at what was going on or taking your interest during your 'Third Emerging Phase' between fifty-four years and fifty-eight years of age (see page 186) or even your 'Second Emerging Phase in your late twenties (see page 164). This is because you may now find that you want to use your time and experience to resurrect or expand upon what was happening at either of these times in your life. Conventional opinion is rather linear in that it fails to recognise that if something does not develop or take off at a certain time, then it never will. Astrological thought, on the other hand, appreciates that, as in the natural world, seeds can lie dormant until they sprout many years later.

Apart from events such as retirement this 'Phase' can also present you with situations or changes that call for some form of Decision. Certain endings in the lives of close friends or relatives may create a shift or alteration in your life too. Whatever the case, observing the 'I can, I must, I want to' rule of all 'Deciding Phases' will be useful (see general description beginning on page 129).

Finally, by way of negative example of how a 'Third Emerging Phase' can be misused with dire consequences come this, the 'Third Deciding Phase', I cite Benito Mussolini and Richard Nixon. During their 'Third Emerging Phase' Mussolini led his country into war and Nixon became the 37th U.S. president. Come their 'Third Deciding Phase' though, 'Il Duce' was shot dead by his own countrymen, and 'Tricky Dickie' resigned following the Watergate scandal (see also 'Third Emerging Phase' on page 186, if you haven't already).

JUPITER GROWTH MODES - 'TAURUS - Gemini - Cancer - Leo"
(see pages 96-102)

3ʳᵈ ADJUSTING Phase   64y 11m to 68y 4m

This 'Phase' coincides with the conventional time of retirement from routine work, like the last two Phases, 'Third Striving Phase' and 'Third Deciding Phase' which, if you haven't already, I recommend you read with regard to this issue. This time could also be viewed as the onset of old age, although in some cases this would not be seen that way. In any case though, there is definitely some Adjusting to be done at this time.

The feeling or prospect of becoming elderly - or the denial of it - is further emphasised by there being two Saturn influences occurring during the 'Phase'. The first, your Third Saturn Waxing Square (see page 233), comes up and taps you between sixty-five and sixty-six years of age, and like many Saturn transits, it can make you feel your age, either physically, psychologically or both. The physical aspect is often all too obvious with stiff joints, aches and pains, less elasticity, etc. being well-known afflictions of even for people considerably younger that this. Diet and exercise, now if not sooner, are what are called for.

Additionally however, it is one's psychological condition which greatly dictates your physical one. A rigid attitude creates or worsens a rigid body, and an inactive life on a mental and/or emotional level can cause the body to be inactive too. And if one is closed to new ideas and circumstances then loneliness and uselessness can tip one down the slippery slope.

As ever, a lot depends upon the previous 'Phase', which in this case was that of deciding to do something worthwhile, new or renewed with one's life. A positive decision to make something out of life with an 'it's never too late' philosophy will have pre-empted any feeling that there is no place in the world for you. Apart from being able independently to make a new life for yourself, there are always things like clubs, charity shops, etc. to keep one from apathy or relying solely upon family for company and meaning. Such practical and useful activities become readily available come the Third Saturn Waxing Trine around sixty-eight (page 234), continuing into sixty-nine and the next 'Phase'.

What you are mainly Adjusting to at this time is those conventional ideas of getting older, either in the sense of not accepting that you have to withdraw and be less in the land of the living, or, that it smacks of being old and infirm when you have to do such things as other retired people do. Of course, if you do not retire, but carry on with some creative avenue of expression, then none of this would apply, except perhaps for having to Adjust what you are creating or doing so that it is ultimately successful - and to any negative attitudes you might encounter from others simply because they cannot positively Adjust themselves.

Two famous examples of the 'Third Adjusting Phase' are Queen Elizabeth II and Margaret Thatcher - both 'leading ladies' of Great Britain. During this 'Phase' the Queen finally had to Adjust to public opinion and agree to taxation of her personal income and open parts of Buckingham Palace. (see also pages 167 and 213). Four years before in November 1990 Thatcher had to make probably her biggest Adjustment so far when she had to resign as Prime Minster after failing to win her party's leadership contest. (see also page 233).

JUPITER GROWTH MODES - 'LEO - VIRGO - Libra - Scorpio - Sagittarius" (see pages 102-110)

3rd REALIZING Phase	68y 4m to 71y 9m

"EMOTIONAL WISDOM" - Here we get to the legendary 'three score and ten' mark which is traditionally regarded as the allotted human life-span, although not as the astrologically regarded one, which is eighty-four years of age (one orbit of the planet Uranus). Furthermore, this time is seen astrologically as a period in your life when some great Realisation can be made, brought about by a wealth of experience and an acceptance of life's great mystery as being ultimately positive. If however, cynicism or narrow-mindedness have been allowed to take hold then such a Realisation is not going to take place. Instead, such Realisation would be seen as 'through a glass darkly', that life was some bad and pointless joke, with only regret and resentment for constant company. A third alternative could be the Realisation that life was not, or just could not be accepted as, such a negative affair - giving rise to the first type of Realisation, that life is something great and that you are now in a better position than most to appreciate this.

Two perfect examples of how the Realisation of this time of life can be a crowning glory is seen in the examples of Nelson Mandela and Emmeline Pankhurst. After having been imprisoned for the rebellious expression of his beliefs and principles for just over the average Lunar Cycle of twenty-seven years and four months Mandela returned to public life, and was recognised by the world as a hero for and of human rights. (see also page 175 for the 'Second Realising Phase' when Nelson was incarcerated). Pankhurst, who could be called the Mother of Female Rights, saw the Realisation of all her dreams and labours when the full and equal vote for women was at last introduced in Great Britain on the day she died in June 1928.

In a strictly relative fashion, you too can rise to the Realisation of being someone unique and useful in this world. Whether this is in a small or large way, the Third Saturn Waxing Trine (see page 234) should help you to make this Realisation through utilising your age and experience, the opportunities and agencies that society offers, or a combination of both.

JUPITER GROWTH MODES - 'SAGITTARIUS - CAPRICORN - Aquarius - Pisces" (see pages 110-116)

3ʳᵈ SHARING Phase   71y 9m to 75y 2m

As the essence of 'Sharing Phases' is that of imparting to others what you have learned and experienced, this one has the advantage of a lifetime of gathering such things. But as with all the 'Phases' that occur in later life, what can be post-retirement years, there can be a disconnection from the world at large for one reason or another. Such isolation, which is more likely to become an issue during your Third Saturn Opposition between seventy-three and seventy-four years of age (see page 235), could have a legion of reasons - from the loss of a lifelong companion to an already made habit of withdrawing yourself, or some other inclination born of resentment, bitterness or simply subscribing to the conventional belief that being elderly is supposed to be a second class state.

Whatever the case, Sharing is the key to making the most of this time in your life, and of resolving any issues or problems. I recommend that you read the general description on page 157, if you have not already, in order to appreciate the full significance of Sharing. One might even say that Sharing is the opposite of being on your own, lacking anyone to Share with. By this it is implied that not Sharing can be the very thing that creates that lack. So if you are lonely, swallow any reservations and muster the courage to Share whatever you can, be it emotionally, mentally or physically. You will then find how Nature, abhorring a vacuum as it does, will bring you what you need. But you have to open the door in order to let in Nature's gifts.

All being well, this can a wonderful time of helping, teaching and entertaining others with the ripeness and wisdom of your personality and its experiences.

JUPITER GROWTH MODES - 'PISCES - ARIES - Taurus - Gemini - Cancer" (see pages 116 and 94-100)

3ʳᵈ UNDERSTANDING Phase   75y 2m to 78y 7m

This is when 'ripe' and 'mature' should turn to wisdom, if it has not done so already. The aforementioned Nelson Mandela, who I used as a positive example of the Second and Third 'Realising Phases' (see pages 175 and 194), also came up trumps with this, his 'Third Understanding Phase'. At the very beginning of this 'Phase' he was inaugurated as the first black president of South Africa. Most significantly for this 'Phase' though was the immediate implementation of his government's Truth and Reconciliation Commission. At the time of writing, this is still seeking to heal the country's past of apartheid and all that it entailed through inviting perpetrators of crimes to come forward and expose themselves to their victims or the friends or relatives of those victims. Rather than create more violence and animosity through revenge and punishment, this wise and Understanding method can only create more Understanding. Astrologically, it is also worth noting that this first year was a Cancer Jupiter Year, the Sign of emotional Understanding and also Nelson's Sun-Sign.

This example is a beautiful testament of how harsh experience, when transmuted with and into Understanding, makes the true human being, which is surely the prime purpose of a human life.

 **JUPITER** GROWTH MODES - 'CANCER - Leo - Virgo - Libra"

(see pages 100-106)

Also occurring during this time...

THIRD SATURN WANING TRINE (see page 236)

3rd RELEASING Phase   78y 7m to 82y 0m

Without being too dramatic about it, and in the awareness that I personally am nowhere near this age, the experiencing of your 'Third Releasing Phase' has about it the ring of surrender and redemption in the face of what must or could be near the end of life. Whatever the case, it is most definitely a time to make your peace with everyone through Releasing anything that you are holding on to which could be regarded as weighing you down. Thus emptied and enlightened, you can proceed toward whatever is in store for you with a transparency that is the passport for crossing the Great Divide.

JUPITER GROWTH MODES - 'LIBRA - SCORPIO - Sagittarius -

Capricorn" (see pages 106-112)

4th EMERGING Phase
3rd LUNAR RETURN
82y 0m to 85y 5m

"YOUR LAST EMOTIONAL ROUND-UP" - Apart form being seen as the Emergence from life altogether - either literally, symbolically or psychologically, this 'Phase' is almost entirely bound up with the significance of your Uranus Return (one orbit of Uranus, 84 years) which symbolically marks the end of an astrological human lifetime, or the whole gamut of Earthly experience.

JUPITER GROWTH MODES - 'AQUARIUS - Pisces - Aries"
(see pages 114, 116 and 94)

Your Saturn Cycle
Life's Lessons & Progression

"Know this, in all the ages past,
I am the one who set your task;
Since first you came unto this Earth
As spirits young to prove your worth"

+	Consolidating	Teaching	Advancing	Cautioning
-	Pressurising	Punishing	Testing	Thwarting

As far as Saturn is concerned, there most definitely is a specific point and purpose to your being here, alive on planet Earth. Possibly, we are most hard-put by Saturn's influence when we are failing to grasp that very point - i.e. that there is one. It is as if many of us are born thinking it's going to be easier than it actually is. Consequently, upon the shock of finding that there is someone or something making it difficult for us, we overreact and commence looking for some way of denying or getting around whatever Saturn appears to be plaguing us with - with the consequence that it then piles on even more pressure. Then again, there are some people who naturally take to the fact that discipline and hard work are central to existence. However, they too may be missing a point.

This is because there are two points inherent in Saturn's dictum, and I describe them below. Interestingly, this dual nature is reflected in the two-faced god, Janus, from which is derived January, the month which is mainly that of the Sign Capricorn, which Saturn rules. Janus is the deity of Doorways and Thresholds, and as you will see, is very relevant to Saturn. Yet another mythological connection between the two is that when Jupiter banished Saturn from the sky, Janus welcomed him in, for Saturn must have resonated with him. As you will see from the following, it will be helpful to appreciate that his two faces allow him to look outwards across the Threshold, the First Point(of view) and inwards across the Threshold, the Second Point(of view): the Threshold simply being the boundary between Inner Reality and Outer Reality. In human physiological terms, this would be your skin. Incidentally, Saturn is also called the Lord of Boundaries and the Dweller on the Threshold.

The First Point or Outer Reality

The Second Point or inner Reality

Saturn's First Point is the point and purpose that the world at large, the status quo, would have us think them to be. This is 'Ground Control' in the sense of being the conventions and controls of the society in which one lives - the 'real world'. These mainly take the form of any external authorities and structures such as the government, teachers, officials, elders, traditions, ancestors, how one is supposed to behave - and initially at least, one's parents (or whoever was responsible for you as a child). All these things - rightly or wrongly, well or badly - provide us with a foundation upon which to build our lives and to make the point and achieve the purpose that this status quo says is a valid point to make or purpose to achieve. Caution and conservatism are fundamental to the nature of Point One because tradition and material stability depend upon such things. The First Point is also that of the concrete, physical world which we are, by and large, bound and limited by - the world of form. This Point sensibly states that one has to fit into society and be materially stable, to have a 'job definition' and status in the eyes of that status quo.

Saturn's Second Point has more to do with what you are learning in terms of your more fundamental and internal reason for being here, something the overseer of which is your Conscience. This is also Ground Control in that there are certain forces and circumstances which keep us to that path of learning, doing what our Conscience deems to be 'right', whether we like it or not, and sooner or later. And if we ignore or fail to listen to our Conscience, then the external authorities of the First Point bear down on us - or some physical condition strikes. This learning entails certain lessons about life itself in the sense that planet Earth is like one enormous school. The key lesson here is that of learning to take full responsibility for what one says, does and even thinks. In turn, this engenders the idea that we have a Grade, a Curriculum, Lessons, Tests and a Timetable.

But then the First Point also obviously engenders these educational factors, but it is just on a different level, involving different criteria. Then again, an important aspect of Saturn is that there is a measure of the First Point within the Second Point - for you cannot very easily start to improve yourself on an inner level if you have nothing to depend upon in the outer world. Conversely, someone who is successful in the outer world has, sooner or later, to come to terms with their inner life. Furthermore, one is probably pursuing more than just one Point at a time. Possibly some people are exclusively involved with the First Point of material status and concrete reality, but there would usually be someone they depend upon who is more concerned with the Second Point. And there are relatively few who subscribe exclusively to the Second Point - like mystics and non-conformists who deny the material world - but even they have to eat and have somewhere to sleep. But the vast majority of us simultaneously subscribe to both to Point One, the conventional values of making something of yourself in the material world; and Point Two, values which state that true success has something to do with personal integrity and spiritual discipline. However, it has to said that in today's world, Point One holds sway. The Monica Lewinsky Affair of Bill Clinton was a testament to the U.S.A.'s majority allegiance to Point One - like 'never mind your personal integrity, Bill - just keep the bucks rolling in!'. Many would agree that Point One is dangerously over-stressed in our world today, and that the personal integrity of Point Two is in need of a resurgence. This is why the Clinton crisis created such a furore, division and confrontation.

Your Grade

This is the calibre or 'form' you have at any given time. From Point Two's point of view, Saturn is 'The Lord of Karma' which means that Saturn keeps the score of how well or badly you are doing so far with regard to your integrity and spiritual standing. Being The Lord of Karma implies that Saturn has something to do with reincarnation - and it does. It dictates the circumstances and limitations we find ourselves in until we have learnt whatever we are supposed to be learning. For instance, if one is learning about the proper value of money, then one would either have a difficult time getting hold of the stuff, or one could have too much of it and be having to learn the value of things that money cannot buy - like love or health. In this case, your Saturn Cycle will test or reward you in this respect; when you have learned something about the true value of money for example, then you would probably not care about it so much, and one way or the other it would cease to be a problem. If you had failed to learn that lesson, the money would continue to be a problem. "For what shall it profit a man, if he shall gain the whole world, and lose his own soul?" (St.Mark ch.8, v.36).

On the other hand, those who subscribe more heavily to Saturn's First Point often prefer to disregard or even ridicule such things as reincarnation and karma. On the very day after writing this, England's football team manager, Glenn Hoddle, spoke out about his belief in reincarnation, saying that disabled people were paying for sins committed in previous lifetimes. The following day he was forced to resign amidst howls of derision. (See also page 242 about Glenn's gaffe - or was it?). This is because the First Point is heavily invested in keeping things 'real' insofar as it is deemed that the only things that exist are those which you can prove to exist - using the very rules for existence laid down by those who preside over the First Point rules - like the abovementioned government, scientific establishment, material standards, etc.. And so then Saturn's influence in your life would be on that level. In other words, you are tested and rewarded in the context of what are conventionally regarded as being socially and materially okay. Using the same example, one would learn how to get, earn and manage money - or not, as the case may be. And from Saturn's First Point of view, making money is making the Grade.

The Curriculum

This, the course which Saturn is running, and upon which you enrolled at birth (or before if you subscribe to the Second Point), has basically two Levels which correspond to the two Points. A simple way of looking at it is to say that one starts off with Point One at Level One and eventually graduates to Point Two and goes on to Level Two. But really it is more complex, because as I have already said, one Point is inextricably bound up with the other. For example, some people might regard themselves as spiritual seekers, or just drop-outs, belonging to Point Two when really they are just woolly-headed dreamers and escapists whose feet have yet to touch the ground, let alone be firmly planted on it. You could say they have jumped the queue and enrolled themselves on the Second Level of the course without having gone through the 'foundation course' of Level One. It can take quite a lot of time, pain and confusion before such individuals realise that they have to put first things first and learn how to manage the material world. And yet it is ironic that the governments of First World countries, the ones who to a great degree run the First Level of the course, subsidise many people who are floundering in this way. But then, as I have said, everyone is dependent upon the First Point to a certain extent. Even genuine Second Point types who have integrated their personalities enough to be virtually self-governing depend somewhat upon the State or Point One.

However, those who have genuinely embarked upon Level Two of the course have qualified by proving themselves able to function in the material world, even if only just. They then set about learning how the world really works. This part of the Curriculum involves the study and practice of Right Thinking and Right Relating, and Saturn's ongoing influence is there to guide and cajole them towards this end. Going back to our Ground Control metaphor, Point One people at Level One are manifest as the ground crew which creates and manages, or in most cases simply works for, what is happening at ground level - the so-called 'real world' or System. Point Two people at Level Two are training to be air crew who eventually qualify to 'take off' in that they become relatively free of the constraints and pressures that most of us are subject to. But, as previously pointed out, even they are still dependent upon the ground crew and practical reality. The 'star' who has risen to fame and fortune still has to pay their taxes and maintain their health. It is only when they are in 'free flight' - utterly self-governing - that they are truly liberated; and like all astronauts and flyers they are relatively few in number. All the same, consciously or unconsciously, these are the heights to which everyone sooner or late aspires - whether it is to be free of the Rat Race owing to material success or because one has risen above it.

The Lessons, Tests and Timetable

When you were born, Saturn - along with the Sun, Moon and other Planets - was positioned in a certain place in one of the Signs of the Zodiac - a depiction of which is called your Birth Chart. The Planets then move on through the Signs, creating their respective cycles, and at certain times in your life reach significant stations or positions. The picture opposite shows Saturn where it was when I was born (A, in Cancer) and where it got to half a cycle or about 15 years later (B, in the opposite Sign of Capricorn). Eventually they return to the positions they were in at birth, the most well-known 'return' being when the Sun returns to where it was on the day you were born - your birthday. In fact, each Planet plays upon all the other Planets, not just upon itself. But this interplanetary interaction- something called Transits - is too complex for this book, but it is very revealing. Refer to the Resources page at the back to inquire into this further if you wish.

Beginning opposite is the actual schedule - determined by these various positions that Saturn makes in relation to where it was when you were born - and thereby lays down when Life's Lessons and Examinations occur in your life and when possible honours are bestowed. Also, as you read these, the Active points in your Saturn Cycle, consider how they are affecting you at Level One or Level Two, that is, on an external level and/or an internal one.

FIRST WAXING SQUARE	Between 6 & 7 Years Old

"THE DIE IS CAST" - The soft and pliable being that you were as a new-born baby and toddler now gets moulded and formed into a product in the image of the expectations of your parents, family and first schooling, and to a lesser or greater degree those of society as they impinge upon the protection of those guardians. Countering or enhancing these expectations and influences that seek to form you would be your own innate personality, your soul. And now that being must find its permanent teeth (quite literally - and lose the milk teeth) and begin to contend with the world as a more independent and accountable ego, all with the assistance or encumbrance that its guardians and teachers lay upon it.

Up until now we often only refer to ourselves by our actual name or pet-

or baby-name. But with the onset of your First Saturn Waxing Square something urges you more and more to say 'I'. In this way you begin that long road of establishing yourself as a separate entity with its very own set of thoughts and feelings. Consequently, at this age you begin to show the calibre and nature of your will. The reaction that you get to this from parents, siblings, teachers and peers causes your will to adjust itself or to assert itself even more - depending upon its innate qualities.

Looking back at this time can be very useful and enlightening with respect to noting the experiences and feelings that happened then. Your importance and potency - whether it shows or not - are the most pressing and sensitive issues then. At age six a client of mine was not told that a house move was about to happen, and one day she came home from school to nothing and nobody. It was only a matter of a few minutes before a neighbour sorted her out but in that time her sense of personal significance was severely damaged. So parents take note - of this and of all the astrology of growing up! Indeed, at and up to this time, the 'die is cast'.

More than anything else, the encouraging of a child to be creative and playful is what really counts now. During these one or two years it forms its more conscious idea of the nature or the world it lives in - especially in terms of the nature of authority. If it finds that authority - in the form or parents, teachers and all adults - is fair-minded, with a balanced sense of the need for work and play, of consideration for itself and others, and stresses the importance of being good at expressing itself as distinct from merely getting it right, then that 'die' will serve it well into a colourful future. If it is made to see authority as rigid, overly conventional and hypocritically 'right/wrong/do as I say not what I do' orientated, then it can be doomed to a black and white, or grey, future - or causes it to rebel. If it experiences very little sense of authority at all, then such an absence of structure will bedevil it with first a false sense of freedom and then a very real sense of insecurity and no sense of discipline. Of course, you could experience and be a product of a blend of these.

Possibly more than anything else, at this time you are made aware of your sense of choice: to choose to look at something in a certain way; to contribute or not to what is going on around you; to choose what kind of world you have been born into. In other words, what you as a unique individual make of it and what you think about is crucial - as too is whether or not anybody asks you to make something or asks you a question, thereby implying that you are a sentient and imaginative being.

JUPITER 'YEAR'   *'Libra-Scorpio'*
for your Growth Mode   *(see pages 106 and 108)*

MOON 'PHASE'   *'First Striving Phase' to 'First Deciding Phase'*
for emotional Attunement   *(see pages 147 and 149)*

FIRST WAXING TRINE	Between 9 & 10 Years Old

"RELEASING YOUR CREATIVITY" - The nature of the creative impulse that is the birthright of all human beings now has a chance to burst forth. A great deal though, depends upon the degree to which it has been previously nurtured. If as a child you were at first dammed up by the ignorance and narrow expectations of others, then this release will be to little avail. But where originality of mind and personality has been encouraged, the child positively flourishes, tumbling over adversity with ebullient enthusiasm. In either case however, there is still the possibility of some helpful and sympathetic teacher or friend appearing on the scene. The very best should be made of any such occurrence, because the inhibited child can be given a chance to loosen up their repressed creativity, whereas the uninhibited one can be shown how to be more creative still - and even be generous with their gifts.

This can be a time when the authority of parents, teachers or adults generally can be a positive influence just when it is needed - like for instance during a change of school. There is no guarantee here though, as the Trine influence needs to be made conscious use of, something which the child itself is obviously not that able to do.

Parents should take serious note of the above, not least of all because at this time the growing child, rather that just accepting or reacting to authority as before, is actually on the look out for a form of authority that it can respect and appreciate, but will reject one that it cannot. This is further emphasised by the ninth year being a 'Capricorn' Jupiter Year.

 'YEAR'   *'Capricorn-Aquarius'*
for your *Growth Mode*   *(see pages 112 and 114)*

MOON 'PHASE'   *'First Deciding Phase' to 'First Adjusting Phase*
for emotional *Attunement*   *(see pages 149 and 151)*

FIRST OPPOSITION	Between 14 & 15 Years Old

"ME VERSUS THE REST" - During this time, the impressions you get of how life works for you can be very far-reaching. On a purely natural level, puberty is forcing you to erupt from the matrix of parents and family - be that matrix like a warm, secure nest or a cold and sticky mud-pit. At the same time, you are also probably having your first 'serious' interaction with others on a sexual or emotional level. On top of all this, or more likely underlying it, there can occur some kind of 'karmic confrontation' at this time. Thrilling and energetic as this time can be for many - courtesy mainly of sex hormones - its impact is often experienced as anything but a groovy teenage picnic. If it was for you, then count yourself very lucky or karmically clean, meaning that your soul's course was still aligned to a natural one.

However, astrologically speaking, and if my friends, acquaintances and clients are anything to go by, the First Saturn Opposition is when you are basically made aware of what you are in for - particularly on a social and emotional level. It is rather as if one embarks on the first round of the roller-coaster that is life and kind of freewheels through the first downhill half with the sheer impetus of being born. Come this, the halfway point of the first round, kinetic energy ebbs and one is made aware of an equal and opposite force coming in the opposite direction. The world and life comes at you like an uphill gradient.

How you relate and receive this has everything to do with the type of person you essentially are. For me personally it was a time when I was just about getting the hang of making out with the opposite sex in quite a pleasant neighbourhood. Then all of a sudden, for financial reasons, my father had to sell up and move away to a cheaper area sixty miles away. This place is a social wasteland, and my social and sexual development is put on ice, with repercussions that I shan't go into here. Also at that time, my mother and father were both having affairs with other people, and had little time for little old desolate me. But suffice to say, these years were 'formative' - a good old Saturnian adjective that describes for many the effect of this time only too well.

Unless you happened to have, or had, a 'Happy Days' type of First Saturn Opposition, you will find that a lot can be gleaned from your experiences now in terms of that Grade I referred to in the introduction to this section. This is that 'karmic confrontation' in that you are made aware of what you have on your plate this lifetime. For me, I was driven into my interior which ultimately bred in me an intense awareness of how myself and others tick - but I paid the price of such introversion by being very hard to reach emotionally for a large part of my life. At that time I also learnt to play the guitar, rather than with girls, and that too formed an important part of my curriculum vitae.

This time can, not surprisingly, be rather alienating - hence the "Me Versus the Rest" tag. The basic thrust of this time, as I initially pointed out, is to pull away from parental influence and become a healthy adolescent. Unfortunately, owing to the alienating and unnatural quality of modern society, more often than not such a natural, hormonal process backfires on itself. Teenage gang warfare is an example of this alienation looking for something it can identify with. Furthermore, a group other than family that also embodies this alienation and one's emotional denial and has a similar group (the opposing gang) to project one's hate and frustration upon, fits the bill nicely.

But every picture tells its own story, and I'm sure each teenage gangster has his or her own reason for feeling split within themselves in this way. A client of mine, for example, got to snog with the 'catch' of her group, but the only thing she caught from him was glandular fever which did wonders for her sexual confidence. Thereupon she enters into a relationship with someone who abuses her, and she puts up with it because it seems to be all she deserves in terms of love and attention. Breaking out of this negative sexual self-image and an obsession with health was the main part of her 'form' which she had to contend with in life. Yet another client went to work for someone who fancied her and so she unwittingly antagonised his wife. This is a pattern of behaviour she has to this day, some sixty years later - that is, she is always relates to men in a way which offends the women they are with, evidencing a karma of unstable but unsure sexuality.

Whatever it is that is a focal issue at this time is going to be a focal issue in your life as a whole. It is not necessarily got to be sexual in nature, but it usually is. For instance, it can also be concerning issues of belief, school, family life, a younger sibling being born, shyness or self-consciousness, or any event, person, change or thing that makes you aware of how different you feel from those around you. For this reason, running away from home is a popular expression of this time. Anything that gives you an intense impression of yourself, whether you want it, like it, or not.

Your First Saturn Opposition is so typical of Saturn itself because it makes you starkly aware of the difficulties and challenges of life at a time when you are supposed to be having fun, according to popular belief. Then again, sometimes 'having fun' is the antidote or counterbalance to Saturn's heaviness, and such is a positive and natural response that you would be wise to adopt if you are experiencing it now. If you are viewing this time in retrospect, then understanding the hard bits and what they posed, and not forgetting the good bits, would be your antidote against it still dogging you to this day. Also, on a more esoteric note, this time can likened to chapter in your life when you come very close to finding your mission in life, hopefully grasping it fully later on. This is reflected in the myth of Parzival who on his quest for the Holy Grail came upon the Grail Castle in his youth. The trouble was he did not know what to say or do when he got there and had to wander off to gain the experience he needed before he eventually came back properly equipped years later. So if you are having your First Saturn Opposition now or are looking back on it, try to focus upon any near misses, for they could hold a valuable piece of information.

Finally, if you are a parent reading this with regard to your teenage offspring - then read it again!

JUPITER 'YEAR'	'Gemini - Cancer'
for your Growth Mode	(see pages 98 and 100)
MOON 'PHASE'	'First Realising Phase'
for emotional Attunement	(see pages 154)

FIRST WANING TRINE	Between 19 & 20 Years Old

"FINDING YOUR NICHE" - This is a time when you are inclined to settle into some form of situation or relationship. This is not to say that it is ideal or that it will last forever, but that it is more like a friendly port where you can feel relatively 'at home'. Statistically, this is a popular time for getting married, probably because this Saturn Trine gives an underlying feeling that emotional stability is at hand. Similarly, the kind of work you are doing now reflects a feeling or material stability - or it simply feels like the right road to be on. Personally, at this time I left my steady job to go on the road with my band; not particularly secure, but it felt right. I also started my first proper relationship which lasted seven years. Others, probably most others, will settle for job security now, especially if they are tying the knot as well.

Another common feature of this period is that you can attract an older person or older people who support or guide you in some way. This may be a trainer or teacher, someone who houses you, or simply a workmate. They may also be someone in authority who gives you that vital step up.

 **'YEAR'**   *'Scorpio - Sagittarius"*
for your Growth Mode   *(see pages 108 and 110)*

 **'PHASE'**   *'First Sharing Phase' to 'First Understanding*
for emotional Attunement   *Phase' (see pages 157 and 160)*

FIRST WANING SQUARE	Between 21 & 22 Years Old

"COMING OF AGE" - Although traditionally this is when the world confers 'adulthood' upon us, it is really more a case of the world challenging us to cut the mustard, to shape up in the face of its tests and opportunities. This can take many forms and be the consequence of any number of situations. Leaving or going to university or college, the ending of something, leaving home, changed circumstances - these are some of the things that can manifest Saturn's call to 'get it together'. But whatever the case may be, you are probably going to have to pile on more effort, endure harder circumstances, do without in some way, acclimatise yourself to an alien environment, or anything that tests your mettle as a young adult setting out on the hard road of life. The types you encounter may well be unobliging or unsympathetic. Beware Scrooges, too.

However, despite the fact that this is a Square influence, it is also a time of significant honours and events. Celebrated examples of this abound, but here are a few. Grace Kelly, Greta Garbo and Brigitte Bardot all made their successful film debuts at this time in their lives - while Howard Hughes first begun to invest in films then. Another kind of debut was that of Queen Elizabeth II of England's maiden speech to the nation on television. There are also significant graduations: Gandhi qualified as a barrister then, Thatcher and Jackie Onassis graduated from college, and Yuri Gagarin got his pilot's licence. Gorbachev joined the Communist Party. An important point here is that all these honours or events are underwritten by effort, commitment or tradition. Saturn never rewards when these elements are absent.

JUPITER 'YEAR'
for your Growth Mode

'*Capricorn - Aquarius'*
(see pages 112 and 114)

MOON 'PHASE'
for emotional Attunement

'*First Understanding Phase'*
(see pages 160)

FIRST SATURN RETURN	Between 29 & 30 Years Old

"YOUR FIRST LIFE PROGRESS REPORT" - Saturn is the shape or mould that your life is supposed to take. Its first impression is made at birth, and when it has completed an orbit around the Sun it comes back, impresses itself upon you again, and checks out whether or not you are realising your potentials and living up to your responsibilities. Depending on how you are doing, it will impose tests and/or promote or consolidate your position in life. Over the previous few years you may well have been experiencing endings and beginnings as your fate set you up for this time of reckoning - especially as decreed by your 'Second Emerging Moon Phase' or First Lunar Return (see page 164).

Using our 'all the world's a stage' metaphor, Saturn is seen as the

Producer - that is, the one who makes sure that the material wherewithal is in hand and that practical considerations and demands are met and maintained. Saturn is all about the shape and form we give to life and ourselves, not just notions and ideas. So if you have some dream or ambition, then at this time you must really make the effort to act upon it and take the time to see if it works. If it does not work, then you will have to rethink and try again - and again if necessary. At the same time however, it is important to stress that the fantasies, ideals and 'crazy ambitions' of your youth and twenties are also necessary in order to withstand the external pressures and doubts that the world at large presents you with during this time. Without that dream, Saturn can make things crushingly dull and meaningless. Just think of a well-financed and well-produced play that has a poor script and second-rate acting! This is a case of Level One pressures being withstood, balanced out, and eventually influenced by Level Two energies (See the introduction to this Saturn section concerning Level One and Level Two).

If after several good attempts to realise an ambition (possibly over a period of years previously) there is, under Saturn's influence, still no success, then you can be sure that your dream is only that, or, that the efforts you have made will come in useful at some later date. But if no effort is or has been made to fulfil some ambition or to live up to some inner belief or standard, then you will obviously gain neither achievement nor experience, and possibly become unstuck during this time.

On the other hand, if you have been making the effort and are made of the right stuff, then Saturn will see to it that you are crowned with the laurels of success. At the very time of writing this, I note an example of striving and succeeding coming at the Saturn Return of Jana Novotna (29) who after years of competing has just won the Wimbledon 1998 Women's Tennis Championship, and also an example of striving and failing at the Saturn Return of her opponent, Nathalie Tauziat (30). Saturn puts us to the test, and rewards or otherwise.

But your Saturn Return is not just about material success or failure on a professional level. Much as the Producer might deem it necessary to inject the play with a new character or element, at this time life may well present you with an event which imposes greater responsibility (=ability to respond), forcing you to measure up or develop in some way. The classic event for this is having a baby. Other such events could be moving into or buying a new home, getting married, starting a demanding job, or some other responsibility that effects you for years to come. It could also mean losing or having your job threatened in some way. Again, rather than just experiencing Level One events such as these, you would also probably be given extra responsibilities on Level Two - that is, such will involve moral decisions and emotional judgments.

In any event, Saturn forces you to establish your correct position, be it professionally, socially or emotionally, often by having to make your boundaries a lot more definite. This means determining a balance between what you do and do not owe anyone, and vice versa. More particularly, it poses you knowing your own ground - a Level Two situation - as distinct from the ways, views and territories of others' - possibly Level One situations. Not knowing your own space - that is, where responsibilities and expectations should begin and end - could bring you quite low and make you feel very insecure. So, not least of all, relationships can at this time go through the mill in some way, meaning that stronger commitments have to be made - to either stay in a relationship or get out of one once and for all. If you attract a new relationship now, you can be sure that it will test you emotionally and materially, giving you experiences that will serve and/or affect you for the rest of your life.

Speaking of 'boundaries' points us to that other major Saturnian issue: Structure. During this period of your life it is vitally important as to how you organise your activities, that you formulate a plan or task. A lack of structure becomes very evident now, because the pressures of life can implode upon if you have little or none. In turn, this all leads to another Saturnian factor, that of time. How you use or misuse your time is another critical issue. Time is the instrument of Saturn, for it is through time well spent that something is achieved, and through it being wasted or procrastinated with that nothing is accomplished. You may well feel that there is very little time to do what you have to do - but this would really be that heavy Saturnian sense of importance and urgency making itself felt. So read the writing on the wall. Also, bear in mind That not respecting or wasting others' time could attract coldness and a lack of response.

At a more karmic or psychological level, the Saturn Return can bring something or someone into your life that challenges you to confront or overcome some major issue that does not involve just you and those close to you. Again you may fail or succeed. Again still, what may have appeared a failure could at a later date prove essential to success. Examples of each of these are, in the first case, Lt.Paula Coughlin who single-handedly took on the US Navy in a sexual harassment case and won, and in the second, Karen Silkwood who blew the whistle on a nuclear scandal only to be mysteriously killed in a car 'accident' on the exact day of her Saturn Return. Both these cases could be described as Level Two values clashing with Level One values, as individuals standing testament to superior moral standards in the face of the System which is inclined to be guided my purely financial/political considerations and the lowest common denominator of morality.

Another crisis that Saturn can bring, as the 'jelly mould' of your fate hits the 'jelly' of your life-so-far, is one of health. But this would usually be because you had evaded or not consciously taken on some challenge, only for it to re-present itself on a cellular level. It could also be the result of some event from the distant past, that still had not been addressed, surfacing as some complaint. Accidents and other physical traumas would also fall into this category.

Naturally, your Saturn Return is not too likely to be as dramatic or drastic as the examples given above, but relatively speaking, it will feel very important and of weighty significance to you. As such, it will be taken seriously - or it had better be - for in many respects your First Saturn Return is the beginning of the rest of your life. At this time you are more yourself than at any other time because you are feeling the difference or similarity between what you are meant to be and what you have so far turned out to be. Taking the time and exercising the discipline to accomplish something is highly important. But possibly more important is your determining quite what 'success' really means to you personally (Level Two), rather than in the eyes of the world (Level One) or according to some naïve fantasy (Level Two 'posing'). At my own Saturn Return I was striving to become a singer/songwriter, having been in the music business nearly all my working life so far. But it was at this time that I took up astrology - which is now decidedly my profession, while music is now a pastime. But I was not really aware of this ending and beginning until some years later when I became a fully-fledged professional astrologer. So have your ear to the ground and your nose to the air, for during your First Saturn Return you should be picking up the essential plot of your life. And, like me, you can, in retrospect, see how you did this.

People have often asked me, after their Saturn Return has technically ended, things like "Why do I still feel Saturn's effect?" or "Have I handled it okay?". The answer here is that any Planet's effect, but especially Saturn's, is a bit like punching a pillow. Take your fist away and the dent in the pillow is there for some time, or until it is plumped up. In other words, you will feel Saturn's pressure as long as you need to, until you have achieved, learnt or straightened out something. In many ways, your First Saturn Return is when you truly become, or have to become, an adult and 'put away childish things'. You have gone through the 'grounding' of 'Ground Control', and now you have to recognise the existence of Level Two and make the effort to aspire to its values. A positive statement that I heard from someone soon after the end of their First Saturn Return was "I am now building myself up to make a better person".

To help you manage and make the most of your First Saturn Return, on the following page you will see a FLOWCHART of 'Your First Life Progress Report', which gives you a graphic idea of what Saturn is bringing into your life, and what the various ways of responding to it can bring you. Just follow the instructions in the top panel in order to steer your way onward and upward, rather than standing still or going down.

A MAJOR INFLUENCE occurs through AGE 29 TO AGE 30

YOUR FIRST SATURN RETURN
"Your First Life Progress Report"

Flowchart below shows how the Positive and Negative Saturn Traits (left), that you may or may not have, encounter Saturn's influence (arrow on the right), which in turn consolidates the Positive Traits into a Positive Outcome (top) and/or relegates the Negative traits to a Negative Outcome (bottom). Negative Outcomes can be made Positive through developing the Positive traits

POSITIVE OUTCOME

Order and control over life situations.
Clear perspective. Practical realisations.
Material development. Promotion.
Stable home and family.
Financial stability.
New beginnings.

POSITIVE TRAITS

Industriousness.
Past efforts to achieve.
Discipline and readiness to try.
Maturity and reliability.
Acumen. Moderation.
Caution. Responsibleness

Make or break
issues and events.
material factors.
The elderly. Ageing.
Extra responsibilities.

SATURN

Laziness and apathy. Impatience.
Lack of discipline and effort.
Irresponsible and bad behaviour.
Lack of enterprise or commitment.
Feebleness. Indecisiveness.
Fanciful, unrealistic ideas.

Authority figures.
Lessons & Teachers.
The Hand of Fate.
Relationship tests.
Entropy

Money problems.
Reduced circumstances.
Confinement. Downfall.
Lack of direction/purpose.
Relationship break-downs.
Major rethink. No progress.
Stagnation. Depression. Lethargy.

NEGATIVE TRAITS

NEGATIVE OUTCOME

Now here follows a 'Saturn Return Gallery' of celebrated examples of this super-significant planetary event...

People who gained honours at this time include Marlon Brando winning his first Oscar for 'On the Waterfront' and Liz Taylor winning hers for 'Butterfield Eight' a month after almost dying from pneumonia - now that is dramatic, Liz! (see pages 154,167 for more about Liz). Howard Hughes set a new air speed record of 351 mph (see also page 213). Marie Curie discovered a new element, Polonium. Muhammad Ali regained his honours as World Heavyweight Champion when the U.S. Supreme Court reversed his conviction for draft-dodging (see also pages 163 & 169).

Another individual who made a highly significant career move at both his First and Second Saturn Returns was Boris Yeltsin; he joined the Soviet Communist Party at the first one and resigned from it at his Second. Other singularly significant professional landmarks were Che Guevara when he led his group against the troops of Batista in Cuba (see also page 244). And a big one for John Lennon - the Beatles broke up (see also pages 167, 245 and 249 concerning John).

Marilyn Monroe married the much older Arthur Miller, probably in the hope of gaining the father figure she never had (Saturn rules father figures) but was divorced five years later - see also pages 167, 172 and 220).

A notorious example of the luck of the Devil(Satan=Saturn) looking after his own, was Al Capone who peaked at $30m dollars from his various illegal activities that year. This peak of his evil was also marked by his ordering the infamous St. Valentine's Day Massacre. But as is the nature of peaks, it was downhill all the way after this for Capone.

Finally, a significant but tragic event concerning ordinary people; in December 1998 six friends were involved in a climbing accident. The 29 and 30 year olds were killed along with two 28 year old (see pages 164 & 279), whereas the ones that survived were 'Saturn-free' and 'Moon-free' 24 and 25 year olds.

JUPITER 'YEAR'   *'VIRGO - Libra'*
for your Growth Mode   *(see pages 104 and 106)*

MOON 'PHASE'   *'Second Emerging Phase' to 'Second Striving*
for emotional Attunement   *Phase' (see pages 164 and 168)*

SECOND WAXING SQUARE	Between 36 & 37 Years Old

"HAVING YOUR WHEELS TAPPED" - As this marks the end of the first stage of your Second Saturn Cycle after that all-important First Saturn Return, we could see this as a kind of minor test of how well you handled the major test. So this 'seven-year itch' of Saturn's cycle can be particularly itchy. Basically this test is there to see what and how well you learnt your lessons from seven years back, if you are still on the right road, here likened to the engineer who taps the wheels of trains to see if they are sound. Did you manage to stand on your own two feet then - or begin to - and how are you doing now? Or are you again unconsciously looking for someone or something to lean on? Are you still looking for a scapegoat upon whom to blame any difficulties?

This influence could be regarded as a time when one really should go from Level One to Level Two if you haven't already (see Saturn introduction). This means that the time has come to begin taking full responsibility for your thoughts, feelings and actions. And so Saturn, in order to make this point, will load certain issues in your life that reflect this and challenge you with it. Personally, I suffered a major collapse in the form of a relationship ending and losing tenure on a house, both of which I had felt very secure in. Saturn was saying to me 'You are getting too comfortable with all this and you're not really getting your act together'. And so they had to go. In retrospect I can see Saturn's wisdom in this - but at the time I was bereft, and had to limp along for a year or two until my Uranus Opposition forced a more radical and conscious move (see page 239).

A client of mine thought she had 'arrived' after having moved into a far better house and neighbourhood than she'd ever had previously, only to get involved in an extramarital affair with a younger and insecure man. This was her own unlooked at insecurities being visited upon her via another person to whom she became attracted. This was Saturn's way of 'tapping her wheels', showing that her issue was not just one of material stability(Level One), but also emotional stability (Level Two).

Two famous examples of people who did not quite qualify at this time of Level One to Level Two transition were Marilyn Monroe and Princess Diana. Marilyn's dependency upon barbiturates and unreliable men was amounting to a quite spectacular flunking of Saturn's test, and she knew it - or rather felt it, could not understand it or deal with it, and withdrew from it in the most complete way that is possible. Suicide is a very 'Level One' phenomenon because on it one fails to see beyond the physical realm and the material world. So there seems to be only one way out. And if, as conspiracy theorists have it, she was murdered, then it amounts to the same thing for such assassins could be regarded as Level One Enforcers.

The same could be said, more or less, for that other female icon of the Twentieth Century, Princess Diana, who also died at thirty-six years of age. Diana also had a well-known security problem, but despite appearances of becoming stronger and more self-directing shortly before her death, she was from an astrological viewpoint simply falling into another security trap. This is borne out by the fact that is was the very shaky security systems around her at the time that were responsible for her death: not wearing seat-belts, drunk chauffeur not familiar with that kind of car, the car hire firm not ensuring that there would be a suitable driver, and other factors we will probably never be aware of. And again, like Marilyn, if there was some sort of sinister conspiracy going on, it amounts to the same thing: Level One Enforcers removing what they saw as a loose cannon.

But none of this is intended to imply that you can only expect negative events, and certainly not of the fatal variety - but in most cases Saturn is putting one to a test which one is not likely to pass with flying colours. Two notable exceptions are Marie Curie when she won the Nobel Prize for Physics, and Albert Einstein when he published his Theory of Relativity. Needless to say these two individuals were exceptional in themselves, very disciplined and actually seeing scientifically beyond Level One to Level Two - although of course that is not how they expressed this.

Tests along the way for two other notables were for Martin Luther King organising difficult and dangerous demonstrations for the right of Blacks to vote in Alabama, and Che Guevara protesting against his erstwhile companion-in-arms Fidel Castro, and being under attack from Cuban exiles while speaking at the U.N. headquarters.

This influence also punctuates the beginning of a new Jupiter Cycle, indicating that your next cycle of growth has to be rooted in far firmer ground than ever before, so that there is no going back, and that you might know how well you are running down the rails of you life.

| JUPITER 'YEAR'
for your Growth Mode | *'Aries - Taurus"*
(see pages 94 and 96) |
| MOON 'PHASE'
for emotional Attunement | *'Second Deciding Phase' to 'Second Adjusting*
Phase' (see pages 171 and 173) |

Also possibly occurring during this time...

URANUS OPPOSITION (see page 239)

Very few people have this influence early enough (at thirty-seven) for it to coincide with your Second Saturn Square, but if you do, then the balancing of the radical and conservative sides of life and how you personally live it, is the main issue.

SECOND WAXING TRINE	Between 38 & 39 Years Old

"FOLLOWING YOUR PATH" - This transit is really a continuation of the last one, your 'Second Waxing Square', in that it could give you a much needed respite to make any necessary adjustments, get your bearings, and elect the best path ahead. But really it would be more accurate to say that this Trine works overtime to contend with your Mid-Life Crisis (see page 239) or the years leading up to it. Apart from this consideration, your Second Waxing Trine of Saturn should make things run more smoothly. In either case, what achieves this is either your living skills born of experience or somebody else either in authority or a position to assist you.

In any event, this is a good time to plan or make a move, possibly because you have to because a move is being made for you, or is unavoidable. Saturn is saying you're a big girl or boy now, and you
should be able to manage anything life throws at you - to bend with the wind, to follow the path as the road unwinds.

JUPITER 'YEAR'
for your Growth Mode

'Gemini - Cancer"
(see pages 98 and 100)

MOON 'PHASE'
for emotional Attunement

'Second Adjusting Phase
'(see pages 173)

Also possibly occurring during this time...

URANUS OPPOSITION (see page 239)

This singularly important influence, 'Your Mid- Life Crisis', can rock your boat considerably, so having this Saturn Trine occurring at the same time comes as a useful and welcome stabilising factor. You may even be able to elect for a safe and predictable course, but it is up to you whether such a thing makes your life worth living.

SECOND OPPOSITION	Between 43 & 44 Years Old

"THE OLD VERSUS THE NEW" - During or following upon the super-significant Uranus Opposition (see page 239), Saturn steps in to see if you have revolutionised yourself and your life - or not. It is saying that some kind of realisation should be taking, or have taken, place that effectively ushers in the new while discarding the old. One could even call this juncture in life 'The Last Chance Saloon', it being probably the last real opportunity you get to turn your life around - or rather your Uranus Opposition is or was that; Saturn is sort of rounding up any stragglers. But then again, it's never too late if your heart's in the right place and you're willing to learn.

However, this transit could also have been called 'Level One Versus Level Two' (see Saturn introduction) because from an astrological or spiritual point of view, the time has come to recognise the reality and significance of your inner rules, strengths and values - the New - and leave behind any unnecessary dependence upon the rules and values of the System, Level One or any other external factor- the Old.

Because of this important aspect of the Second Saturn Opposition, it is difficult to find examples of this 'Level One to Level Two' version of 'The Old Versus The New'. A shift of emphasis from outer to inner values is not, by its very nature, that noticeable from the outside - at least, not while that shift is going on, for the rewards (or deserts) tend to come after this transit is over. Instead I can only find glaring instances of this Opposition in figures who were ushering in the new and doing away with the old in a political, world-stage manner, rather than attending to their inner, Level Two, affairs. First we have Adolf Hitler who became German Chancellor at forty-three in 1933, putting him in a position to bring in his 'new order' of the Third Reich, and literally do away with the old thereby displaying an absolute lack of Level Two, inner integrity. As things turned out, the new order was a new Europe (and World) following the disaster and holocaust of World War Two, and it was the

Third Reich that went the way of the dinosaurs. And then there was John Kennedy, the face and voice of a new, young and discrimination-free United States, who was elected president in 1960 at the age of forty-three. Unfortunately, his Level Two condition of moral rectitude was greatly wanting, and it is open to question as to how much that contributed to his assassination three years later (see also page 245 about Kennedy).

A third example of this kind of Second Saturn Opposition, but with an important difference, is Nelson Mandela. In 1962, at forty-three years of age, he was arrested for allegedly conspiring to overthrow the government of South Africa - the 'old'. However, he then had over twenty-seven years in gaol to ponder and look within and discover the 'new' in himself - Level Two. As a consequence of this, the outer world manifested support and opportunity and ultimately he did usher in the new South Africa as its first black president. (see also pages 166,177,180,194,196 and 245 for Nelson).

All the above examples serve to show the vital importance of understanding what 'The Old Versus The New' really means. In more everyday terms, on the outside events can occur that make the 'old' apparent, such as life seeming stale and meaningless, or being tired and lonely, or being stuck in old habits. Work and relationships very much reflect and play out these dilemmas. Your body too can start to show signs of wear and tear now, and exercise and diet could well be important issues. Things seem to want to die, either literally or figuratively - emphasised by the 'Scorpio' Jupiter Year at forty-three.

One asks 'What have I got going for me?' - possibly in desperation. But at The 'Last Chance Saloon' it is definitely a case of 'they that drink of the old wine have no place for the new'. What you really have to identify is the way in which you evaluate your life and experience. Is it cynical, escapist and resistant to inner, and subsequently outer, change? And is this characterised by watching too much TV, not meeting anyone new or different, or overworking to avoid emotional situations, or drinking and smoking too much? If you are a man are you becoming boring? if you are a woman are you becoming neurotic about your looks? Such things or something like them are warning signs from Saturn. You have become a casualty of Level One living, of evaluating and therefore living your life by standards set for you by something external to you, and that is not really interested in how you feel - just so long as you 'fit in'. You are a creative being that can discover its own values and live by them - just so long as they are rooted in something good, true and beautiful.

For myself, at this time I became involved in a relationship that was spelling out the death of a certain way of relating and emotionally responding. I did not know this at first, of course, because I was still on the same old tack of seeking sexual highs and not being aware of how I really felt. It took an actual physical disaster and being unceremoniously rejected to get me painfully to see the light. My father also died at this time. A manifestation of my seeing the light was getting my first book published, and then meeting someone who really 'knew' me. 'The Last Chance Saloon' is quite a dive, but you could say that it gives value for money if you get the message that you are creating your own reality, on Level Two - that's what's 'new' - and that it is psychological suicide to be dictated too much by those 'old' external standards of Level One - what's done and gone.

JUPITER 'YEAR'
for your Growth Mode

'Scorpio - Sagittarius'
(see pages 108 and 110)

MOON 'PHASE'
for emotional Attunement

'Second Realising Phase' to 'Second Sharing
Phase' *(see pages 175 and 178)*

URANUS OPPOSITION (see page 239)

This singularly important influence, 'Your Mid-Life Crisis', is all too suitable an accompaniment to your Second Saturn Opposition because both of them are about a plateau, a realisation and revolution - or they'd better be. Mandela and Kennedy, in two different ways, bears witness to this astro-fact.

SECOND WANING TRINE	Between 48 & 49 Years Old

"FINDING YOUR TRUTH" - These are years when you can expect some kind of 'profit' from any efforts you made during the preceding years that included your Second Saturn Opposition. Failing any attempt at all to have revitalised or developed your inner being, this transit is not going to confer much upon you other than a sense of ease materially that is spoiled by frustration and boredom on an emotional or psychological level.

But assuming that you have turned inward and begun to recognise that the world really is what you make it by the way you're looking at it, and thereby how you respond to it, then this influence can give you a sense of your age, experience and maturity that amounts to a genuine confidence and an incipient wisdom. And the more you recognise and feed this truth, the more you find that it is your truth. You then slowly wake up to how powerful is that inner truth which is your inner being. All being well - which you also realise is something that is entirely up to you - your life becomes more and more a quest for increased wisdom, something which is simply a knowledge of how life and human nature actually interacts. As a result of this you become more and more the true teacher and/or benefactor of others. The 'Aries Jupiter Year' that occurs at forty-eight also marks a new beginning, but how new it is depends upon how much you previously put an end to any stale or rigid ideas and ways.

JUPITER 'YEAR'
for your Growth Mode

'Aries - Taurus'
(see pages 94 and 96)

MOON 'PHASE'
for emotional Attunement

'Second Understanding Phase'
(see page 181)

SECOND WANING SQUARE	Between 51 & 52 Years Old

"SPIRITUAL MATURITY" - The Saturnian imperative to consider seriously that you have to adopt a new outlook on life in order eventually to grow old gracefully, that begun with the Second Saturn Opposition at forty-three to forty-four years of age, now has further weight lent to it. You should continue to identify and discard any old and entrenched attitudes in order to reach a wisdom that befits your age. The one old idea that you should cling to is that which says that if human beings were not supposed to grow wiser as they got older, then in terms of our species' survival, what would be the point of having old human beings?

Yet the irony here is that at this age it is very likely that you have to bear with ageing parents who are well-entrenched in old and inappropriate patterns of behaviour, and are far from wise. It could also be younger people that you have to bear with - and possibly your own children. It would seem that at this time you are challenged to contend with all manner of annoying or demanding circumstances that test your own centredness and self-control. But failing to bear with others and maintain your own integrity is a likelihood at this time, simply because this is the very way in which you are being tested. This means that the test is also about being able to bear with yourself.

Losing your rag and feeling guilty are signs that you need to reconcile yourself with those around you, especially the ones who are close to you. To have a parent die when you are on bad terms can leave a stain that is hard to remove and pollutes your life to come. If you have long since removed yourself from such family members or friends, then Saturn could åbring a heavy feeling of emptiness or hollowness down upon you. Whatever the case here, that imperative still holds sway: to come to an understanding of how you may have inadvertently cultivated a negative or faulty attitude, and to find a way of releasing any bitterness, anger, resentment or regret. Pleading that you are too old to change now does not wash, simply because the negative feelings are shuffled to the bottom of the deck, to be dealt later when you are even less well-equipped.

A positive starting point is to discover for yourself a nobler way of living and a more wonderful reason for being, and try at all costs to live up to them. On an esoteric note, the star-cluster called the Pleiades takes fifty-two years to return to the same spot in the sky. According to that enigmatic and highly advanced civilisation, the Mayans, it is the Pleiades that are the source of Love and Wisdom in our galaxy, the Milky Way. And so this, your Pleiadian Return, is a time when you can tune into this source, and elevate your manner of living and loving. In one way or another, the challenge to do so will certainly be there - in the form of someone or something demanding selfless care and devotion as the best means to manage your life.

JUPITER 'YEAR'
for your Growth Mode

'Cancer - Leo'
(see pages 100 and 102)

MOON 'PHASE'
for emotional Attunement

'Second Understanding Phase' to 'Second
Releasing Phase' (see pages 181 & 183)

SECOND SATURN RETURN	Between 58 & 59 Years Old

"YOUR SECOND LIFE PROGRESS REPORT" - This is a time when you may quite rightly ask yourself what your life has amounted to. A good clue or starting point to answering this question is to cast your mind back to your First Saturn Return at twenty-nine to thirty years of age (see page 213). This is because whatever happened or began then was the seed of where you have got to now. In strictly Saturnian terms, this is the time when you should be able to see what has developed with regard to what you started then. There is no rule of thumb here, because whatever has happened over those intervening years should have an entirely personal message for you.

A celebrated example that was cited for the First Saturn Return was Boris Yeltsin who joined the Russian Communist Party at that time and then resigned from it at this time. One can only guess at what these corresponding events meant to him. Perhaps he felt a sense of disillusionment mingled with a sense of having taken something as far as it could go. But I am sure there were far more intricate feelings involved for him.

Another interesting case was Indira Gandhi who during her First Saturn Return at twenty-nine enjoyed her father becoming the first prime minister of India, while she acted as his political hostess. Come her Second Saturn Return though, she was defeated in general election after having been prime minister herself for eleven years, during which she was convicted for corrupt electoral practices. She was re-elected three years later only to be assassinated four years after that. Here Saturn's judgement seems quite straightforward in one respect, but quite complex in another.

Yasir Arafat had his First Saturn Return shortly after co-founding the Al Fatah terrorist movement. Come his Second Saturn Return he formally renounced terrorism and recognised the state of Israel.

And a poignant mix of experiences befell Mikhail Gorbachev during his

Second Saturn Return when at fifty-nine he won the Nobel peace prize and then resigned as leader Soviet Union four days after its abolition.

The above are what could be called monumental occurrences for 'Second Life Progress Reports', but for so-called ordinary people, events at this time are relatively just as significant. Seeing what your life has added up to is, as I have said, a key feature of this time. From a philosophical point of view - which is really the essential point of view to adopt now - appraising one's life and personality in terms of having stood for something worthwhile is what is recommended. Failure should possibly be seen as having kow-towed too much to the values and figures of the System or Level One (see introduction to the Saturn section), whereas success may best be framed in terms of having been true to yourself and your own individual sense of choice (Level Two), and of having managed to remain relatively free from crystallised attitudes born of convention. Not least of all, having been of help, support and guidance to others should figure highest of all in one's self-assessment.

For many, retirement, or the prospect of it, can be a major issue now. Whether such is seen as a new beginning or a meaningless ending has everything to do with the above-described criteria. Being one's own person would grace you with the former, but having sold one's soul to the System for the sake of a limited form of security would be only too likely to inherit the latter.

On the following page you will see a FLOWCHART of your Second Saturn Return, 'Your Second Life Progress Report', which gives you a graphic idea of what Saturn is bringing into your life, and what the various ways of responding to it can bring you.

JUPITER 'YEAR'   *'Aquarius - Pisces"*
for your Growth Mode   *(see pages 114 and 116)*

MOON 'PHASE'   *'Third Emerging Phase' to 'Third Striving Phase'*
for emotional Attunement   *(see pages 186 & 189)*

A MAJOR INFLUENCE occurs through AGE 58 TO AGE 59

YOUR SECOND SATURN RETURN
"Your Second Life Progress Report"

Flowchart below shows how the Positive and Negative Saturn Traits (left), that you may or may not have, encounter Saturn's influence (arrow on the right), which in turn consolidates the Positive Traits into a Positive Outcome (top) and/or relegates the Negative traits to a Negative Outcome (bottom). Negative Outcomes can be made Positive through developing the Positive traits

POSITIVE OUTCOME

Order and control over life situations.
Clear perspective. Practical realisations.
Material development. Promotion.
Stable home and family.
Financial stability.
New beginnings.

POSITIVE TRAITS

Industriousness.
Past efforts to achieve.
Discipline and readiness to try.
Maturity and reliability.
Acumen. Moderation.
Caution. Responsibleness

Make or break
issues and events.
material factors.
The elderly. Ageing.
Extra responsibilities.

SATURN

Laziness and apathy. Impatience.
Lack of discipline and effort.
Irresponsible and bad behaviour.
Lack of enterprise or commitment.
Feebleness. Indecisiveness.
Fanciful, unrealistic ideas.

Authority figures.
Lessons & Teachers.
The Hand of Fate.
Relationship tests.
Entropy

NEGATIVE TRAITS

Money problems.
Reduced circumstances.
Confinement. Downfall.
Lack of direction/purpose.
Relationship break-downs.
Major rethink. No progress.
Stagnation. Depression. Lethargy.

NEGATIVE OUTCOME

THIRD WAXING SQUARE	Between 65 & 66 Years Old

"RE-FORGING OR SHUNTED TO THE SIDINGS" - Except if you are self-employed or have some ongoing work commitment, by now or at this time, most people have retired or retire from regular work - or at least, your partner has. In any event, in terms of what this influence poses, it is time to take stock of what you do with your time and whether or not you can continue to perform it efficiently or rewardingly enough. One public example of this was Margaret Thatcher, the 'Iron Lady' who seemed pretty immovable, was beaten in the leadership contest for her political party.

There could arise some challenge to take stock of yourself on a more personal level. A dramatic example of this was Marlon Brando whose son Christian was convicted for manslaughter of his sister Cheyenne's boyfriend, leading to her suicide soon after.

These examples are not meant to lead you to expect disaster, but serve to show how a person's 'record' can be visited upon them. Whatever may happen on these fronts, your choice is that of welcoming any change or arrival of something or someone different and breathing new life into your veins, or, of giving in to a quiet but possibly meaningless existence.

JUPITER 'YEAR'
for your Growth Mode

'Virgo - Libra'
(see pages 104 and 106)

MOON 'PHASE'
for emotional Attunement

'Third Adjusting Phase' (see page 192)

THIRD WAXING TRINE	Between 68 & 69 Years Old

"TRUSTING YOUR FATE" - Although this is a Trine and therefore an easy Saturn period, because it is nudging the proverbial 'three-score years and ten' that a human being has been traditionally allotted, it can give rise to anxiety and doubt. Of course, this is not necessarily so, but of this you can be sure: it is your fate to die - but the question of what follows that is the tricky one. If you truly believe that there is no hereafter, that when you die you are no more, and that's it, then any anxiety would obviously be totally unfounded - some regrets maybe, but no anxiety. If there is doubt however (or doubt posing as anxiety), this implies that you are no longer so sure of there being nothing when you die - which lead us on to looking at what 'hereafter' means. To approach it scientifically, according to Newton's Second Law of Physics, the Law of the Conservation of Energy, energy is never born or dies - it only changes the form it is takes. In Quantum Theory, everything is energy, including you and your body. When you die, the energy that was you is going to become something, or part of something, or someone else. But this still leaves us with the prospect of the Great Unknown - which is the real cause for anxiety.

As far as Saturn is concerned, a 'score' has been kept, and when you die there is a reckoning - just as there has been in life, but this time that score will be determined by Level Two and not just Level One criteria (see Saturn introduction). And so I venture to suggest that any anxiety is similar to what most people feel after sitting an examination and they are waiting for their results. But the highly significant point is that you are not dead yet - you are still alive in the examination room! And so your Third and final Saturn Waxing Trine offers you the opportunity to still 'put in a good paper' or at least admit to making a bit of a mess of it and promise yourself you'll do better next time, for this makes alL the difference to the form your energy will take on after you die.

**JUPITER** 'YEAR'
for your Growth Mode

'Sagittarius - Capricorn"
(see pages 110 and 112)

MOON 'PHASE'
for emotional Attunement

'Third Adjusting Phase' to 'Third Realising
Phase' (see pages 192 & 194)

THIRD OPPOSITION	Between 73 & 74 Years Old

"THE OLD VERSUS THE NEW - TWO" - One can have relationship difficulties at any age, and this is one of them. This time however, they could quite likely be because you have lost a partner, or that you have no-one to relate to and be with, or that there are people around you that you would rather not have to relate to. In any event, Saturn is confronting you with your social and emotional state. If all is well in that you are still in the midst of positive relationship, then this Opposition will confer a feeling of satisfaction upon you, possibly enabling you to help those less fortunate or wise than you, be they younger, older or the same age. If though you feel emotionally or socially ill at ease, then either you must search inside of yourself for the reason, and reconcile yourself to it - or you can carry on bemoaning your fate, probably worsening what relationships you do have in the process.

Relationship and relating are the stuff of life. Having the curiosity and humility to interact equally with others, whoever they are, will keep you interested in life, and, more's the point, keep life interested in you.

JUPITER 'YEAR'
for your Growth Mode

'Taurus - Gemini'
(see pages 96 and 98)

MOON 'PHASE'
for emotional Attunement

'Third Sharing Phase' (see page 195)

235

THIRD WANING TRINE	Between 78 & 79 Years Old

"KNOWING YOUR HEART" - The greatest positive power a human being can possess is the power to help other living creatures, be this to one or many, in a small or big way. In the introduction to this Saturn section I put forward the idea that life was like a big school and periodically we have to sit examinations. Under your Third Waxing Square at 65/66 and your Third Opposition at 73/74, described on pages 233 & 235, we saw how one is confronted with a sense of how well one has or has not done in these examinations, and that as long as one was alive there was always a chance to 'improve one's marks', so to speak. This, the time of your Third and probably last Waxing Trine, is one of those chances. And the chance comes in the form of someone or something you can help, possibly because they remind you of yourself at some time in your past when you could have done with some help. Some people meet such an opportunity merely with scorn and bitterness, simply because it does remind them of how no-one helped them when they needed it. This attitude, needless to say, does not earn any marks - quite the contrary in fact. On the other hand, recognising life's poetry in motion, and responding to it with a generous heart that expects no reward other than the pleasure of giving, means you can rest assured.

JUPITER 'YEAR'
for your Growth Mode

'Libra-Scorpio'
(see pages 106 and 108)

MOON 'PHASE'
for emotional Attunement

'Third Understanding Phase' to 'Third Releasing Phase' (see pages 196 and 197)

THIRD WANING SQUARE	Between 80 & 81 Years Old

"FINAL ACCEPTANCE" - All of what has gone before has been done, and nothing can alter that. However, the way you now think and feel about it can. And how you feel and think about it should be focussed solely upon an acceptance of it all - that it was all for the best. Reading through the various influences of the whole of your Saturn Cycle, but especially the more recent ones, and accepting what is written there, may help you in doing this. Doing the same with your Moon Cycle is also a good idea, for this will help you recall and clear away unwanted memories, and polish up the good ones.

JUPITER 'YEAR'
for your Growth Mode

'Sagittarius - Capricorn'
(see pages 110 and 112)

MOON 'PHASE'
for emotional Attunement

'Third Releasing Phase' (see pages 197)

The Uranus Opposition
Your Mid-Life Crisis

First of all, a little bit about the astrological significance of Uranus itself.

+	Awakening	Exciting	Liberating	Reforming
-	Disrupting	Shocking	Destabilising	Ruining

There is in all of us, to varying degrees, an urge to be free - from something or to do something. But as we have seen with the Moon and Saturn in the last two sections, there is also a need for emotional and material security. This compromises that urge to be free because on the face of it security is, of necessity, bound by familiarity, convention and a resistance to change. But all this begs the question as to what freedom is all about anyway. Essentially, freedom is having the space and time to be or find out who you truly are, to explore the unknown, and the urge to do so. And so who you truly are is the very thing that gets constrained by those needs for security, by staying with the 'devil you know'. Consequently, the 'urge to be free to find out who you truly are' often has to find an original, surprising or alternative way of making itself felt in your life. Something has to change or shock us in order to free us - and because we all have that innate desire to be free, we therefore attract change and the unexpected into our lives.

Now, in astrology, when one Planet or point in the sky is OPPOSITE to another Planet or point (see page 205 for a graphic depiction of this), this is seen as making one AWARE of what that Planet or point means in one's life. This can be seen to be the case with respect to any two opposing factors - not least of all Man and Woman. In other words, it usually takes a member of the opposite sex to make us aware of our own sexuality.

And so when Uranus reaches a point in the sky that is in Opposition to where it was when you were born - bingo! - you become suddenly aware of what Uranus means in your life with respect to freedom and change and finding out who you really are. This is...

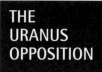

THE URANUS OPPOSITION	Between 37 & 45 Years Old FOR 1-3 YEARS*

"THE MID-LIFE CRISIS" -The message in this 'Memo for Heaven' is so monumental that it is difficult to avoid putting it across in the same way that it can get sent you - by blowing your fuses. By 'fuses' I mean those basic limits we place upon the impressions we receive from the world around us, and upon what we express to that world in terms of our behaviour and personal style. These fuses are first put in place very early on - in the womb, at birth, or sometimes not until early childhood - and so more often than not people do not even know they are there. However, these fuses themselves are more to do the Moon, and not Uranus, because it is the Moon that protects us from shocks, the unfamiliar, chaos, and anything which is too sudden a change - which are the province of Uranus. Other fuses are installed later as we grow up, but they could be regarded as practicality, socialisation or acculturation

*See Mid-Life Crisis Ready Reckoner on pages 252-254 to find out exactly when it occurs for you.

and are governed by Saturn. Using 'fuses' as a metaphor is very appropriate here for Uranus really is electricity, chi, the life-force.

The trouble is that those 'fuses' are not just fuses - they are blockages. Think of your body as an 'appliance' that is vitalised by the life force which is electricity. Up until now you have got along, one way or the other, with your appliance being set up a certain way, with certain specifications. These specifications tell you what you like and dislike, what you feel allowed to do and not allowed to do. These specifications got installed, as I said, early on, and were determined by the values, circumstances, customs and predilections of your parents, culture and the status quo. But actually, these were in themselves determined by what is called your fate - which has something to do with your soul and unconscious mind. Then along comes your Uranus Opposition which is like a power surge that courses through your body, and thereby your life. And if you are not ready for it, that surge quite simply blows one or more of those fuses.

Being 'not ready' means that certain parts of your life have become too attached to those specifications to which you have conformed in order to ensure a secure and stable life - whatever that might be in terms of those specifications. Effectively, you are now being 'upgraded'!

So any elements of your life - job, partnership, lifestyle, location, attitude, values, beliefs, etc. - that are in some way not conducive to your expressing your true identity (as distinct from the version that your fate initially determined for you), now begin to play up, get in your way, and generally seem to limit your freedom. The knee-jerk reaction would be to leave your job, spouse, home or whatever , and possibly become madly involved with something or someone highly unlikely. But this would be owing to an urgent feeling that you had fallen into a rut of predictability, and hadn't really done what you once dreamt you'd do. Be on your guard against this desperate manner of relieving a feeling that life has passed you by, or that you want to relive your adolescence in a fortyish-year old body.

What this highly significant period of your life is actually asking you is "What is unique about you, and how are you going to express that uniqueness?" - and this doesn't mean throwing the baby out with the bathwater by rejecting or ejecting anything or anyone that appears to represent what is stale and unstimulating and blocking your freedom. This would be like throwing away the mirror because you didn't like what you were seeing in it. For one thing, maybe existing elements in your life could do with a shot in the arm themselves. If they don't, and are quite happy with the way things are, then you need to start making some radical changes, which they can accept or reject. But as freedom is presently the name of the game, make sure that everyone has a chance to express themselves freely too. Bringing things out in the open is a very constructive way of dealing with this influence. Study very carefully any other planetary influences that are also occurring now, for they indicate in what ways and areas of your life changes may or must be made - and where you could be fooling yourself too. Overall, this is a great time to introduce something fresh and far-reaching into your life - particularly anything that furthers an ideal. So having a goal or aspiration is your truest guiding star right now. An example - current at the time of writing - of a celebrity doing nearly all these things during his Uranus Opposition - that is, saying and doing something despite his better judgment, and bringing something into the open, and making a fool of himself, all at the same time - is ex-England Football Manager, Glenn Hoddle. His proclamation that disabled people are paying for sins committed in past lives didn't go down at all well. But he did start a ball of debate rolling, and I daresay it will create waves for some time in quite subtle ways - even though he scored an own-goal at first. (See also page 203 regarding Glenn and Saturn).

But then again - back to that 'electricity', that 'power surge'. What I have said in the above two paragraphs is all very well as long as you are able to keep things mentally under control. This is a bit like fuses being blown when someone knows how to replace them - but not everyone does. In other words, being able to respond spontaneously in an appropriate fashion to a need for change, as and when it hits you, is quite rare and not so easy. So this is where astrology comes into its own at, or preferably before, this time (Uranus rules astrology, by the way). By knowing in advance that this is coming up for you or someone you know, changes can be made that facilitate or 'ride' that wave of increased power, that wind of change, when it arrives. So if you are stuck in a boring and unfulfilling job, start looking around or preparing yourself for something more 'you' - and this may mean going it alone. If you are living in a situation where you do not feel at home or able to lead you life in the way that want to, then plan that move. If you are in a relationship that is deadlocked and unhappy, then make some sort of temporary or permanent break from the relationship or make a radical change within it.

The trick is to be alive to what is wanting to shift, and use Uranian 'chance means' to do so. For example, prior to the onset of my own Uranus Opposition, it became more and more obvious that where I was living and what I was doing was not taking me in the direction I wanted to go. Furthermore, the relationship I was in at the time reflected all of this. The trouble was that I did not know where to go.

So I drew up a list of options and experimented with each one, eliminating them until there was only one left, having already agreed to myself that I would follow that last remaining option by the onset of my Uranus Opposition. On the face of it, this last option was the least attractive to my ego, but as things panned out it was the right one - and in an unexpected way. This is an important point, for Uranus is 'anti-ego' in that it is the force that really drives us as distinct from what we think is doing the driving. Again, think about the electricity(the force) and the appliance(the ego). A toaster, say, is totally dependent upon the electricity for its functioning, whereas the electricity exists in its own right. Or to put it another way, think of the electricity of transmitted television waves. They determine what pictures the TV can display, not the other way around.

So what other kinds of change can you expect during this time - or if you are in the middle of it, what signs of change should you be alive to, and subsequently of acting upon.

On a physical level there is the possibility of the need for change manifesting as panic attacks, apparently unfounded feelings of insecurity, hot flushes, the shakes, or any other kind of spasm or sensory distortion. Or then again, such anxieties can be projected on to the collective with over-concern for what is happening in the world at large as seen in the media. These are all signs that one or more of those fuses are blowing or are about to blow. Nervous complaints and conditions such as M.E. are also possible if the system is being overloaded. Each individual case will tell its own story, so I cannot go into them here, but generally speaking, any one of these indications are pointing to a urgent need to change the way you live or look at life. Using again the television analogy above, it is as if a new channel is being beamed at the 'receiver' of your personality (which includes your physical body) but you are refusing to upgrade that receiver so that it can channel or express it. This all poses the necessity of 'taking the back off' through having some form of therapy or consultation to discover and replace that 'dud component', that outmoded part of your personality and life-style.

Another, and important, arena of Uranian focus is that of 'rights', which is the concern of social change, personally or collectively. At this time, if there is any situation that is severely abusing the rights of yourself or someone close to you, then you will be called to resolve it in some way.

This could be on a strictly personal level, such as being in a unacceptably confining relationship, or, more to do with some abuse of power by an external authority. The Uranus Opposition can be quite a time of reckoning in this respect. There is a 'Famous Five' here that dramatically demonstrates this point. At the time of their Uranus Oppositions the following five champions of human rights were subject to crucial experiences (four of them fatal) as part and parcel of their respective crusades.

One who could be called an 'icon of freedom', Che Guevara, was assassinated by Bolivian troops at the age of thirty-nine. This was not such a surprising fate for the radical and high-profile activist for ending poverty in Latin America that Guevara was. See also page 219 about Che.

Similarly, Martin Luther King, champion of racial equality and harmony, was also a target of the hatred that opposes such truth and virtue. Although unlike Guevara in that he espoused non-violence, he met a violent end, also at the age of thirty-nine. King was possibly more of a classic hero of freedom that Guevara; a few years before his assassination, while preaching in church when gunfire was heard outside, he declared "It may get me crucified. I may even die. But I want it said even if I die in the struggle, that 'He died to make me free'." For more about Martin see pages 166 & 222.

Robert Kennedy, an outspoken champion of truth and justice, was also assassinated. He was forty-two years of age.

John Lennon was assassinated at the age of forty, during his Uranus Opposition. Ironically, he was killed by the kind of working-class nonentity that he consciously strove to encourage. Other aspects of John's life are covered on pages 167, 218 & 249)

The fifth of these 'Famous Five' is the happy exception to this rule of assassination, Nelson Mandela. He was arrested for allegedly conspiring to overthrow the then racist and oppressive South African government when he was forty-four years of age. But he lived to become his country's first black president thirty-one years later (see also pages 166,177,180,194,196 & 225 concerning Mandela).

Continuing with theme of freedom and rights, John F. Kennedy who was also assassinated, was experiencing his Uranus Opposition when he was elected president, very much on that kind of Uranian 'freedom and rights' ticket. See page 225 also about JFK.

These examples seem to indicate that the Uranus Opposition is a key point in one's 'freedom stakes'. Obviously, they are exceptional in that these men all lived and died (except Mandela) to show us how important a thing freedom is, even so - or is it all the more because? - they took quite a few liberties themselves!

One more example of a 'freedom-fighter' experiencing the ultimate during his Uranus Opposition was Billy Giles, ex-member of the Ulster Volunteer Force, a Protestant group in Northern Ireland. His story is remarkable in that following upon his assassinating a Catholic friend in 1982 as an act of retaliation for an IRA murder of a Catholic girl, he, in his own words 'lost a part of myself that I'll never get back. ...Before I would have been classed as a decent young man. Then suddenly I turned into a killer. That's Northern Ireland'. Sixteen years later, a year after being released from prison, and during his Uranus Opposition, this inner truth of his being drove him to execute himself. Hopefully, this act of a man who was honest enough to admit that - apart from what he had done to his friend and his loved ones - he had abused and damaged his own humanity, will stand as a poignant example to others involved in the Peace Process.

Returning to more personal issues and the Uranus effect, any kind of situation or relationship that sets the proverbial cat amongst the pigeons is a 'favourite'. If something in your life needs stirring up, then Uranus will see to it that someone or something arrives on the scene to do the stirring - intentionally or not. When those fuses are blockages they will attract something to free it up. Such blockages can often be the result of social or religious indoctrination. Enormous conflicts can arise from feelings of 'forsaking a parent' or 'denying God' when a person is unavoidably drawn into something that challenges such allegiances. This is especially so when it is a case of one 'truth' opposing another.

But the simple formula for truth as far as Uranus is concerned is that it "should make you free" rather than make you feel guilty or judgmental. As Thomas Paine, author of 'The Rights of Man' wrote "... and my religion is to do good". Mind you, one had better be sure that what's seen as good is good. There is nothing worse than the 'Rights Blight' where people foist their idea of truth upon others when all they are really doing is trying to camouflage their own inadequacies. This too is something one may have to contend with, or be found guilty of, during the Uranus Opposition.

Going back to 'electricity' and the life force' again, Uranus is the sexual impulse itself , and as such it is the most basic function of any living creature's 'wiring' to 'interface' with the wiring of another creature - usually, but not always, of the same background, creed, race or even species (remember that Uranian impulse to shock, experiment and step beyond the norm). This can be appreciated in the fact that electricity always seeks to go to earth - that is, we need another's body to absorb our 'charge' - or to 'charge' us up. In the same sense, it is Uranus that sparks anything into action - like the 'electricity' you feel when encountering someone or something that is 'electrifying'; like the semi-conscious impulse to do or say something against one's 'better judgement'.

And so your Uranus Opposition will focus upon this in some way or other. Sexual energy is like electricity, and an electrical current will always seek to go to earth. And so it is as if, at a very primal level, we simply want to make sexual contact to 'earth' ourselves through the body of another. This sounds very unemotional and lacking in romance, but that is because Uranus is only concerned with the fundamental forces that drive us, not how we dress them up afterwards. None of this precludes sentiment and finer feelings, but unless one understands that this takes second place under the influence of Uranus, you are in for a shock - or rather another one.

During my own Uranus Opposition I personally became involved with a white witch who initially was purely interested in me for my male sexual energy, which she 'earthed' very well - in fact, her 'craft name' meant 'Earth'. But later we fell out because the emotional side was lacking. However, the point is that there was the mutual desire to earth or charge up one another in this way, and romance had to take a back seat . How or if your Uranus Opposition gets to you on a sexual level is, as ever with Uranus, down to your own unique personality and circumstances. But the point that I am trying to make here is that you will be primarily dealing with the energy that brings people closer together, often in spite of, or rather because of, their reservations. This Uranian energy is no respecter of your social standing, romantic illusions, sexual conventions or marital status. If there is a message 'bubbling under' that intends to blow your cobwebs away through some wild and off-the-wall affair that unsettles your settled life, then that is what it will happen! Uranus is very much the 'anything can happen' planet.

On a more psychological or esoteric level, the sexual call is to become (more)aware of what is called your 'anima' if you are a male, or your 'animus' if you are a female. The anima is the feminine being inside of a man, and the animus the male being inside of a woman. The experience of these 'opposites within' can be particularly acute between two people at this time, or occasionally through experimenting with cross-dressing or the same or group sex. But at a more intellectual or spiritual level, a man getting in touch with his anima (which means 'soul', that which earths the charge) is him becoming familiar and at one with his vulnerability, receptivity and passivity. Conversely, a woman getting in touch with her animus (meaning 'spirit', that which charges the earth) is her getting a handle on the more dynamic, objective and creative side of her being. However, the usual way this is played out is through what is called 'anima or animus projection'. You can think you've fallen madly in love with someone when really you have been 'plugged in' to your anima or animus through being respectively earthed or charged up by someone whose sexual energy resonates rather well with yours. If you are aware of this and take on board the fact that you are getting to know your other half through the sexual electricity between you and someone else then you will become a more mature and whole person as a result. Furthermore, you can then build a lasting a relationship upon such a foundation of self-completion - but not necessarily with that same person. On the other hand, if you insist on thinking you are 'in love' rather than becoming more sexually and psychologically aware, then don't be surprised if you become suddenly 'unplugged' as your opposite number gets a nasty attack of mismatched voltages or mistaken identity through feeling either suffocated, over-stimulated or emotionally neglected. Never forget that Uranus is there to wake you up, not make you feel cosy and romantic. If, as I have stressed in the introduction, your paths are destined to intertwine, then well and good - but it is Uranus that sets you off on that path.

To close on this crucially important influence, when all is said and done, the so-called 'Mid-Life Crisis' is a crisis because we are, as Lennon himself so cutely put it, "busy making other plans". So whatever happens comes as a shock - big or small. And as I have warned previously, the bigger the resistance to Uranus's charge, then the bigger that explosive charge shall be. A tragic example of this was Paula Yates whose 'other plans' were shown, during her Uranus Opposition, to be sheer fantasies when her lover Michael Hutchence hung himself. And maybe John Lennon also needed to experience a shock, but it was so great it killed him. And, like Martin Luther King, his Uranian intuition foresaw it, and in a remarkably similar fashion - proclaiming in one of his own songs that sooner or later they would 'crucify' him.

Naturally, do not expect such drastic and tragic events now - but expect the unexpected. Uranus rules, okay?!

On the following page you will see a FLOWCHART of your Uranus Opposition, 'Your Mid-Life Crisis', which gives you a graphic idea of what Uranus is bringing into your life, and what the various ways of responding to it can bring you.

JUPITER 'YEAR' *for your Growth Mode*	Having ascertained the actual years of your Uranus Opposition from the Ready Reckoner on pages 252-254, then refer to the Age Index on page 293 for the Jupiter 'Years' and Moon 'Phases' and any Saturn transits occurring during that period. If applicable, also see below.
MOON 'PHASE' *for emotional Attunement*	

SECOND REALISING MOON PHASE (see page 175)

As this influence accentuates certain issues that you have been previously

A MAJOR INFLUENCE occurs Between*AGE 37 TO AGE 45

THE URANUS OPPOSITION
"Your Mid-Life Crisis"

Flowchart below shows how the Positive and Negative Uranus Traits (left), that you may or may not have, encounter Uranus's influence (arrow on the right), which in turn transforms the Positive Traits into a Positive Outcome (top) and relegates the Negative traits to a Negative Outcome (bottom). Negative Outcomes can be made Positive through developing the Positive traits

POSITIVE OUTCOME

Progressing to a better lifestyle.
Release from tension or confusion.
Smooth transitions. Calm under pressure.
Stimulating and rewarding sex-life.
Clarity of mind. Improved intuition.
Becoming a leading light to others

POSITIVE TRAITS

Awareness of blocks and the desire to remove them.
Willingness to take a calculated risk and change.
Being prepared for change before the need for it arrives
Being more open and psychologically aware regarding sexuality.
Honest desire to get to the truth of the matter.
Openness and a resolve to aspire to higher value

Power surge from your
unconscious mind.
New values & directives.
Destabilising over-rigidity.
Encouraging uniqueness

URANUS

Ignorance of your inhibitions and the power they exert.
Inflexible attitude. Refusal to make necessary changes.
Narrow or uniformed sexual attitude and lifestyle.
Sticking to your version of reality, no matter what.
Being closed to the idea of elevating your standards.

Sudden chances and change
The Wheel of Fortune.
The Moment of Truth.
Unusual encounters.
Desire for freedom.

Being subjected to shocking events.
Feeling unbearably tense and struck
Creating more chaos than you were in.
Sexual frustration or confusion.
Disharmony in relationships or your body.
More entrenched in the Rat Race

NEGATIVE TRAITS

NEGATIVE OUTCOME

*See Tables on pages 252-254
for when it is for you.

unaware of, the wake-up call of the Uranus Opposition can be particularly acute. How you experience all this has great deal to do with whether you value an 'enhancement of your reality' or find it threatening and disturbing. Nelson Mandela, alluded to above, had these two powerful influences coinciding.

SECOND SATURN WAXING SQUARE (see page 220)

Be prepared to be confronted with whatever needs renovating or refreshing in your life, and then take appropriate action. Letting the grass grow under your feet at this time could find you up to your neck in undesirable commitments later on. This combination of influences is particularly critical because caution is just as necessary as the changes.

SECOND SATURN WAXING TRINE (see page 223)

Here you'd have a sobering or steadying influence that could possibly prevent you from overreacting to the Uranian wind of change. A welcome handrail.

SECOND SATURN OPPOSITION (see page 224)

Being another Opposition this stresses the 'writing on the wall' factor. Having to be practical and responsible and at the same move with times and ride the wave of Uranian excitement could prove very testing. The secret of success here would be to cut out non-essentials - once you had determined what those non-essentials are. Again, not easy, but it helps to know that these are your priorities.

Where your month and year of birth intersect you will find the ages during which you experience the Uranus Opposition..

m/y	1920	1921	1922	1923	1924	1925	1926	1927	1928	1929
JAN	41-42	41-42	41-42	41-42	41-42	40-41	40-41	40-41	39-41	39-40
FEB	41-43	41-43	41-43	41-42	41-42	41-42	40-42	40-42	40-41	40-41
MAR	42-43	42-43	41-43	41-42	41-42	41-42	40-42	40-42	40-41	40-41
APR	42-43	42-43	42-43	42-43	41-42	41-42	41-42	41-42	41-42	41-42f
MAY	42-44	42-43	42-43	42-43	42-43	41-42	41-43	41-42	41-42	41-42
JUN	42-44	42-43	42-43	42-43	42-43	41-43	41-43	41-42	41-42	41-42
JUL	42-43	42-43	42-43	42-43	42-43	41-43	41-43	41-42	41-42	41-42
AUG	42-43	42-43	41-42	41-42	41-42	41-42	41-42	41-42	41-42	41-42
SEP	41-42	41-42	41-42	41-42	41-42	41-42	41-42	41-42	41-42	41-42
OCT	41-42	41-42	41-42	41-42	41-42	41-42	41-42	41-42	40-41	40-41
NOV	41-42	41-42	41-42	41-42	41-42	41-42	41-42	40-42	40-41	40-41
DEC	41-42	41-42	40-42	40-41	40-41	40-41	40-41	39-41	39-40	39-40

m/y	1930	1931	1932	1933	1934	1935	1936	1937	1938	1939
JAN	39-40	39-40	39-40	39-40	39-40	39-40	38-39	38-39	38-39	38-39
FEB	39-41	39-40	39-40	39-40	39-40	39-40	38-39	38-39	38-39	38-39
MAR	40-41	39-41	39-40	39-40	39-40	39-40	39-40	39-40	38-39	38-39
APR	40-41	40-42	40-41	40-41	40-41	40-41	40-41	39-40	38-40	38-40
MAY	40-42	40-42	40-41	40-41	40-41	40-41	40-41	39-40	39-40	39-40
JUN	41-42	40-42	40-41	40-41	40-41	40-41	40-41	39-40	39-40	39-40
JUL	41-42	41-42	40-41	40-41	40-41	40-41	40-41	40-41	40-41	40-41
AUG	41-42	41-42	40-41	40-41	40-41	40-41	40-41	40-41	40-41	40-41
SEP	40-42	40-42	40-41	40-41	40-41	40-41	40-41	40-41	40-41	40-41
OCT	40-41	40-41	40-41	40-41	40-41	40-41	40-41	40-41	40-41	40-41
NOV	39-40	39-40	39-40	39-40	39-40	39-40	39-40	39-40	39-40	39-40
DEC	39-40	39-40	39-40	39-40	39-40	38-39	38-39	38-39	38-39	38-39

m/y	1940	1941	1942	1943	1944	1945	1946	1947	1948	1949
JAN	38-39	38-39	38-39	38-39	38-39	38-40	39-40	39-40	39-40	39-40
FEB	38-39	38-39	38-39	38-39	37-39	38-40	38-40	38-40	38-40	38-40
MAR	38-39	38-39	38-39	38-39	37-39	37-39	38-39	37-39	37-39	38-39
APR	38-39	38-39	38-39	38-39	38-40	37-39	38-40	38-40	38-40	38-40
MAY	39-40	39-40	39-40	39-40	38-40	38-40	38-40	38-40	38-40	38-40
JUN	39-40	39-40	39-40	39-40	39-40	38-40	38-40	38-40	38-40	38-40
JUL	39-40	39-40	39-40	39-40	39-40	38-40	38-40	38-40	38-40	38-40
AUG	39-41	39-41	39-41	39-41	39-41	39-41	39-41	39-41	39-41	39-41
SEP	39-41	39-41	39-41	39-41	39-41	39-41	39-41	39-41	39-41	39-41
OCT	39-41	39-41	39-41	39-41	39-41	39-41	39-41	39-41	39-41	39-41
NOV	38-39	38-39	38-39	38-39	39-41	39-40	39-41	39-41	39-41	39-41
DEC	38-39	38-39	38-39	38-39	39-40	39-40	39-40	39-40	39-40	39-40

Where your month and year of birth intersect you will find the ages during which you experience the Uranus Opposition..

m/y	1950	1951	1952	1953	1954	1955	1956	1957	1958	1959
JAN	39-40	38-40	38-40	38-40	38-40	38-40	39-41	39-41	40-41	39-41
FEB	38-40	38-40	38-40	38-40	38-40	38-40	38-40	38-40	40-41	39-41
MAR	37-39	38-39	38-39	38-39	38-39	38-39	38-39	38-39	39-40	39-40
APR	37-39	38-39	38-39	38-39	38-39	38-39	38-39	38-39	38-39	38-40
MAY	37-39	38-39	38-39	38-39	38-39	38-39	38-39	38-39	38-39	38-40
JUN	38-39	38-39	38-39	38-40	38-40	38-40	38-40	38-40	38-40	38-40
JUL	38-39	38-39	38-39	38-40	38-40	38-40	38-40	38-40	38-40	38-40
AUG	39-41	39-41	39-41	39-41	39-41	39-41	39-41	39-41	39-41	39-41
SEP	39-41	39-41	39-41	39-41	39-41	39-41	39-41	40-41	40-41	40-41
OCT	39-41	39-41	39-41	39-41	39-41	39-41	39-41	40-41	40-41	40-41
NOV	39-40	39-40	39-40	39-40	39-41	39-41	39-41	40-41	40-41	40-42
DEC	39-40	39-40	39-40	39-40	39-41	40-41	40-41	40-41	40-41	40-42

m/y	1960	1961	1962	1963	1964	1965	1966	1967	1968	1969
JAN	40-41	40-41	40-41	40-41	40-42	40-42	40-42	41-43	41-43	41-43
FEB	40-41	40-41	40-41	40-41	40-42	40-42	40-42	41-43	41-43	41-43
MAR	39-40	39-40	39-40	40-41	40-41	40-41	41-42	41-42	41-42	42-43
APR	39-40	39-40	39-40	39-41	39-41	39-41	41-42	41-42	41-42	41-42
MAY	39-40	39-40	39-40	39-40	39-41	39-41	40-41	40-41	40-41	40-42
JUN	39-40	39-40	39-40	39-40	39-41	39-41	40-41	40-41	40-41	40-42
JUL	39-40	39-40	39-40	39-40	39-41	39-41	40-42	40-42	40-42	40-42
AUG	39-41	39-41	39-41	39-41	39-41	39-41	40-42	40-42	40-42	40-42
SEP	40-41	40-41	40-42	40-41	40-42	40-42	41-42	41-42	41-42	41-43
OCT	40-42	40-42	40-42	40-42	40-42	40-42	41-42	41-42	41-42	41-43
NOV	40-42	40-42	40-42	40-42	40-42	40-42	42-43	42-43	42-43	41-43
DEC	40-42	40-42	41-42	41-43	41-43	41-43	42-43	42-43	42-44	41-43

m/y	1970	1971	1972	1973	1974	1975	1976	1977	1978	1979
JAN	42-44	42-44	43-44	43-44	43-44	43-44	43-44	43-45	43-45	43-45
FEB	42-43	42-43	43-44	43-44	43-44	43-44	43-44	43-44	43-45	43-45
MAR	42-43	42-43	42-43	43-44	43-44	43-44	43-44	43-44	44-45	44-45
APR	41-42	41-42	42-43	42-43	42-43	42-43	42-43	42-43	43-44	43-44
MAY	41-42	41-42	41-42	41-42	41-43	41-43	42-43	42-43	42-43	42-43
JUN	40-42	40-42	41-42	41-42	41-43	41-43	41-43	42-43	42-43	42-43
JUL	40-42	40-42	40-42	40-42	41-43	41-43	41-43	42-43	42-43	42-43
AUG	41-42	41-42	41-42	41-42	41-43	41-42	42-43	42-43	42-43	42-43
SEP	41-43	41-43	41-43	42-43	42-43	42-43	42-43	42-43	42-43	42-43
OCT	42-43	42-43	42-43	42-43	42-43	42-43	42-43	42-43	42-43	42-43
NOV	42-44	42-44	42-44	42-44	42-44	42-44	42-44	42-44	42-44	42-44
DEC	42-44	43-44	43-44	43-44	43-44	43-44	43-45	43-45	43-45	43-45

Your Mid-Life Crisis Ready-Reckoner

Where your month and year of birth intersect you will find the ages during which you experience the Uranus Opposition..

Your Mid-Life Crisis Ready-Reckoner

m/y	1980	1981	1982	1983	1984	1985	1986	1987	1988	1989
JAN	44-45	44-45	44-45	44-45	44-45	44-45	44-45	44-45	44-45	44-45
FEB	44-45	44-45	44-45	44-45	44-45	44-45	44-45	44-45	44-45	44-45
MAR	44-45	44-45	44-45	44-45	44-45	44-45	44-45	44-45	44-45	44-45
APR	44-45	44-45	44-45	44-45	44-45	44-45	44-45	44-45	44-45	44-45
MAY	43-44	43-44	43-44	43-44	43-44	43-44	43-44	43-44	44-45	44-45
JUN	43-44	43-44	43-44	43-44	43-44	43-44	43-44	43-44	43-44	43-44
JUL	42-43	42-43	42-43	42-43	42-43	42-43	42-43	42-43	42-43	42-43
AUG	42-43	42-43	42-43	42-43	42-43	42-43	42-43	42-43	42-43	42-43
SEP	42-44	42-44	42-44	42-44	42-44	42-44	42-44	42-44	42-44	42-44
OCT	42-44	42-44	42-44	42-44	42-44	42-44	42-44	42-44	42-44	42-44
NOV	43-44	43-44	43-44	43-44	43-44	43-44	43-44	43-44	43-44	43-44
DEC	43-45	43-45	43-45	43-45	43-45	43-45	43-45	43-45	43-45	43-45

m/y	1990	1991	1992	1993	1994	1995	1996	1997	1998	1999
JAN	43-45	43-45	43-45	43-45	43-45	43-45	43-44	43-44	43-44	43-44
FEB	44-45	44-45	44-45	44-45	43-45	43-45	43-44	43-44	43-44	43-44
MAR	44-45	44-45	44-45	44-45	44-45	43-45	43-45	43-44	43-44	43-44
APR	44-45	44-45	44-45	44-45	44-45	43-45	43-45	43-44	43-44	43-44
MAY	44-45	44-45	44-45	44-45	44-45	44-45	43-44	43-44	43-44	43-44
JUN	44-45	44-45	44-45	44-45	44-45	44-45	43-44	43-44	43-44	43-44
JUL	43-44	43-44	43-44	43-44	43-44	43-44	43-44	43-44	43-44	43-44
AUG	43-44	43-44	43-44	43-44	43-44	43-44	43-44	43-44	43-44	43-44
SEP	42-44	42-43	42-43	42-43	42-43	42-43	42-43	42-43	42-43	42-43
OCT	42-44	42-44	42-44	42-44	42-44	42-43	42-43	42-43	42-43	42-43
NOV	43-44	43-44	42-44	42-44	42-44	42-44	42-43	42-43	42-43	42-43
DEC	43-44	43-44	43-44	43-44	42-44	42-44	42-43	42-43	42-43	42-43

m/y	2000	2001	2002	2003	2004	2005	2006	2007	2008	2009
JAN	42-43	42-43	42-43	42-43	42-43	42-43	41-43	41-42	41-42	41-42
FEB	42-44	42-44	42-44	42-43	42-43	42-43	41-43	41-42	41-42	41-42
MAR	43-44	42-44	42-44	42-43	42-43	42-43	41-43	41-42	41-42	41-42
APR	43-44	43-44	43-44	43-44	42-43	42-43	42-43	42-43	42-43	41-43
MAY	43-44	43-44	43-44	43-44	42-43	42-43	42-43	42-43	42-43	41-43
JUN	43-44	43-44	43-44	43-44	42-43	42-43	42-43	42-43	42-43	41-43
JUL	43-44	43-44	43-44	43-44	42-43	42-43	42-43	42-43	42-43	42-43
AUG	42-43	42-43	42-43	42-43	42-43	42-43	42-43	42-43	42-43	42-43
SEP	42-43	42-43	41-42	42-43	41-42	41-42	41-42	41-42	41-42	41-42
OCT	41-42	42-43	41-42	41-42	41-42	41-42	41-42	41-42	41-42	41-42
NOV	41-43	41-43	41-42	41-42	41-42	41-42	41-42	41-42	41-42	41-42
DEC	41-43	41-43	41-42	41-42	41-42	40-42	40-42	40-41	40-41	40-41

5. PLANETS OF LOVE

The Sun. Moon and Planets work and play together like a team. They relate perfectly. The Solar System is like a family or society that is living, moving and changing in dynamic equilibrium - constantly. And so Astrology can show us how to do the same by modelling ourselves on this greater whole, for each Planet represents and reflects a part of us as individual human beings. "As above, so below" - the Greater is mirrored in the Smaller. This is plainly seen in the fact that the structure and movement of the Solar System is identical to an Atom - a nucleus or central body orbited by electrons or other bodies - and that, between the two, a human being is exactly midway in size (see diagram overleaf).

In order that you may identify and identify with these perfectly relating entities, these Planets of Love, they are here described, both as they stand alone and in relationship. Words in bold italics are keywords for that planet. Remember that all of these Planetary Laws apply to ALL Sun-Signs as universal guidelines to living and loving. However, you may well identify more with one Planet than another, or the one which rules your Sun-Sign. If you do not know your Sun-Sign's ruler, here they are...

Sign	Ruler	Sign	Ruler
Aries	Mars	Libra	Venus
Taurus	Venus	Scorpio	Pluto
Gemini	Mercury	Sagittarius	Jupiter
Cancer	Moon	Capricorn	Saturn
Leo	Sun	Aquarius	Uranus
Virgo	Mercury	Pisces	Neptune

✪ Planet Positions or Profiles - Sometimes I refer to the meaning of a planet in your own birth chart. These positions offer a further wealth of information, and I refer you to my two other books "Do It Yourself Astrology" and book/CD "The Instant Astrologer", and to the Resources on page 290 of this book.

THE SUN
love of Life

The Sun is the Creator of everything - "Life-Truth blazed in the sky". The dying words of the celebrated painter William Turner were "The Sun is God". Remember that we, our physical bodies, are literally made up of stardust, the same stuff as our Sun, as originally created at the Big Bang. Furthermore, the Solar Wind that sprinkles out from the top of the Sun affects our DNA, the basic building blocks of life, and it varies according to what part of space the Sun is shining from - that is, according to what Sign it is in. So, type of Solar Wind means type of DNA means type of human being - or for that matter, type of any life-form.

Astrologically, the Sun therefore represents your life itself, and what is generating it - your heart and spirit - which is more than you know. The twelve Signs of the Zodiac are rather like the twelve chapters in a year of the Sun's life as experienced here on Earth (see The Zodiacal Life-Stream on page 33). So your Sun-Sign is a general indication of what kind of life you have to lead and play out. As the Sun touches every planet in its System with its rays, so too does the Sun in your chart affect every part of your being which the Planets represent.

IN RELATIONSHIP, the Sun can be the warm light of your heart that shows the way, or it can be the harsh light of your ego which obscures it. Being true to the Sun, that is, following the deepest dictates of your heart, will enable you to manage not only your relationships strongly and successfully, but all other areas of your life too. Following the path that is illuminated by your Sun-Sign will help you do just this. Regard this as a directive from the highest command.   Merely following your ego - that is, a false sense of what you are - will blind you to who you truly are. If you are blind to who you really are, then you will also be blind to who Other is and what they are doing in your life. The ego is a false god who has usurped the real thing. It is the author of most, if not all, of Humanity's problems. Humanity is, after all, a gigantic set of relationships. Any relationship of yours is therefore contributing to the state of Humanity, in the same way that the Sun shines on all, vitalising or dominating, warming or burning.

Your Sun is the light which sheds itself upon Other. It is powerful and effective, whether you know it or not. Someone with a weak will and little confidence may not have such an obvious effect as someone who is a stronger individual, but they do have a most significant influence because they elicit a response from the 'strong'. The 'strong' can dominate the 'weak' or protect them, overwhelm them or strengthen them. If you feel you are the weaker half of a relationship it is probably because you have not yet noticed the effect that you have on Other. The more you observe this, then the more conscious you become of your life in terms of its significance and importance. You may not like some of what you see - but that is probably why you never felt like looking! But persist and you will progressively see how you can be more positive and creative in the way that you relate, and be someone in your own right. The Sun for many people is rather like a torch they do not realise that they are holding. This is very likely owing to some authority in your life - often your father - that has given a negative impression and/or suppressed your own self-expression.

Good examples of the Sun in the form of generosity and dignity, respect and strength, go a long way to giving Other a better idea of life and people generally. Your own father will have probably given you a mixture of both the bad and the good examples, but this would be entirely in accord with your own Sun Profile (the condition of the Sun in your individual birth chart). For instance, a tyrannical father would indicate that your inner core was in need of strengthening or purifying itself. A kind father would be someone to look up to - but he may have been weak too, indicating that you would need to be more sure of yourself. Your relationship with your father strongly affects how you manage your relationships, or whether Other does that, or whether you do it together like two equal Suns shining as One.

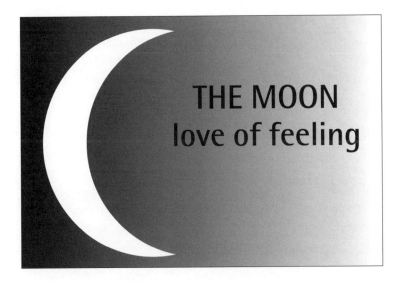

THE MOON
love of feeling

The Moon is your soul - the realm of feelings, dreams and memories . It is your personal unconscious, your past, your eternal and inner child. It is also the care of such tender things in yourself and others, and also meeting the need for security, familiarity and comfort. The Moon is the Mother - whether you are male or female, an actual mother or not. The Moon can also be looked at metaphorically, or literally if you wish, as being the Sun in the chart from your previous lifetime. So, if I have my Moon in Aries now, that means I had Sun in Aries then. Whether you believe in reincarnation or not, this gives a good feel of what the Moon is - a memory or how and who you once were filtering through as a predisposition to the present.

IN RELATIONSHIP, how your Moon behaves, responds and reacts is vitally important. Love of Feeling means recognising and nurturing these Lunar qualities in yourself and Other - but without becoming a victim or slave to unmet childhood needs in yourself or Other. True Love of Feeling cannot exist without an awareness of the state of the soul - be it of an adult (which means his or her Inner Child) or of an actual child. Without this awareness, which unfortunately is poor in most cases, relationships become a battleground where your hurt and unrecognised feelings from the past vie in vain for attention and concern from Other, who is doing exactly the same thing with you. Needless to say, negative childhood feelings surfaced in this manner turn into resentment, defensiveness and alienation. When functioning positively in a relationship, our Moons can, like children, spontaneously play together - hence the 'baby-talk' of people in love.

The child, inner or actual, is the fragile membrane between the person and their soul. Love of Feeling is to be aware of and sympathetically in touch with this membrane. If the membrane has been damaged, feelings will either be denied and hardened (like a blocked waterway), or become over-sensitive (like an unchecked flood). As a result, relationships become unstable, or dependent upon one person doing most or all of the caring. To halt this negative pattern of behaviour, recourse to therapy or counselling may well be necessary.

Love of Feeling needs to exist for a healthy relationship to do so too. To create it - or simply maintain the feeling of care and tenderness that is felt upon most initial encounters that are emotionally significant, like falling in love or having a baby - we must consciously focus upon what we and Other are feeling, with tenderness in our hearts. This means consistently showing a gentle consideration for Other, but at the same time not allowing our own possibly hurt inner child to get sucked into any drama more than it has to.

Women are usually far more in touch with the Moon than men are, if only for the simple reason that their bodies are attuned to the Moon by the menstrual cycle. It is highly important at this time in human evolution for men to recognise and attune to the Moon - their feelings - but without falling into a dependency upon the woman as Mother. The male obsession with breasts is symptomatic of a need for emotional nurture that is being denied and displaced into sexuality. If you think how large breasts appear to a suckling baby then you get some idea of why our preoccupation with them being big rather than small came into being. The reason why it is more so of late, is possibly because we are more insecure than we have been for a long, long time. This would account for there also being a female obsession here, but in addition this would be owing to the need to be attractive towards men, or to be too caring by way of compensation.

How two people's Moons interact is super-significant - more so than your Sun-Signs, in fact. Disharmonious interactions usually denote a need for both people to become more aware of their feelings, made imperative by the emotional discomfort and incompatibility involved. Harmonious interactions make for a ready recognition of and attunement to one another's inner child, with an ensuing Love of Feeling.

MERCURY
love of communication

Mercury is how you communicate - which would include how you listen and interpret the words being said to you. We learn to communicate from very early on in life, particularly with brothers and sisters, and of course at school. Mercury is the mental way in which you perceive, map out, identify and categorise your thoughts, feelings, sensations and intuitions. In myth, Mercury is the Messenger of the Gods - and as such would often edit and present messages according to his own agenda. This means to say that what we make of life, ourselves and others, is only that - what we make of them - not necessarily the thing itself. What they actually are is usually far more complex and indeterminate than our faculties of perception and reason are able to appreciate. So, communication is entirely dependent upon how accurate our perception of what we are trying to communicate or have communicated to us.

IN RELATIONSHIP, saying the wrong thing or the right thing can at times be utterly critical. It may only be one inappropriate word being used at a crucial moment that will make the difference between accord and discord, success or failure. On the other hand, we can sweet-talk or be sweet-talked, and be totally seduced purely by what someone is saying. Words are like fingers pushing buttons. Get the right combination and 'Open sesame!' - you have talked your way into someone's emotional and/or mental interior. Whether your actions and style can live up to this is another matter - so too can be whether or not you want to stay in the place you so cleverly talked your way into. In the end then, it is your inner state rather than what you say that matters - or rather it is how much in touch you are with that inner state that determines how you verbally express it. If there is little or no connection of this kind, someone with the 'gift of the gab' can make an impression on someone, but like a single coat of paint, it won't last very long. All of this is only too apparent when we consider that if a bond of trust is broken, nothing you say, however well-informed or well-put, will make much difference towards re-establishing that contact with Other.

Ultimately, the trick with Mercury is being able to listen to yourself - before expecting anyone to understand what you are trying to communicate to them. So often, the trouble is that our sense of our real inner selves and feelings are perceived a bit like over-hearing one end of a telephone conversation. This is reminiscent of the scientific finding that we say 60% of what we mean, and of this, 60% is understood by Other. This means that most communications are only 36% (60% of 60%) effective. The most Mercurial way of increasing this rate is to improve that first 60% by writing down what you think you feel. In the process, you will invariably find that what you thought was one thing is really another, and what you thought was clear-cut resembles reading a newspaper at the bottom of a well. The effort used to really read what is written deep inside of you is well worth it. When you speak from the heart - for that is precisely what this is - you clarify how both you and Other see and feel, dispelling illusions as you do so.

A disinclination to take the trouble to make contact with yourself, in this or some other way, would indicate a reluctance to know yourself. This amounts to a reluctance to know Other. This is how people lose touch with one another - through losing touch with themselves. In myth, Mercury is a mischievous sort of guy. He would sometimes edit what one god was saying to another for his own reasons, or just for laughs. In our reality, this is equivalent to rationalising our feelings to the point of not recognising what or how we feel. We also sometimes make fun or light of how we feel or Other feels - because we cannot emotionally accommodate it. It is well worth remembering to 'clip Mercury's wings' regularly by resisting the impulse to label how we feel. Let the feeling have its head - but without letting it run away with you - then you will know how to express it, verbally or otherwise.

VENUS
love of harmony

Venus is beauty and pleasure - which can be merely skin-deep, or which has more to do with an inner quality of being. In both cases, harmony is what creates the beauty or the pleasure. In the first case it is a harmony that is merely superficial, like room-spray masking a bad smell, or pretty wall-paper covering cracks - or more to the point, good looks hiding a weak personality. In the second case, it has more to do with grace. Grace is a state of being that is socially and/or artistically attuned to what truly constitutes harmony, whether it is between two people or in a musical composition. The pleasure side of Venus can also become perverted into sheer indulgence and affectation, or be something which has been bought for a price, rather done out of love. Positively, it is appreciativeness, generosity and affection. In the end, Venus is all about value and values, and whether or not they are sound or questionable. A good example of this is a painting by a celebrated artist that has sold for a fortune, only to find later that it is a fake. Something about the 'real thing' is what stands the test of time and scrutiny.

IN RELATIONSHIP, Venus is the planet which is actually running the show, for Venus represents harmony, and harmony is what relating and relationships are mostly about. Having said this though, it is always important to bear in mind that sooner or later one has to go though conflict in order to reach or establish true harmony, or grace as described above. Falling in love with love, just being nice and wanting to please and be pleased, or to have peace at any price - these are some of the expressions of Venus which are not harmony of the true and tried variety. This version of Venus could be called 'fancy', for such notions of love and harmony are fanciful and not based upon sincere feelings or real values. Unfortunately, western culture is currently infected with these superficial values - that anything can be got for a price and/or immediately -

and the difficulties that most relationships find themselves in bear witness to this state of affairs.

And so it is very much an issue of 'false' Venus/values or 'true' Venus/values - something which is only too commonly the case with relationships. A lover, friend or family member can be false, or they can be true. Everything depends upon the worth you are ascribing to another person, a relationship, or most of all, yourself. Venus is about attracting and being attracted, so if you feel worthwhile as a person, then to the same degree you will attract a worthwhile partner and relationship. If you have little or no sense of your emotional or physical worth, then only too often you will attract someone who undervalues and fails to appreciate you. But it should be pointed out here that Venus is also very good at compensating for such things by making out that someone is not good enough, when really one's own sense of inadequacy is the issue.

Venus is also symbolic of female sexuality, the hallmarks of which are sensuous appeal and mysterious allure. This stresses that femininity is something which draws things to it as distinct from masculinity (Mars) which goes and gets it. This is not to say that Venus is exclusive to females, any more than Mars is exclusive to males. The presence of what Jung called the 'anima', or the feminine nature within a male, is something that the position of Venus (along with the Moon) indicates the nature of. The anima is what determines for a man the kind of females he is attracted to. Conversely, the 'animus' or the masculine within a woman, and the kind of male to whom she is attracted, is revealed by her Sun and Mars position.

Another important facet of Venus is that of not putting all one's eggs in one basket. Negatively, this would be expressed in either smothering someone with affection, or conversely, being teasing and capricious as one plays the field in an attempt to have one's cake and eat it. Such is again an indication of an individual lacking self-worth. Also they probably feel unlovable, even if they are attractive. Developing one's artistic, aesthetic and social talents, is a sound way of increasing your sense of self-esteem and being worthy of someone's love. Above all, the best way to find harmony with Other is through sharing both one's light and shadow.

MARS
love of action

Mars is the impulse to act and get. Mars is raw energy, desire, decisiveness and self-assertion. Before anything can happen in life, something has to move in the direction of making it happen. There are people who make very little happen of their own volition, depending upon others to make things happen. But even they would have to want something before long. Even moving their hand or just saying something would entail the desire to do so, then the decision to do so, and finally the energy and muscles to do so. Such people are very possibly lacking in the courage to accept the consequences for their own actions. There is probably a good reason for this in their personal history, like doing too much, or violence or abuse - given or received. It is quite possible that physical disability falls into this category, and the non- or negative activity that caused it may be seen to have originated in one or more former incarnations. If one does not believe in re-incarnation then it would have to be ascribed to some other reason, like 'bad luck' or heredity. Whatever one's philosophy, Nature has a way of putting on hold anything that has got out of control. Unfortunately, such thwarting of desire eventually leads to anger - for anger is simply the troublesome residue of unexpressed or frustrated desires. And so...

IN RELATIONSHIP, the expression of Mars, possibly more than any other planetary energy, determines whether there is going to be strife or satisfaction. It is not that it creates these states all on its own - it is just that the wrong move, or the lack of any move at all, can lead to offence or misunderstanding. And the moves we make, or do not make, are determined by our thoughts and feelings - which are represented by every planet and astrological influence in the book. But it is Mars that makes that move - or again, doesn't make it.

Mars is the planet of masculinity, which obviously does not mean to say that it only exists in men. Everyone has a Mars in their chart. Masculinity is simply another word for all these Martian attributes, and because of this, the male of the species is traditionally or biologically expected to act first, or to 'be a man'. As someone once said "Men do, woman are". Proverbially, the male usually makes the move towards the female, taking the risk of being accepted or rejected. But then there is many a woman who is 'twice the man', being far more decisive and effective than many men. But whatever the gender, there is always a doer and a done to. In any relationship, deciding or being instinctively aware of who should be active and who should be passive, and when, is a critical issue. Because Mars is so important in relating, a good general rule is: Whoever acts or reacts, or does not act at all, should take full responsibility or credit for it.

SEX.It would be inaccurate to say that Mars is entirely representative of sex, for the whole personality (that is, all astrological influences) have some bearing on it. However, it is again a case of it being the actual act, and not necessarily the thoughts and feelings that are behind it. There may be little or no thought or feeling behind it at all - just lust, the physical desire to gratify the senses, or the primal urge to procreate. Then again, there are very few people who are so primitive as to have no premeditation at all concerning sex. On the contrary, today this would be impossible considering that we are bombarded constantly with sexual words, sounds and images that inflame the senses - or offend them.

When another human being affects us sexually in some way, it ultimately means that they are reaching more than just our Mars, that is unless one is a mindless sex machine! Sex, like Mars, is the first or decisive move that sets in motion a whole lot else; the fire that ignites. Sex is Cupid's bow and arrow; the hearts and flowers are delivered later - or not, as the case may be.

JUPITER
love of 'God'

Jupiter is the Law Giver. In life there are laws which are quite obvious, like, for example, the Law of Gravity. But there are laws that govern everything, some of which are not so provable as the one which states that if you fall you hit the ground. Science has taken over much of our sense of there being laws other than scientifically provable ones. But these laws still exist, and without an awareness of them we are like falling aeroplanes, and we will hit the ground! This book is comprised of laws of this kind.

These less obvious laws were traditionally ascribed to 'God'. I put this word in inverted commas because it needs its meaning clarifying. For many people, 'God' is associated with the stuffy world of churches and bible-bashers or whatever might be the name of the place of worship and its priests.

Such things are the result of 'God's' Laws getting interpreted by people who did so with their own little laws - that is, their ambitions and egos - getting in the way. In other words, they used our natural sense of there being a deity or Higher Power, to hoodwink and frighten us into believing something that had more to do with their own intent rather than 'God's'. This, combined with science's upstaging of 'God', has rendered 'God' dead, unacceptable or unbelievable to many people. What's really happening here though is that it is not so much 'God' that so many are no longer accepting or believing in, but that perversion of 'God' that got stuffed down their throats. The trouble is that those 'false priests' will have succeeded if we throw the baby out with the bath-water. And now we need that baby, that something that is divine and beyond what mere science has told us and sold us. Fortunately it appears we are beginning to return to 'God' - but a new and more intuitively and personally defined version.

IN RELATIONSHIP, Jupiter takes on a particularly subtle importance which is owing to the above-described demise of 'God'. Because human beings have an innate need to find 'God' - that is, a sense of greater meaning, a sense that there is some greater being or plan that is ultimately managing life, the Universe and everything - we will still unconsciously look for It even when science has told us that It never existed. And so we will look for It in our two primary areas of interest: money and sex. Obviously, money is worshipped as evidenced by our dangerously materialistic culture. With regard to sex, we look for 'God' in our mate. This is why we expect far too much of them, attach the wrong sort of importance to them, and feel the world has ended if we lose one.

Jupiter is also important in relationships because it represents qualities that are often omitted from relationship, or at least are not consciously acknowledged and therefore fall by the wayside with our romantic or idealistic intentions - or marriage vows. These qualities go beyond immediate physical desires and emotional needs, and include virtue, pledges, morality and a belief in and reverence for some Higher Good. All in all, Jupiter is about growth - particularly in terms of the development of better character and relationship.

Jupiter is the 'bigger picture'. There are far-reaching reasons for relationships that have to do with such things as having inner connections with certain people that must be explored and experienced for reasons that often escape a more limited viewpoint that is defined by some romantic or average expectation. For instance, a relationship's path could entail great suffering and endurance, the experience of which took the couple to a level of understanding they could not have reached without taking that journey. On the other hand, a limited concept would prompt one to give up and go for pastures new only to find that the same old issues arise (Saturn!), but in different guises. Of course, sometimes 'pastures new' may be the correct course of action - but it will have been taken as the result of having acquired the wisdom from the experience.

Each person's respective opinions and religious and cultural beliefs (or lack of them) - and how they are shared or accepted, rejected or imposed - can be critical to a relationship's stability and harmony.

SATURN
love of duty

Saturn teaches us our lessons and confronts us with what we cannot get away with doing, or leaving undone, any longer. Saturn puts us on notice that the time has come or is coming when we must get ourselves together, grow up, and generally be more objective and mature about whatever the issue might be. Saturn is not interested in or impressed by our emotional reactions, so whenever we are under the Saturnian pressure to learn and take stock of a situation, no amount of wheedling, complaining, blaming or evading will pass its test or excuse us from it. In fact, Saturn is more liable to pile more pressure on when we insist on remaining emotional babies who expect some easy way out, or that someone else will sort it out. Saturn is therefore our purpose and duty - whether it be to ourselves, others, or to some external authority. A good example of Saturn is the force of gravity, for it imposes limitations, puts the weight on us, and is what we have to rise and grow against. (The Law of Gravity referred to on the previous page under Jupiter, appertains to just that, the 'law' of gravity, not gravity itself).

IN RELATIONSHIP, Saturn is particularly important because it governs what many people feel either denied or afraid of where relationships are concerned: commitment. Commitment could be described as an equal blend of Love and Duty - but these two things often seem to be poles apart. If we say to someone we do such-and-such for them out of a sense of duty, they may well feel 'unloved' by this. But the word 'duty' simply comes from the word 'due'. To be dutiful to someone or something is to render what is due to them. This can be done purely because you know in your own mind what must be done and that you must do it, or, because some external pressure or condition forces you to discover your duty and perform it. It may also be a mixture of the two. In either case, time and circumstances will be the elements that restrict or pressurise you until you realise what is 'due'. It is also important to appreciate that such elements can also be the very things that equip you to establish your duty and fulfil it.

And so, the primary objective with Saturnian, that is, difficult or onerous relationship situations, is to recognise and establish what your duty is to Other. The ultimate objective is to perform that duty with love. If when we reluctantly recognise and grudgingly accept what our duty is, we are not doing it with love. The reason for this is that the inadequate or irresponsible part of us is still looking for an easy way out of or through the relationship. Of course, there is also the case when one does not recognise or fulfil one's duty at all. If this is the case, you can be sure that in the fullness of time Saturn will re-present one with the bill, so to speak. And it being 'overdue', the pressure will be all the greater. On the other hand, gladly committing yourself to the tasks and obligations that relationship imposes will progressively establish a foundation upon which a real and lasting love can be built. This is not easy, for it rather like the alchemist who through hard work and trial and error transmutes lead (called 'Butter of Saturn', the weight of basic reality) into gold (heart-love, spiritual enlightenment, the Sun).

However, because Saturn is, by its very nature, to do with setting limits and allotting responsibilities, it poses the necessity of knowing your own ground if you are to know where your duties end and someone else's begin. In other words, having a purpose or position all your very own is essential if you are to prevent impossible demands being made of you by those to whom you are responsible. A time and a place of your own is something worth striving to establish or maintain. Nature abhors a vacuum, which means to say that if you have not developed that duty to yourself, then your time and space will be invaded by someone else. Drawing such lines of demarcation is made difficult because we may feel that we will not be liked or loved for doing so. In truth, we are loved all the more - given time - because Other then knows where they stand.

Then again, one may draw one's lines too far out, allowing few or no people into one's increasingly cold, lonely and overly controlled space. Saturn says "Render what is due - no more and no less".

URANUS
love of freedom

Uranus is the truth that sets you free. This means that if you were able to look at things for what they truly are - free from egotistical distortions and emotional agendas - then every little bit of you would know that the 'where, what, why and who with' of your life were exactly as they should be. This is because you are caught up in a process called Evolution that has got to where it has got to and nowhere else - that is, NOW. There is no alternative to this, because the alternative would be NOW too. Of course, for most people, this is merely an abstract, esoteric or incomprehensible concept. Then again, this is what Uranus is about - a detached overview of life as a process that revolves and evolves onwards and onwards, like the Planets themselves.

Inside all of us is this 'program' that is searching for our unique identity and place in the scheme of things. Pitted against this program however, is our ego with its own vain and fanciful idea of what this should be. And underlying the ego (Sun), is our need for safety and security (Moon) that limits what we truly are or could be. And so, more often than not, we need the freedom to find the freedom, in order to find out who we really are! We are chained to the 'devil we know' (Saturn), whereas Uranus is the 'god we don't know', the great unknown.

IN RELATIONSHIP, where ego and security needs are particularly rife, Uranus - the unknown, the urge to be free to find out who you really are - can have a field day, or be like an ongoing bomb-scare. If Uranus is a strong influence in a relationship, resisting it by trying to keep yourself and/or your partner to some convention or security agenda is asking for trouble. If we do not consciously grant one another the freedom and space to do our own thing, then Uranus will suddenly introduce a shock, accident or coincidence that rocks what we thought was our safe little boat. Such surprises are sometimes the only way to free us from set patterns of behaviour - Uranus's main target. Instances of this would be when a partner, out of the blue, ups and goes off with some unlikely lover, or say, when a disruptive element interferes with domestic harmony. Healthy Uranian relationships - that is, ones in which flexibility and space are allowed one another - are 'usually unusual'. This means that they are as unique as the individuals involved.

In terms of actual types of relationship, Uranus is more attuned to groups and friendships. This is because we allow our friends far more latitude to do their own thing, and without being constantly accountable, than we would with family or lovers. The reason why we so often find this hard to do with those with whom we are more emotionally involved is simply because we are more dependent upon them. Conversely, we cannot just do our own thing when others are depending upon us. But Uranus is no respecter of such emotional considerations and investments. If Uranus is in play, the process of social, cultural and personal evolution must proceed at all costs, whatever the emotional conditions - or rather because of them.

Uranus has been called 'The Great Awakener', and this is borne out in relationships where one person provokes the other in some way, or is actively introducing them to a new way of living or looking at life. More often than not, this will be mutual. Using unusual or alternative means to breathe new life into a relationship would also come under the Uranian heading of awakening or quickening. Such can also be the case in relationships where the two people are separated in age by a generation. The differing values rub against one another, constantly challenging and thereby quickening what each person believes, thinks and feels.

There is always a 'false' expression of any planetary energy, and with Uranus it is a pretence of liberated behaviour. For example, someone might want an 'open' and 'honest' relationship, but what they really want is to avoid commitment and emotional confrontation. The real key is to be true to yourself and maintain a healthy relationship. The poet Kahlil Gibran's perfectly advised on relationship in a patently Uranian fashion: "Let the winds of the heavens dance between you".

NEPTUNE
love of all

Neptune has been called the Lord of Unseen Realms, which is a mysterious title for a mysterious planet. Perhaps this could be described as that dimension of life, both in space and time, which we cannot discern with the usual five senses or with conventional means. It can only be perceived or appreciated psychically, in the imagination, with the heart, or with the aid of some kind of metaphysical or mystical awareness or drugs or alcohol. As such, it is also difficult to prove its existence with scientific or rational means, simply because it is subject to laws that are outside of the physical ones. The sea, of which Neptune is the mythological God, perfectly represents this strange and different Realm of Oneness, where we all sprung from, and to where it is said we will all return. We are as many, many drops making up one great ocean. And Neptune, like the sea, has no boundaries of its own making. This sense of oneness, or at least togetherness, can be seen when people gather in water or near it, and how all waters return to the sea.

A few more examples of specific areas of Neptune's Realm are re-incarnation, for it poses no separation between one (life)time and another; 'faith' healing, which utilises a subtle energy that recognises no barrier between the inside and outside of the body; music which is common to all levels and classes of society, and defies rational explanation. And so through metaphor and association - which, rather than facts and figures, are Neptune's language - we can eventually see that we are all One on a more sublime or elevated level. And by entering this Realm and immersing ourselves in it completely - perhaps through meditation or surrender of ego attachments - we are healed and redeemed, the slate wiped clean. Through saving one individual, we are are ultimately saving all. Through a sacrifice of the higher, we benefit the lower.

IN RELATIONSHIP, Neptune, because it represents Oneness and Salvation, takes on a powerful but subtle importance. This is simply because, for the individual human being, the most common experience of entering Neptune's Realm is what we call 'falling in love'. This would also include any other state where we feel at one with the other person, when their charisma draws us to them like a whirlpool, or when we painfully identify with others, consciously or unconsciously. Addiction to a person or thing is also Neptunian. Furthermore, it is all too often that what we see as the loved one, at a later date, turns out to be something quite different. Neptune also governs wishful thinking and subsequent disappointment and feelings of being deceived. How often is it that high hopes evaporate into acute emotional pain and embarrassment? But this can be an illusion within an illusion, for although the mirage of the beloved disappears when subjected to the harsh light of mundane reality or the ego's desires, it is only that: the mirage of the beloved. The actual person is, or could be, who we are spiritually joined to by unseen ties for mysterious reasons. Such reasons may include mutual salvation - or for that matter, damnation. Perhaps we feel we have met before in another time, and must now come together again to resolve a past split or misunderstanding, or settle a score. But we often fail to see this because the 'beloved' suddenly fails to match up to our romantic, glamorised or idealised conception of what that beloved should be. It is hard to sacrifice this conception, or rather illusion, of love. It is harder still to reveal to Other that we too are vulnerable, damaged and in need of saving and redeeming. Strangely, disappointment is regarded, more often than not, as the lesser of these two types of pain.

Neptune is therefore a higher or spiritual love - an unconditional, and sometimes platonic, love. Through loving another in such a selfless way we are loving ourselves more completely. This is because we are not pulling any strings or making any claims, but trusting that Love itself will inevitably put things right - as surely as rivers eventually meet the sea. Neptune is the Love of All for it is through loving one person, or any number of any creature, in this higher, unconditional way, that the great 'pool' of love is added to, for other seekers of redemption to draw from, to be refreshed and healed by.

PLUTO
love of depth

Pluto is Lord of the Underworld, where all things of Earth have their physical origins. To know the seeds of things is to know all things, and therein lies true power. To varying degrees, we all have a sense of this something deep and dark within us. This something is like a root memory 'that in the darkness binds us'. It is also the place to where our physical bodies will inevitably return, as ash or rotting matter, to feed the life to come. Pluto is therefore the Planet of Death and Regeneration. It is the omega, the end of all things, the Judgment Day. And so it can give rise to obsessions or convictions, depending on the consciousness around such fixed feelings. This can express itself at one end of its dark spectrum as 'completion compulsion' where one feels driven to bring things to any sort of conclusion, or simply being bent on destruction. At the other end however, it can forge the kind of individual who is able to penetrate to the core of things and destroy what is negative, thereby bringing about healing and transformation.

IN RELATIONSHIP, Pluto is intimacy, which encompasses the intense pleasure of deep union and sexual passion as well as the sheer hell of depravity or desolation. It is the urge to get to the bottom of things, no matter what pain or loss is incurred in the process. Once Pluto's great millstones of deep desire or emotional hunger have been set in motion, then inevitably things will no longer be able to remain the same. It draws innocent and fiend alike down its tunnel, through the extremes of subjugation and omnipotence, to a point in time and space where something dies. This will usually be the death of something like a fixed idea or attitude, a pattern of behaviour, or a sexual preoccupation - or it may be even be the death of a relationship or even an actual person. But whatever it is that is getting in the way of union - it must perish.

The most common manifestation of Plutonian behaviour in a relationship is one person manipulating the other. The word 'manipulation' has a negative connotation for many people, when in actual fact it can be extremely positive. For example, a chiropractor or osteopath will manipulate one's skeletal structure to bring it back into alignment and thereby alleviate suffering and create better health. The problem on a personal level, as opposed to a professional one, is that too often one person will manipulate another motivated by selfish or even evil intent. The deep sense of being joined or involved with another can give the impression to one person that if the other person changed in a certain way things would be a lot better. And this is made possible because one person will submit to the other's manipulation when there is an unconscious movement towards profound change. A negative example here would be that of a jealous person convincing their partner that certain people are bad for them, when the real reason is because they are a threat to the jealous person. Their partner is manipulatable possibly owing to their fear of ugly scenes where deep and dark emotions surface. This is typical of how one can be emotionally blackmailed because of some deeply-seated social or cultural taboo. But if the partner could be more positively Plutonian themselves and recognise that having such secrets makes them more vulnerable than the substance of the secrets themselves, then their opposite number would have no power over them. This does, of course, necessitate them delving more deeply into their own make-up and confronting old fears. But that is par for the course in a Plutonian relationship.

A positive form of Plutonian manipulation on the other hand, is occasioned by the one person having an accurate insight into the true but hidden nature of the other person - the 'seeds' of their being. Guided by this psychological insight, and through ruthlessly identifying and eliminating any dubious motivations of their own, awesome transformations can occur - and not just in the one person, but both. This is because through the gruelling process of self-scrutiny and the deep psychological probing necessary for making the manipulation positive, the manipulator positively transforms themselves too.

THE EARTH
love of being

When considering so-called Planetary influences, one may well ask where the influence of the Planet that we are living on comes into the picture. The answer to this is that a Birth Chart is set out as a view from Planet Earth - from exactly where you are born, in fact. From this viewpoint the sky is then divided up into twelve segments, radiating out from that spot where you were born, or the point of observation. These twelve segments are called the mundane Houses for they represent areas of Earthly experience - of Being on Earth. The Earth's rotation on its own axis is seen symbolically as the unfoldment of an individual's life.

This begins with the most important of the Houses, the First, which is always that segment of sky just below the Eastern Horizon, or where the Sun rises at Dawn. This is therefore the House that symbolises the first experience of life - your Birth, when you came into Being. It is the most important House because it represents the one who is doing the experiencing, without which there would not be any other experiences! The Eastern Horizon which is the beginning or Cusp of the First House, the House of Being or Self, is also called the Ascendant, and the Sign that it is placed in is called the Rising Sign, which symbolises how you continue to be 'born' or emerge into the present moment - your persona or mask. Of the eleven other Houses of Earthly experience, three of them are almost as important (or arguably, as important) as the First House or Ascendant.

Two of these are the Fourth House (positioned on the Nadir or where the Sun is at Midnight), representing Roots, Background, Home-life, etc., and the Tenth House (positioned on the Zenith or where the Sun is at Noon), representing Worldly Position, Status, Profession, etc..

And then there is the Seventh House (positioned on the Western Horizon or where the Sun sets), representing...

RELATIONSHIP, for it is always directly opposite the First House or Ascendant, that is, the Self. The Seventh House (which begins with the Western Horizon, the Seventh House Cusp or Descendant) is every bit as important as the First House or Ascendant. In other words, the Self or Being (Ascendant), is made more distinct and aware through experiencing Other beings, to whom it has to Relate (Descendant). There is no Self without Other, just as there can be no East without West, or Sunrise without Sunset. There can be no true Love of Being without there being a Love of Other, and you can only really love Other as much as you love your Self. Furthermore, astrology goes on to describe the kind of Other and nature of Relationship that you will attract because of the type of Being that you are.

The Three Ages of Man

In terms of time passing, the cycle of the twelve Houses last 28 years, and there are three of these cycles - the Three Ages of Man. The first cycle is for the development of the personality, the second for the development of oneself as a being who creatively contributes to society, and the third is one of spiritual development, preparing oneself for the next world. This symbolic Life Span is equivalent to one orbit of Uranus, the planet that governs astrology itself (see pages 239 & 272). The numerology of these three 28 year cycles runs like this... The whole subject of Houses is central to Astrology, for it takes into account what Houses all the Signs and Planets fall in, and the effects these Sign and

From	0-28	=	2+8	=	10=	1+0=	1st Age
From	29-56	=	5+6	=	11=	1+1=	2nd Age
From	57-84	=	8+4	=	12=	1+2=	3rd Age

Planet energies have upon those House experiences. Unfortunately though, it is not something that can be gone into in detail without a more technically complex approach than this book uses. If you wish to know more about the the calculation and personal meaning of the Ascendant and Houses, etc. this is made easy in my book/CD 'The Instant Astrologer'. I also refer you to the astrological resources on page 290.

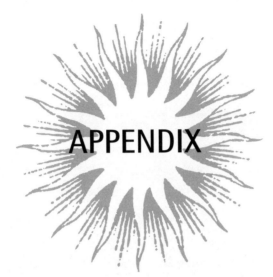

APPENDIX

APPENDIX

THE JUPITER-SATURN BALANCE OF POWER

"And with Joy we'll Persevere"

**Managing to live healthily and successfully in the midst
of the experiences that the Planetary influences
symbolise can be greatly assisted by understanding how to
balance the effects of these,
the two biggest planets in our Solar System.**

You Are a Physical Being

Much as the above statement seems obvious, we tend to forget what being physical actually means. One of the most important aspects of physical existence is PRESSURE. We can appreciate this by thinking of an automobile tyre. The tyre itself has an internal air pressure to counteract the external air pressure of our atmosphere. When the internal pressure is too low or too high in relation to the external pressure then the vehicle becomes unstable while travelling.

Relating all this to being human is quite simple. We travel around, or live, with an internal sense of life and ourselves. This 'internal pressure' is what we need in order to respond to and contend with the pressures of living in the world of people and things - the 'external pressure'. Astrologically, Jupiter represents the internal pressure, while Saturn stands for the external pressure. And you cannot, and should not, consider the one without the other. When our internal pressure or faith in ourself is too low then the everyday pressures of our daily lives becomes too hard to bear - eventually it can even crush us or put us 'off the road'. Alternatively, when our internal pressure is too high or we have an inflated idea of our capabilities and prospects, then through ignoring the limitations placed on us by the external pressure (which includes your physical body) we can burn-out, or external pressure has to compensate in some way - like, for instance, causing us to run foul of someone in authority, or someone who has an emotional hold on us.

The tyre metaphor again applies here in that with lower tyre pressure it is more secure as there is more grip on the road surface (like for wet weather driving) but it uses up more energy and so limits how far we can go. With higher tyre pressure there is less grip and less energy used - but driving is more precarious. In both cases there is far less control over the vehicle (you, that is!), especially if an emergency or the unexpected should happen.

The principle of pressure can also be seen in terms of something highly applicable to our own physical health and existence: blood pressure. With low blood pressure we feel weak and faint, so, psychologically speaking, we need 'pumping up' with a stronger sense of ourselves in order to cope with life. This can also mean feigning humility (being a victim) in order to avoid asserting oneself. With high blood pressure we are overcompensating for what we feel the pressures of the outside world to be - and so need to calm down, or be let down. This could also mean feigning being full of oneself as a defence mechanism.

All of the above can actually be seen in the original symbols or glyphs for Jupiter and Saturn...

Both are comprised of two other symbols: the Crescent for the Moon and the Cross for Matter. The Moon represents, as you know, your emotional being - that is, your personal sense of existing. So, Jupiter, on the left, the Crescent on top of the Cross, is the personal, emotional sense taking

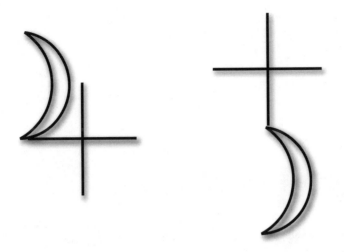

precedence over the material world and its pressures and considerations. Saturn, on the other hand, is those material pressures and considerations taking precedence over your emotional or personal state of being.

On the following two pages is a table of various states experienced through having either too much Saturn and not enough Jupiter, or the reverse, along with the remedies that they can be met with.

TOO MUCH SATURN AND NOT ENOUGH JUPITER*

♦ REMEDY (Of the below, adopt one or more that appeals to you)

♦ Cultivate optimism; look on the bright side; accentuate the positive, attenuate the negative. Laugh - a sense of humour is a sense of proportion.

♦ Fill your life with a faith in someone or something, but preferably yourself. Follow you dreams.

Feeling sluggish and/or depressed. Feeling intimidated by life and others. A sense of hopelessness. Lacking in confidence. Fearfulness. Worry and anxiety. Low Blood Pressure.

♦ Be more assertive and ebullient. Be theatrical, outgoing and larger than life.

♦ Attract JOY into your life by being true to your responsibilities, exercising impartiality, and protecting the sanctity of your inner being (Moon).

♦ Do yogic breathing exercises. This literally 'pumps' you up, filling you with the spirit of enthusiasm - pneuma , as in pneumatic, is the Greek for 'spirit' or 'breath of life'.

♦ Acquire a philosophy of life than enables you to see the bigger picture, thereby cutting your perceived problems down to size or putting them into a more meaningful perspective.

♦ Be more adventurous; feel the fear and do it anyway. Get out, do something different. Let experience be your teacher rather than worry be your tormentor.

♦ Be more open and spontaneous; have less agendas and rigid expectations.

♦ Take vigorous physical exercise, let off steam, have a good scream and shout.

♦ Make the most of your Jupiter 'year' or Growth Mode.

* These effects can result from compensation, that is, too much Jupiterian behaviour can eventually attract more Saturn influences in to your life, or conversely, too much Saturnian behaviour will attract more Jupiter influences. For example, High Blood Pressure(too much Jupiter) could be a condition compensating for feeling inhibited (too much Saturn).

TOO MUCH JUPITER AND NOT ENOUGH SATURN*

◆ REMEDY (Of the below, adopt one or more that appeals to you)

◆ Give yourself readily achievable goals, rather than pie-in-the-sky projects.

◆ Ask yourself why you are trying to please or impress others more than yourself. Make the distinction between what you expect of yourself and what you have been led to believe others expect of you (but probably do not).

Over-optimism resulting in deflation or not being taken seriously by others Over-commitment; promising more than you can deliver. Excessiveness and indulgence, giving rise to health or weight problems, lack of control and wasted time and energy.
False confidence created by alcohol, drugs, delusions of grandeur, etc.
Lack of discipline.
High Blood Pressure.

◆ Remember that actions speak louder than words. DO IT, don't just think about it. Walk your talk.

◆ That which is not written down does not exist.

◆ Practise the Art of Humility. True greatness veils itself.

◆ By your works shall they know you - not by your intentions.

◆ Identify the 'gap' in your life that you are trying to fill, and then you will know how to successfully fill it. This would be 'creatively indulging' yourself.

◆ Channel excessiveness into a productive pursuit to benefit yourself and others.

◆ Use your time constructively - draw up a plan and schedule and KEEP TO IT.

◆ Become aware of how you overreact to/overcompensate for what you feel to be inadequacies, rather than being clear what those actual shortcomings are.

◆ Take up a program of exercise, study or relaxation - preferably one involving others that make sure you stay the course.

◆ Give actuality to words of wisdom.

* These effects can result from compensation, that is, too much Jupiterian behaviour can eventually attract more Saturn influences in to your life, or conversely, too much Saturnian behaviour will attract more Jupiter influences. For example, High Blood Pressure(too much Jupiter) could be a condition compensating for feeling inhibited (too much Saturn).

APPENDIX

SUN-SIGN QUOTATIONS

ARIES - "Courage is not merely one of the virtues, but the form of every virtue at its testing point" - Cyril Connolly (Palinurus) from *The Unquiet Grave*

TAURUS - "Nature does nothing without purpose or uselessly" - Aristotle from *Politics* bk.1, 1256b

GEMINI - "Hail to thee, blithe Spirit!" - Percy Bysshe Shelley from *To a Skylark* (1819)

CANCER - "Home is where the heart is" - Proverb

LEO - "All the world's a stage" - William Shakespeare from *As You Like It* act 2. Sc.7, l.34

VIRGO - "Man will err while yet he strives" - Johann Wolfgang von Goethe

LIBRA - "Beauty is Truth, Truth Beauty" - John Keats from *Ode to a Grecian Urn*

SCORPIO - "Yea, though I walk through the valley in the shadow of death, I shall fear no evil" - Psalm 123, The Holy Bible.

SAGITTARIUS - "It never matters how hard the road ahead might look, for it is still road, and roads go places!"- Author from *Do It Yourself Astrology* p140

CAPRICORN - "The opposite to the devil you know is the god that you don't" - Author

AQUARIUS - "A paradox is the truth standing on its head to attract attention" from *The Cynics Encyclopaedia*

PISCES - "Obstacles - I either use them or go around them" - Sir Michael Caine

RESOURCES – If you wish to take your interest in astrology further I recommend that you contact:

AUSTRALIA

AUSTRALIAN SOCIETY OF ASTROLOGERS INC: President –Renee Badger.
Tel : + 61 7 5445 8017. Australian Society of Astrologers,
PO Box 7120, Bass Hill, New South Wales 2197.
Tel/fax: + 61 2 9754 2999
Email: GJdeMAS@bigpond.com.au.
Website: www.angelfire.com/journal/asainc/index.html.

CANADA

CANADIAN ACADEMY OF ASTROLOGY AND RELATED DISCIPLINES
(CAARD): Margaret Day.
Tel: + 1 613 722 5975. Fax: + 1 613 567 0797.
Email: cyclespeak@home.net/cyclespeak/

NEW ZEALAND

ASTROLOGICAL SOCIETY OF NEW ZEALAND (ASNZ): PO Box 5266, Wellesley
Street, Auckland C1, New Zealand.
Tel: + 64 9 480 8019.
EMAIL: clearavu@ihug.co.nz.

SOUTH AFRICA

ASTROLOGICAL SOCIETY OF SOUTH AFRICA (ASSA): Elena van Baalen, PO B
ox 1953, Saxonwold 2132, South Africa.
Tel: + 21 0 11 646 3670. Fax: + 21 011 646 5477.
Email: elena@kallback.co.za.
Website: www.naturalhealth.co.za/assoc/ass_216.html.

UNITED KINGDOM

ASTROLOGICAL ASSOCIATION, Unit 168 Lee Valley Technopark, Tottenham
Hale, London, N17 9LN.
Tel: + 44 (0) 20 8880 4848. Fax: + 44 (0) 20 8880 4849.
Email: astrological.association@zetnet.co.uk
Website: www.AstrologicalAssociation.com

USA

AMERICAN FEDERATION OF ASTROLOGERS: Executive Secretary
Robert W Cooper, PO Box 22040, Tempe, AZ 85285-2040.
Tel: + 1 480 838 1751. Toll-free: + 1 888 301 7630.
Fax: + 1 480 838 8293.
Email: afa@msn.com/.

FOR ALL OTHER COUNTRIES, GO TO

www.uraniatrust.org

◆ Any other queries or correspondence for Lyn Birkbeck to be sent (enclose
SAE if from UK) to:
Lyn Birkbeck (AW)
c/o O Books, John Hunt Publishing Ltd, 46a West Street,
New Alresford, Hampshire SO24 9AU, United Kingdom

Or e-mail to
lynbirkbeck@btopenworld.com
Or via his website:
lynbirkbeck.com

Other Books by Lyn Birkbeck:
Do It Yourself Astrology (Thorsons) 1996
The Astrological Oracle (Thorsons) 2002
The Instant Astrologer + CD (O Books) 2003
Dynamic Synastry (O Books) 2004(scheduled)

APPENDIX

7. THE AGE INDEX

The Age Index gives you an overall view of all the Planetary Cycles that are covered in this book. The name of any actual influence is given in the box that intersects a PLANET column and the row corresponding to your AGE (given in first column).

For Jupiter, the year 'Sign' or 'Growth Mode' is given along with the page number that you will find that Year/Mode. Before reading the description of any Jupiter influence first digest the Jupiter introduction on page 91.

For the Moon, the various 'Phases' are depicted as shaded strips of graduated density; the densest shade is at the beginning, indicating when that 'Phase' is at its most powerful, while the actual name of the 'Phase' is given along with the page it is described upon. I recommend that you read the introduction to the Moon beginning on page 119 as well as the General Interpretation of each type of 'Phase' starting on page 125.

For Saturn and Uranus, the names of the critical points in their cycles are given along with the page number where their effects are described. With Saturn, as a rule, the darker the shade, the stronger the influence. Introduction to Saturn is found on page 199 and to Uranus on page 239.

So for example, at age 29 you would have a 'Virgo' Jupiter Year or Growth Mode (described on page 104, be mid-way through your Second Emerging Moon 'Phase' (described on page 164),and reached your First Return of Saturn (described on page 213),

Bear in mind that any influence might have to get 'under way' before you feel its effect, or it could kick in a bit earlier - so don't expect it to start on your birthday!

Note that the three pages the Age Index is set out upon correspond to the Three Ages of Man (see page 279).

AGE	JUPITER Lucky Years	MOON Emotional Tides	SATURN Lessons & Progression	URANUS Mid-Life Crisis
0	'Aries'-94	1st Emerging		
1	'Taurus'-96	p144		
2	'Gemini'-98			
3	'Cancer'-100	1st Striving		
4	'Leo'-102	p147		
5	'Virgo'-104			
6	'Libra'-106		1st Waxing	
7	'Scorpio'-108	1st Deciding	Square p205	
8	'Sagittarius'-110	p149		
9	'Capricorn'-112		1st Waxing	
10	'Aquarius'-114	1st Adjusting	Trine p207	
11	'Pisces'-116	p151		
12	'Aries'-94			
13	'Taurus'-96			
14	'Gemini'-98	1st Realising	1st Opposition	
15	'Cancer'-100	p154	p208	
16	'Leo'-102			
17	'Virgo'-104	1st Sharing		
18	'Libra'-106	p157		
19	'Scorpio'-108		1st Waning	
20	'Sagittarius'-110		Trine p211	
21	'Capricorn'-112	Understanding	1st Waning	
22	'Aquarius'-114	p160	Square p212	
23	'Pisces'-116			
24	'Aries'-94	1st Releasing		
25	'Taurus'-96	p161		
26	'Gemini'-98			
27	'Cancer'-100	2nd Emerging		
28	'Leo'-102	(1st Return) 164		

AGE	JUPITER Lucky Years	MOON Emotional Tides	SATURN Lessons & Progression	URANUS Mid-Life Crisis
29	'Virgo'-104	p164	1st Return	
30	'Libra'-106		p213	
31	'Scorpio'-108	2nd Striving		
32	'Sagittarius'-110	p168		
33	'Capricorn'-112			
34	'Aquarius'-114	2nd Deciding		
35	'Pisces'-116	p171		
36	'Aries'-94		2nd Waxing	
37	'Taurus'-96	2nd Adjusting	Square p220	Opposition
38	'Gemini'-98	p173	2nd Waxing	p239
39	'Cancer'-100		Trine p223	(See table on
40	'Leo'-102			pages 252-254 for the
41	'Virgo'-104	2nd Realising		1-3 yesr period when
42	'Libra'-106	p175		this occurs for you
43	'Scorpio'-108		2nd Opposition	personally)
44	'Sagittarius'-110	2nd Sharing	p224	
45	'Capricorn'-112	p178		
46	'Aquarius'-114			
47	'Pisces'-116			
48	'Aries'-94	Understanding	2nd Waning	
49	'Taurus'-96	p181	Trine p227	
50	'Gemini'-98			
51	'Cancer'-100	2nd Releasing	2nd Waning	
52	'Leo'-102	p183	Square p228	
53	'Virgo'-104			
54	'Libra'-106			
55	'Scorpio'-108	3rd Emerging		
56	'Sagittarius'-110	(2ndReturn) 186		

AGE	JUPITER Lucky Years	MOON Emotional Tides	SATURN Lessons & Progression	URANUS Mid-Life Crisis
57	'Capricorn'-112	p186		
58	'Aquarius'-114	3rd Striving	2nd RETURN	
59	'Pisces'-116	p189	p230	
60	'Aries'-94			
61	'Taurus'-96	3rd Deciding		
62	'Gemini'-98	p191		
63	'Cancer'-100			
64	'Leo'-102			
65	'Virgo'-104	3rd Adjusting	3rd Waxing	
66	'Libra'-106	p192	Square p233	
67	'Scorpio'-108			
68	'Sagittarius'-110	3rd Realising	3rd Waxing	
69	'Capricorn'-112	p194	Trine p234	
70	'Aquarius'-114			
71	'Pisces'-116			
72	'Aries'-94	3rd Sharing		
73	'Taurus'-96	p195	3rd Opposition	
74	'Gemini'-98		p235	
75	'Cancer'-100	Understanding		
76	'Leo'-102	p196		
77	'Virgo'-104			
78	'Libra'-106	3rd Releasing	3rd Waning	
79	'Scorpio'-108	p197	Trine p236	
80	'Sagittarius'-110		3rd Waning	
81	'Capricorn'-106		Square p237	
82	'Aquarius'-114	4th Emerging		
83	'Pisces'-116	(3rdReturn)		
84	'Aries'-94	p198		RETURN